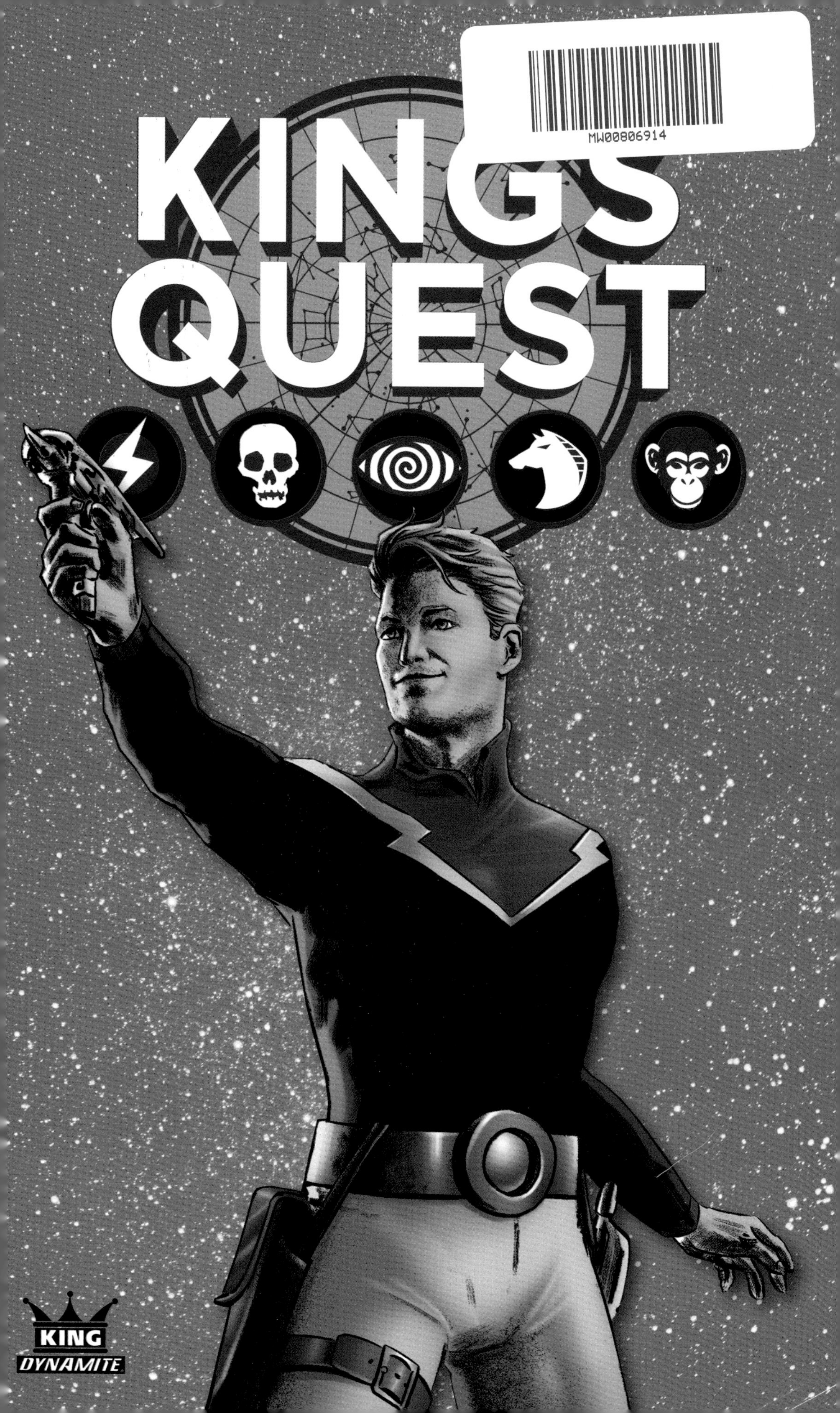
KINGS QUEST™
KING
DYNAMITE

KINGS QUEST™

Nick Barrucci, CEO / Publisher
Juan Collado, President / COO

Joe Rybandt, Executive Editor
Matt Idelson, Senior Editor
Anthony Marques, Associate Editor
Kevin Ketner, Editorial Assistant

Jason Ullmeyer, Art Director
Geoff Harkins, Senior Graphic Designer
Cathleen Heard, Graphic Designer
Alexis Persson, Production Artist

Chris Caniano, Digital Associate
Rachel Kilbury, Digital Assistant

Brandon Dante Primavera, V.P. of IT and Operations
Rich Young, Director of Business Development

Alan Payne, V.P. of Sales and Marketing
Keith Davidsen, Marketing Director
Pat O'Connell, Sales Manager

FIRST PRINTING 10 9 8 7 6 5 4 3 2 1   ISBN13: 978-1-5241-0220-3

Online at www.DYNAMITE.com
On Facebook /Dynamitecomics
On Instagram /Dynamitecomics
On Tumblr dynamitecomics.tumblr.co
On Twitter @dynamitecomics
On YouTube /Dynamitecomics

For information regarding press, media rights, foreign rights, licensing, promotions, and advertising e-mail:
marketing@dynamite.com

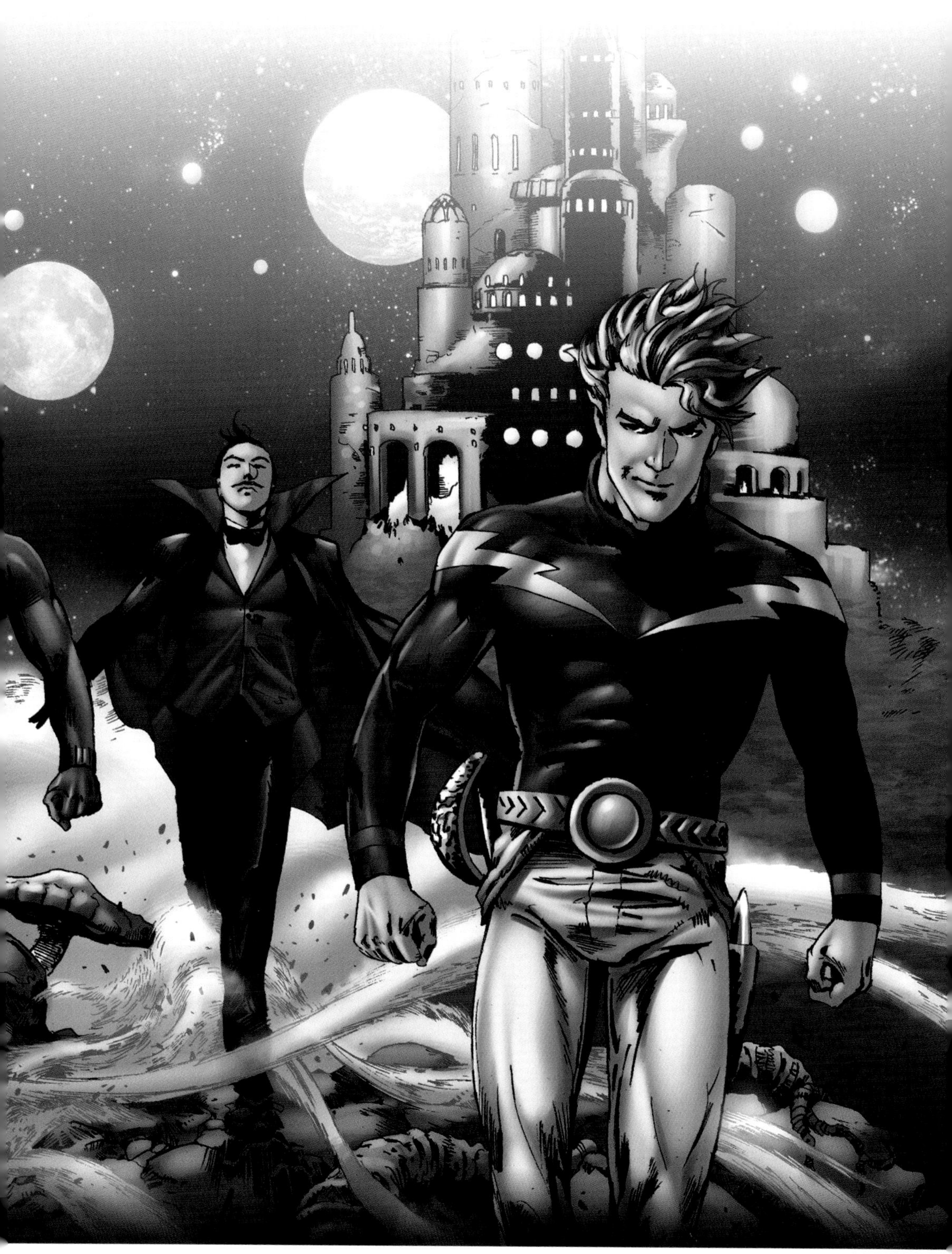

Written by **Ben Acker** & **Heath Corson**
Art by **Dan McDaid** & **Bob Q**
Colors by **Omi Remalante** with **Bob Q**
Letters by **Simon Bowland**

Collection Cover by **Marc Laming** & **Lara Margarida**
Collection Design by **Bill Tortolini**

Special Thanks to **Brendan J. Burford**

Packaged & Edited by **Nate Cosby**

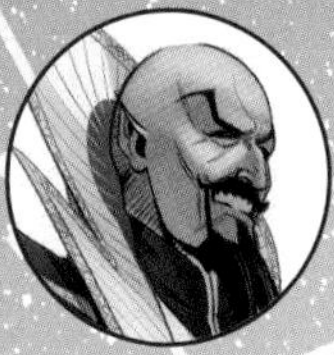

MING THE MERCILESS™
conqueror of worlds, failed to conquer Earth, thanks to its mightiest champions!

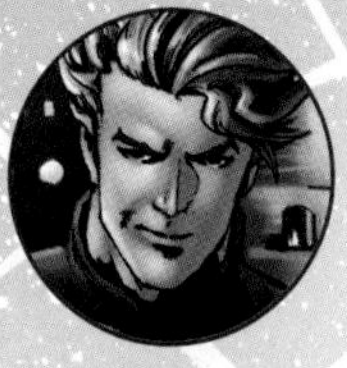

Three cheers for
FLASH GORDON™

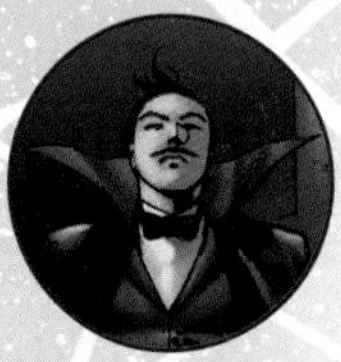

MANDRAKE THE MAGICIAN™

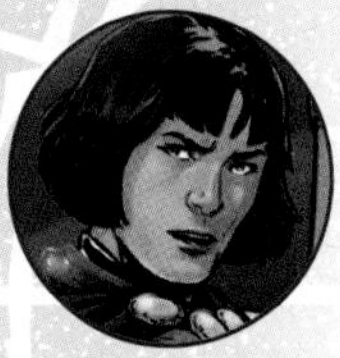

PRINCE VALIANT™

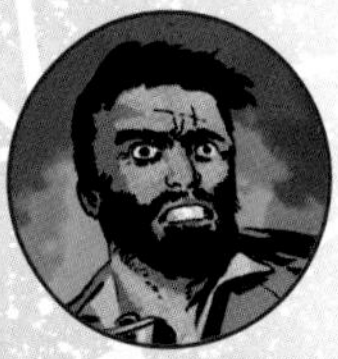

PROFESSOR ZARKOV™

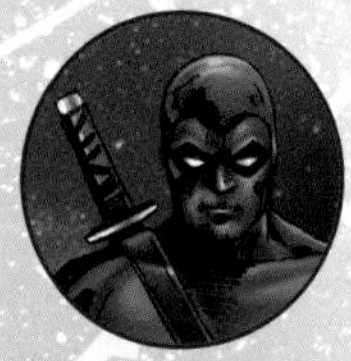

THE PHANTOM™

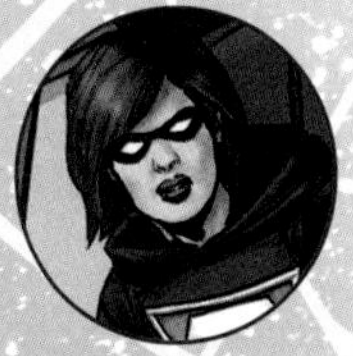

And...THE OTHER PHANTOM!?

Their home saved, our heroes strike out upon a new daring, spacefaring quest: Save one of their own from MING's dastardly clutches: The intrepid science reporter, DALE ARDEN!

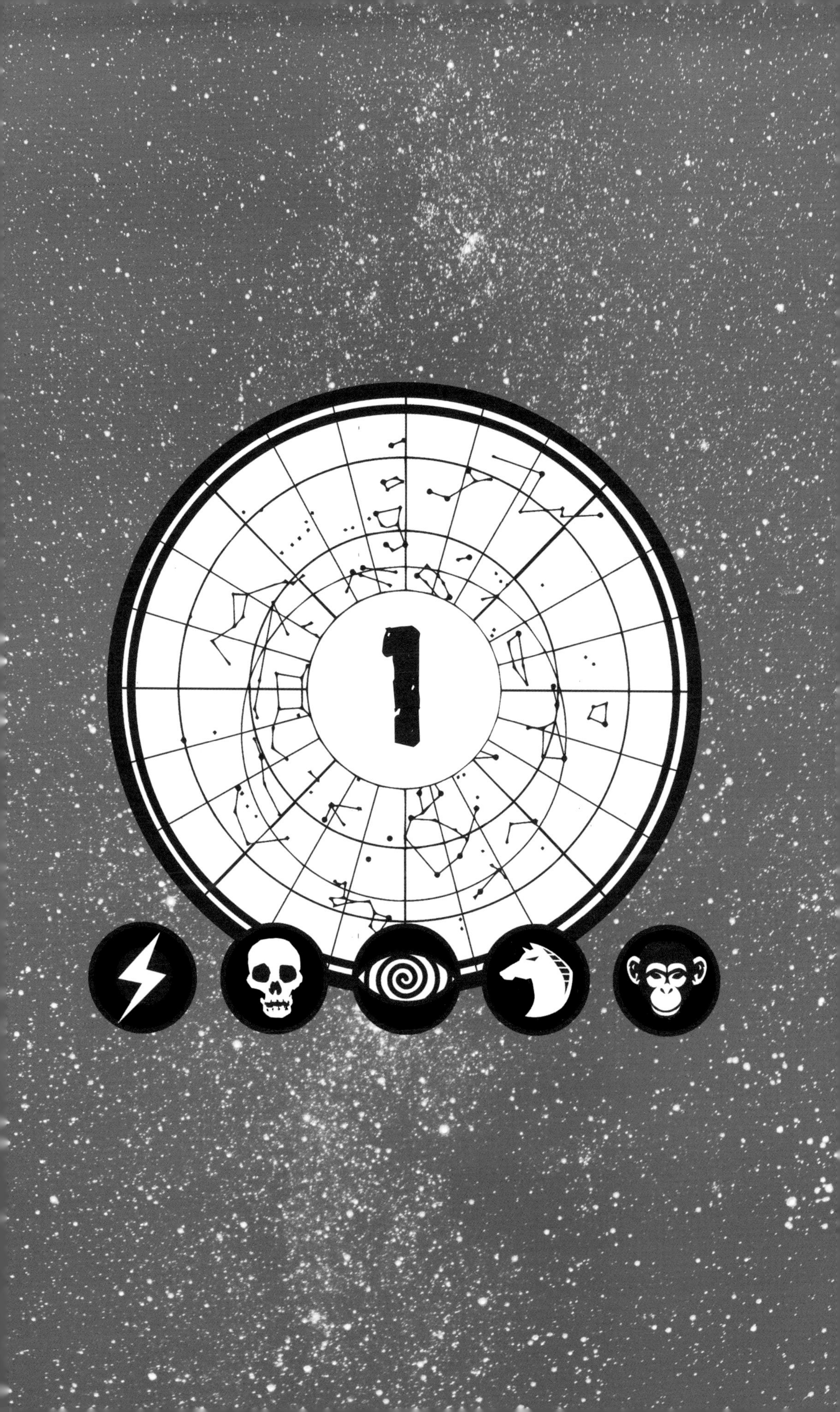
1

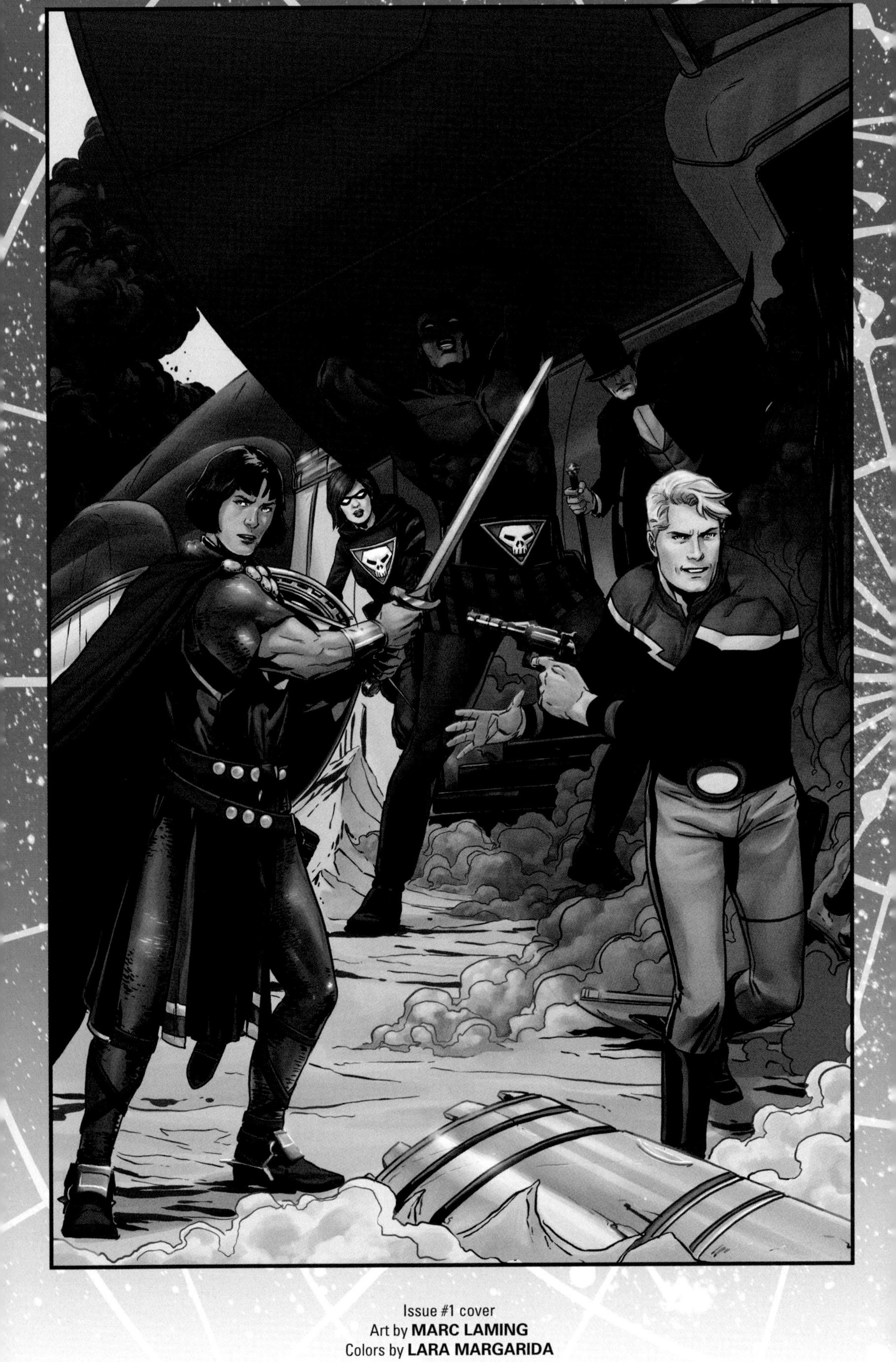

Issue #1 cover
Art by **MARC LAMING**
Colors by **LARA MARGARIDA**

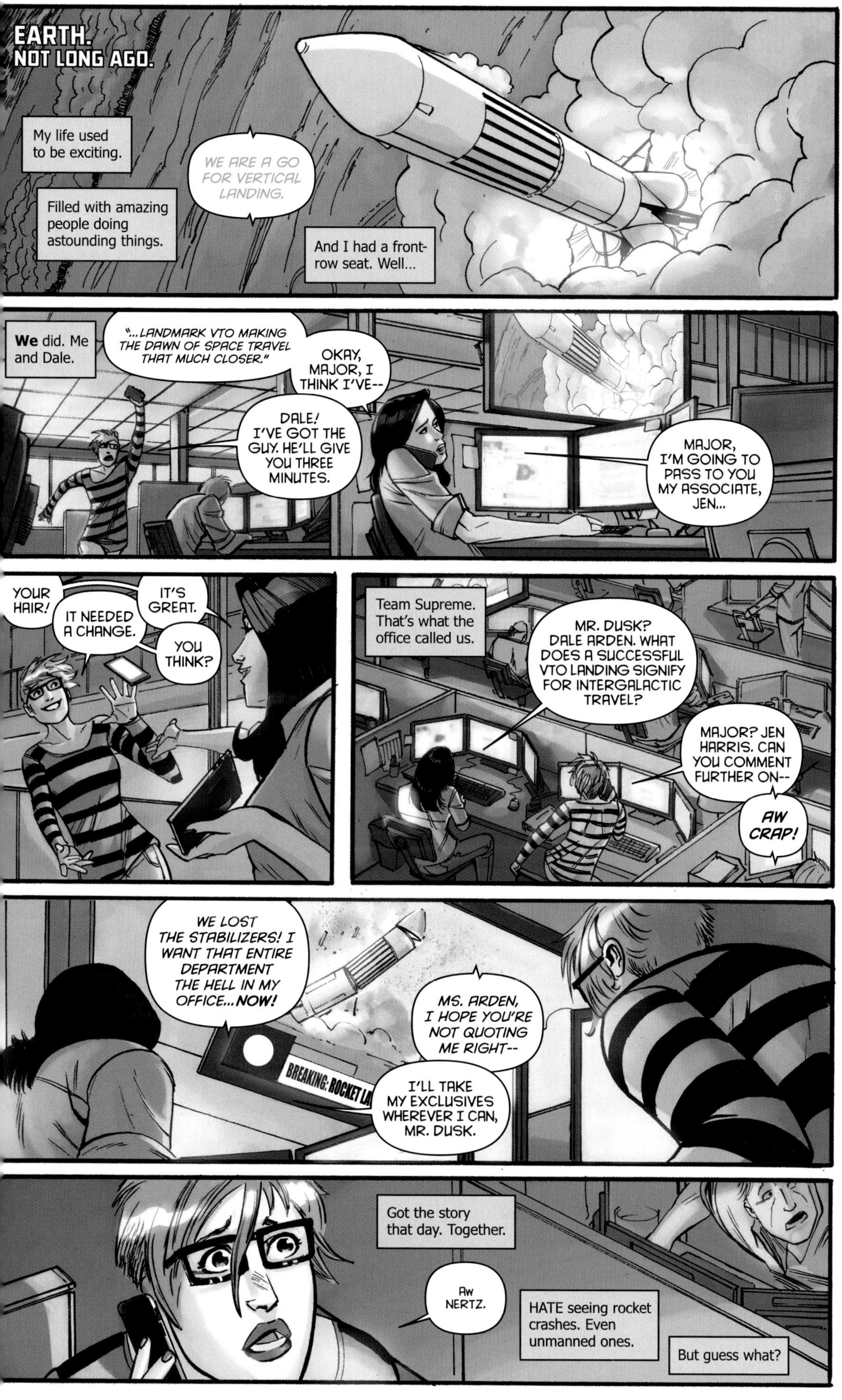
EARTH.
NOT LONG AGO.
My life used to be exciting.
Filled with amazing people doing astounding things.
WE ARE A GO FOR VERTICAL LANDING.
And I had a front-row seat. Well...
We did. Me and Dale.
"...LANDMARK VTO MAKING THE DAWN OF SPACE TRAVEL THAT MUCH CLOSER."
OKAY, MAJOR, I THINK I'VE--
DALE! I'VE GOT THE GUY. HE'LL GIVE YOU THREE MINUTES.
MAJOR, I'M GOING TO PASS TO YOU MY ASSOCIATE, JEN...
YOUR HAIR!
IT'S GREAT.
IT NEEDED A CHANGE.
YOU THINK?
Team Supreme. That's what the office called us.
MR. DUSK? DALE ARDEN. WHAT DOES A SUCCESSFUL VTO LANDING SIGNIFY FOR INTERGALACTIC TRAVEL?
MAJOR? JEN HARRIS. CAN YOU COMMENT FURTHER ON--
AW CRAP!
WE LOST THE STABILIZERS! I WANT THAT ENTIRE DEPARTMENT THE HELL IN MY OFFICE...**NOW!**
MS. ARDEN, I HOPE YOU'RE NOT QUOTING ME RIGHT--
BREAKING: ROCKET LA
I'LL TAKE MY EXCLUSIVES WHEREVER I CAN, MR. DUSK.
Got the story that day. Together.
AW NERTZ.
HATE seeing rocket crashes. Even unmanned ones.
But guess what?

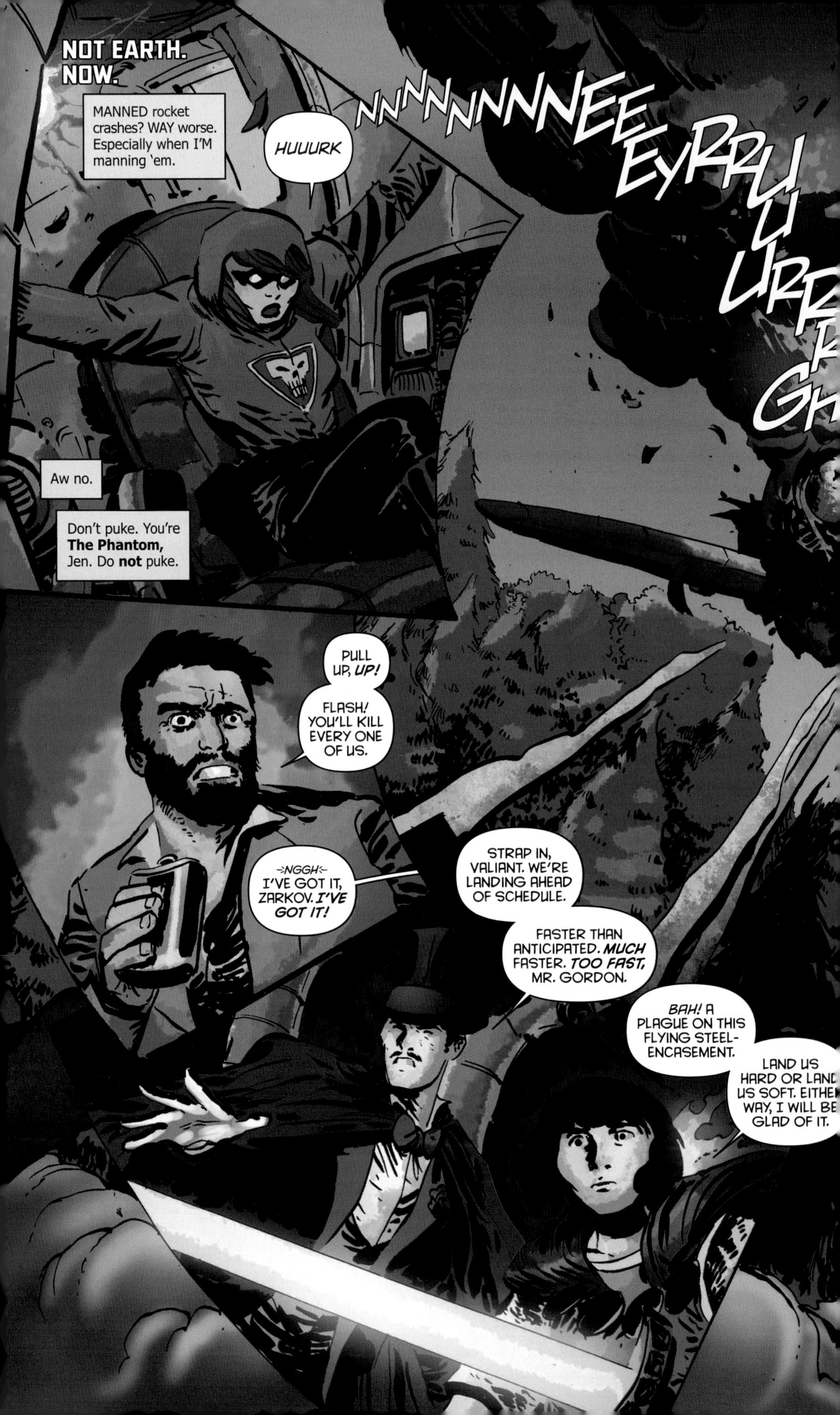
NOT EARTH.
NOW.
MANNED rocket crashes? WAY worse. Especially when I'M manning 'em.
HUUURK
NNNNNNNNNEEEYRRUUURRRGH
Aw no.
Don't puke. You're **The Phantom,** Jen. Do **not** puke.
PULL UP, *UP!*
FLASH! YOU'LL KILL EVERY ONE OF US.
NGGH I'VE GOT IT, ZARKOV. ***I'VE GOT IT!***
STRAP IN, VALIANT. WE'RE LANDING AHEAD OF SCHEDULE.
FASTER THAN ANTICIPATED. ***MUCH*** FASTER. ***TOO FAST,*** MR. GORDON.
BAH! A PLAGUE ON THIS FLYING STEEL-ENCASEMENT.
LAND US HARD OR LAND US SOFT. EITHER WAY, I WILL BE GLAD OF IT.

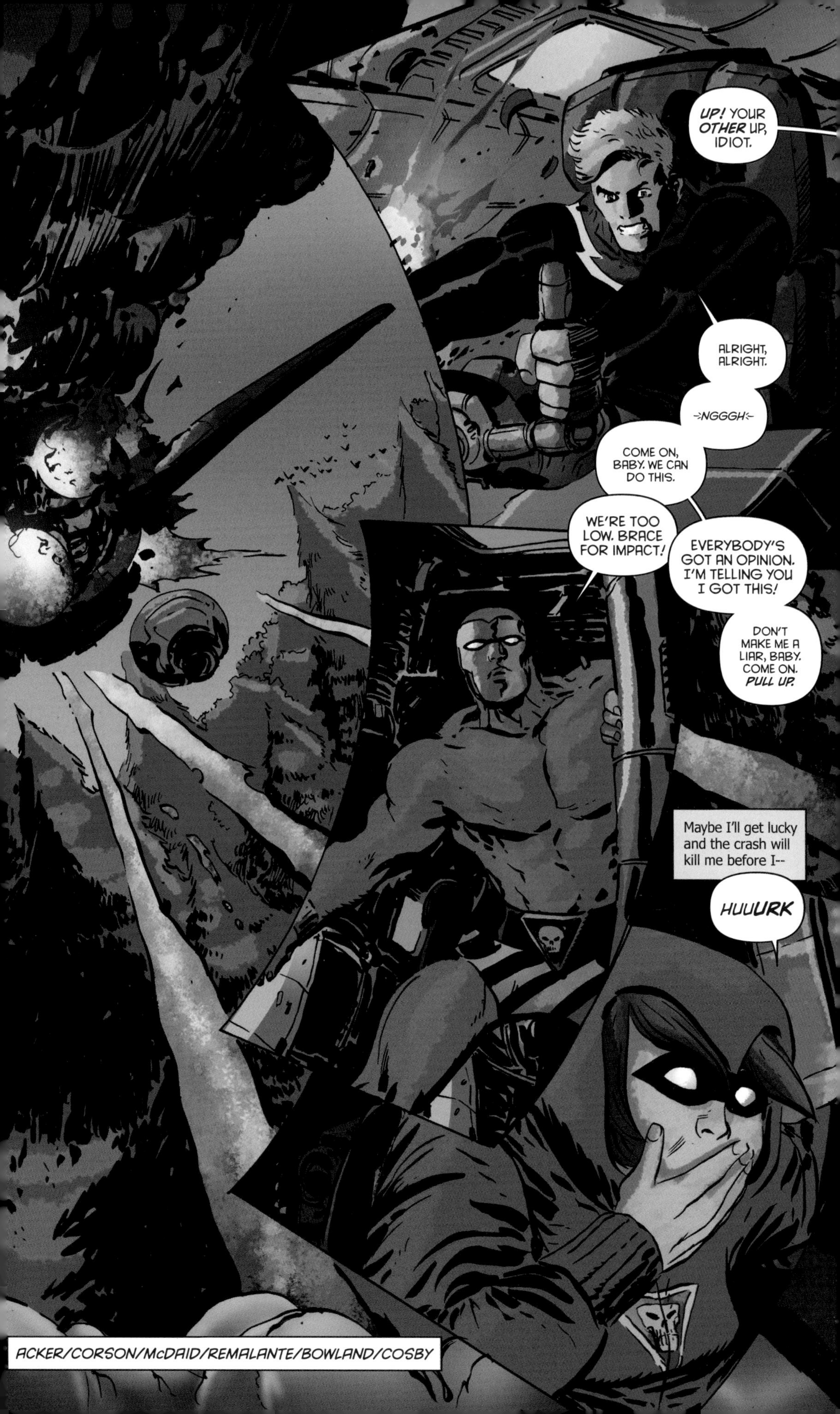

UP! YOUR *OTHER* UP, IDIOT.
ALRIGHT, ALRIGHT.
NGGGH
COME ON, BABY. WE CAN DO THIS.
WE'RE TOO LOW. BRACE FOR IMPACT!
EVERYBODY'S GOT AN OPINION. I'M TELLING YOU I GOT THIS!
DON'T MAKE ME A LIAR, BABY. COME ON. *PULL UP.*
Maybe I'll get lucky and the crash will kill me before I--
HUUURK
ACKER/CORSON/McDAID/REMALANTE/BOWLAND/COSBY

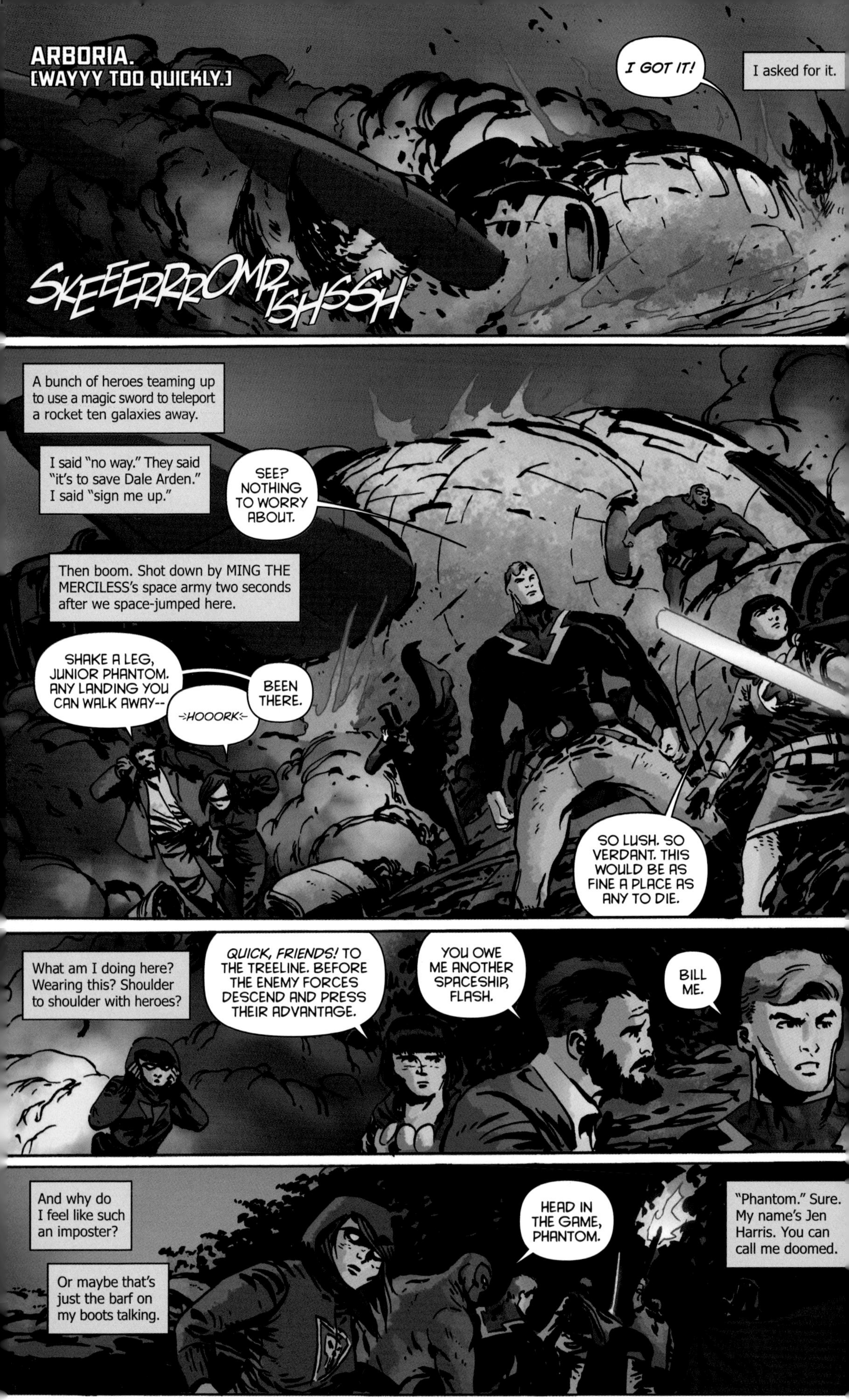
ARBORIA.
[WAYYY TOO QUICKLY.]
I GOT IT!
I asked for it.
SKEEEERRRROMPISHSSH
A bunch of heroes teaming up to use a magic sword to teleport a rocket ten galaxies away.
I said "no way." They said "it's to save Dale Arden." I said "sign me up."
SEE? NOTHING TO WORRY ABOUT.
Then boom. Shot down by MING THE MERCILESS's space army two seconds after we space-jumped here.
SHAKE A LEG, JUNIOR PHANTOM. ANY LANDING YOU CAN WALK AWAY--
BEEN THERE.
HOOORK
SO LUSH. SO VERDANT. THIS WOULD BE AS FINE A PLACE AS ANY TO DIE.
What am I doing here? Wearing this? Shoulder to shoulder with heroes?
QUICK, FRIENDS! TO THE TREELINE. BEFORE THE ENEMY FORCES DESCEND AND PRESS THEIR ADVANTAGE.
YOU OWE ME ANOTHER SPACESHIP, FLASH.
BILL ME.
And why do I feel like such an imposter?
Or maybe that's just the barf on my boots talking.
HEAD IN THE GAME, PHANTOM.
"Phantom." Sure. My name's Jen Harris. You can call me doomed.

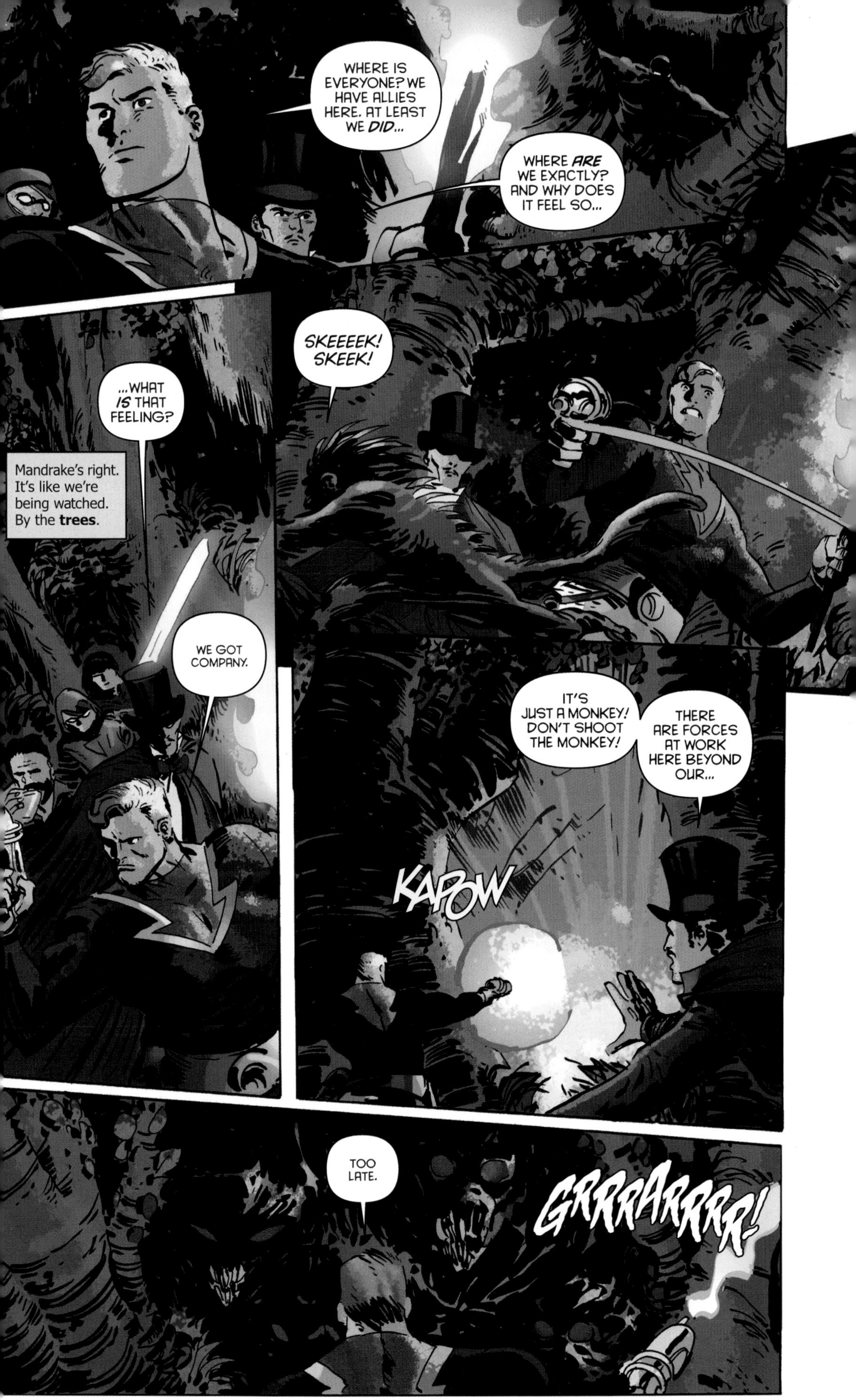
WHERE IS EVERYONE? WE HAVE ALLIES HERE. AT LEAST WE *DID*...
WHERE *ARE* WE EXACTLY? AND WHY DOES IT FEEL SO...
...WHAT *IS* THAT FEELING?
Mandrake's right. It's like we're being watched. By the **trees**.
SKEEEEK! SKEEK!
WE GOT COMPANY.
IT'S JUST A MONKEY! DON'T SHOOT THE MONKEY!
THERE ARE FORCES AT WORK HERE BEYOND OUR...
KAPOW
TOO LATE.
GRRRARRRR!

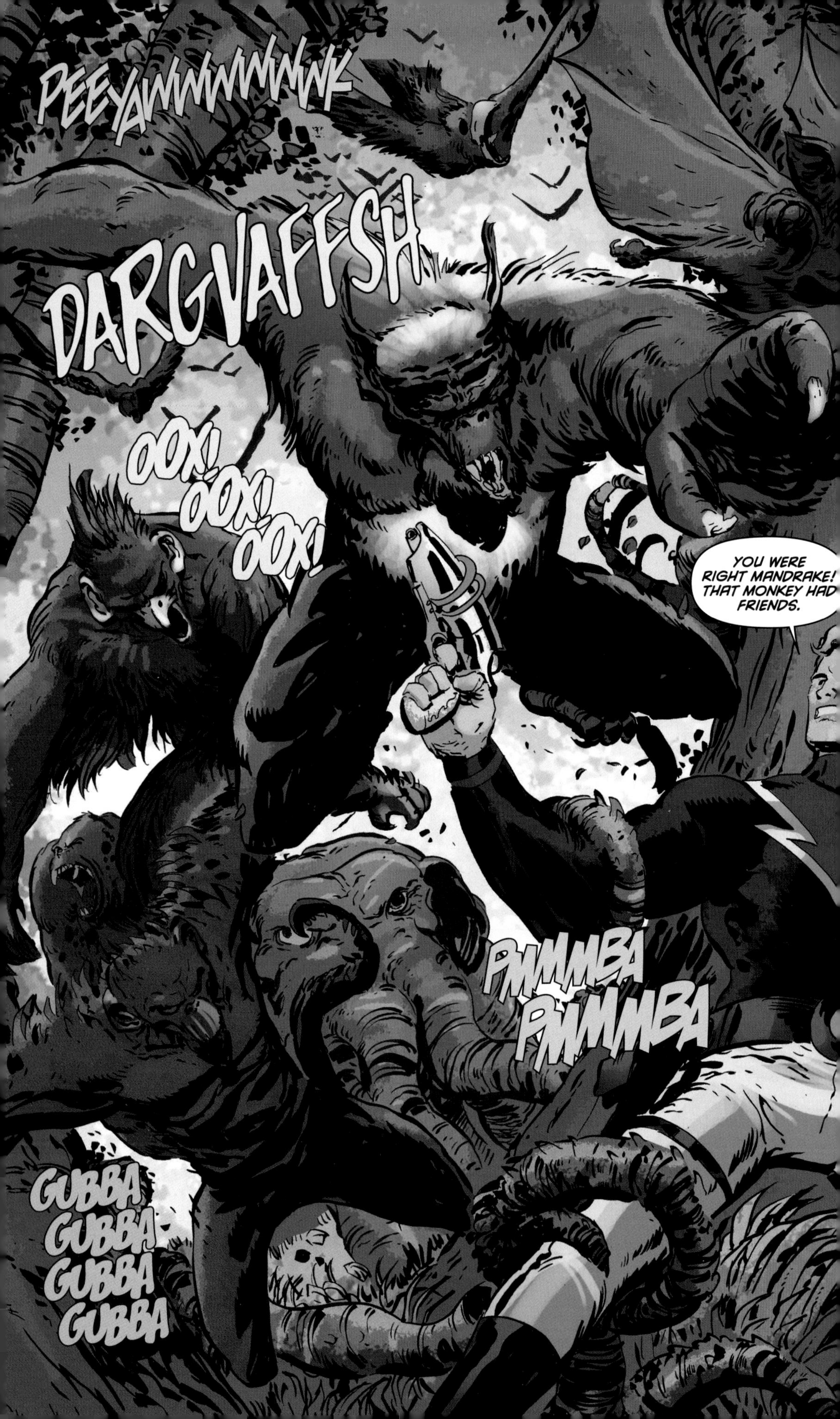
PEEYAWWWWWWK
DARGVAFFSH
OOX! OOX! OOX!
YOU WERE RIGHT MANDRAKE! THAT MONKEY HAD FRIENDS.
PWWMBA PWWMBA
GUBBA GUBBA GUBBA GUBBA

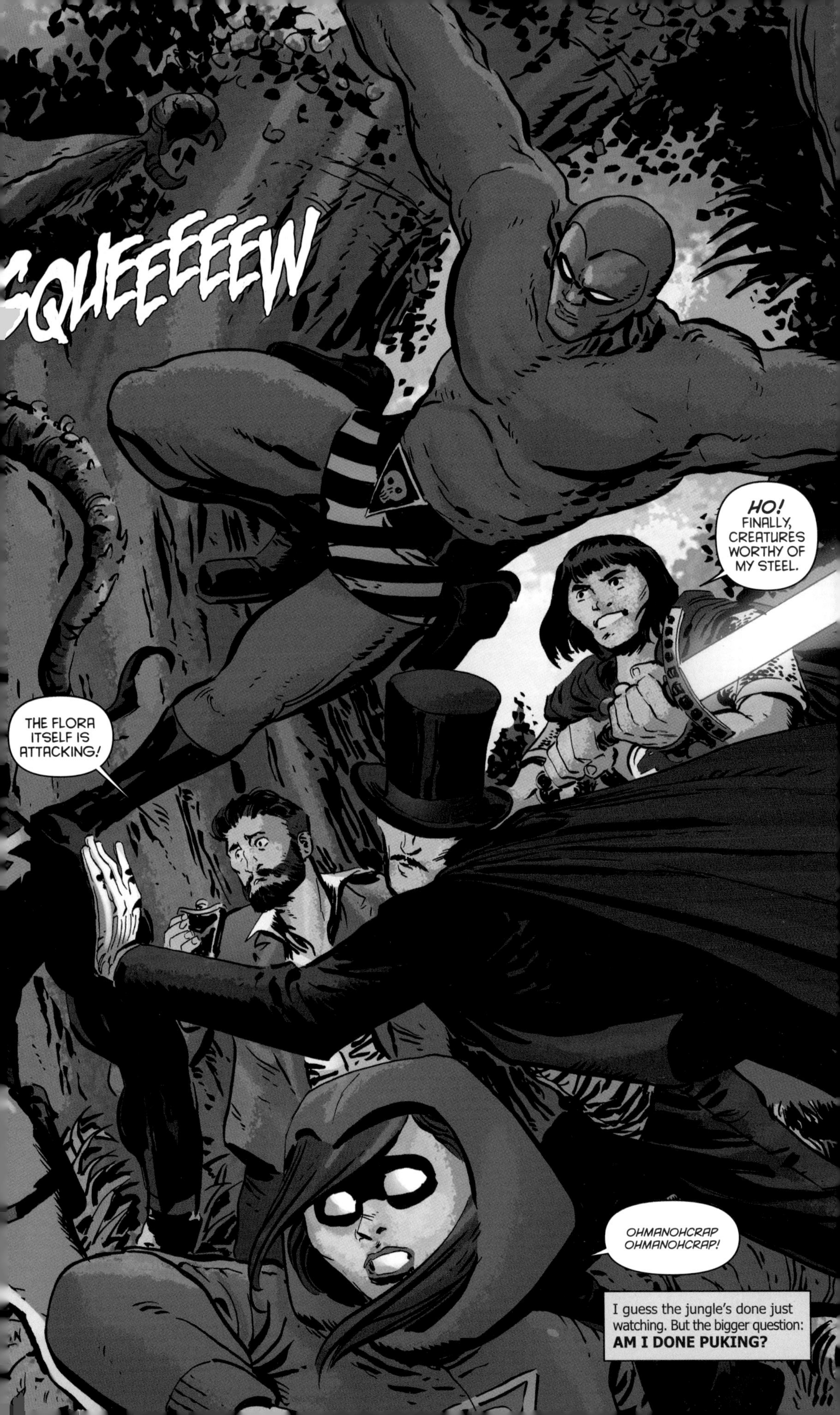
SQUEEEEEW
HO! FINALLY, CREATURES WORTHY OF MY STEEL.
THE FLORA ITSELF IS ATTACKING!
OHMANOHCRAP OHMANOHCRAP!
I guess the jungle's done just watching. But the bigger question:
AM I DONE PUKING?

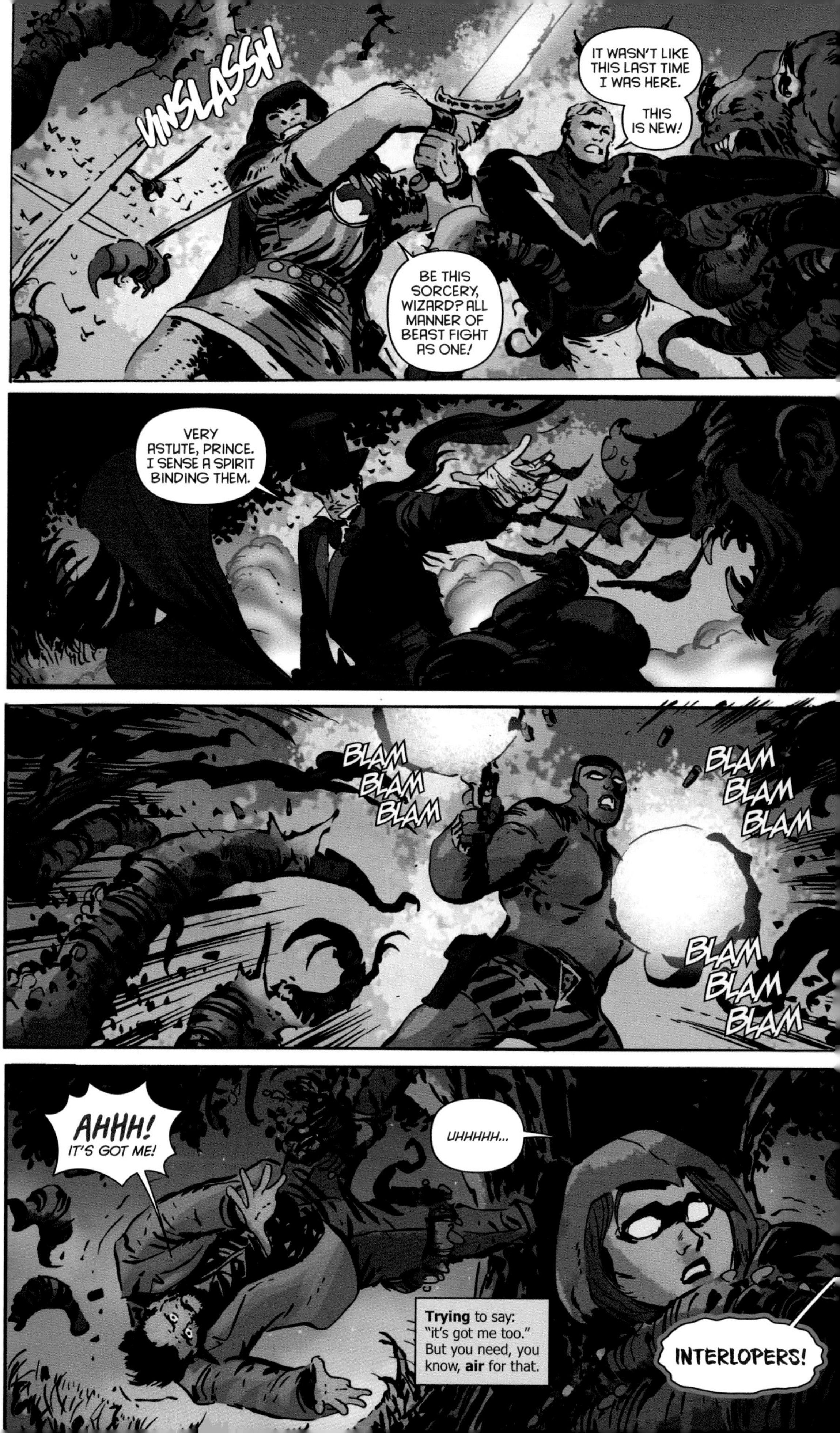

VINSLASSH
IT WASN'T LIKE THIS LAST TIME I WAS HERE.
THIS IS NEW!
BE THIS SORCERY, WIZARD? ALL MANNER OF BEAST FIGHT AS ONE!
VERY ASTUTE, PRINCE. I SENSE A SPIRIT BINDING THEM.
BLAM BLAM BLAM
BLAM BLAM BLAM
BLAM BLAM BLAM
AHHH! IT'S GOT ME!
UHHHHH...
Trying to say: "it's got me too." But you need, you know, air for that.
INTERLOPERS!

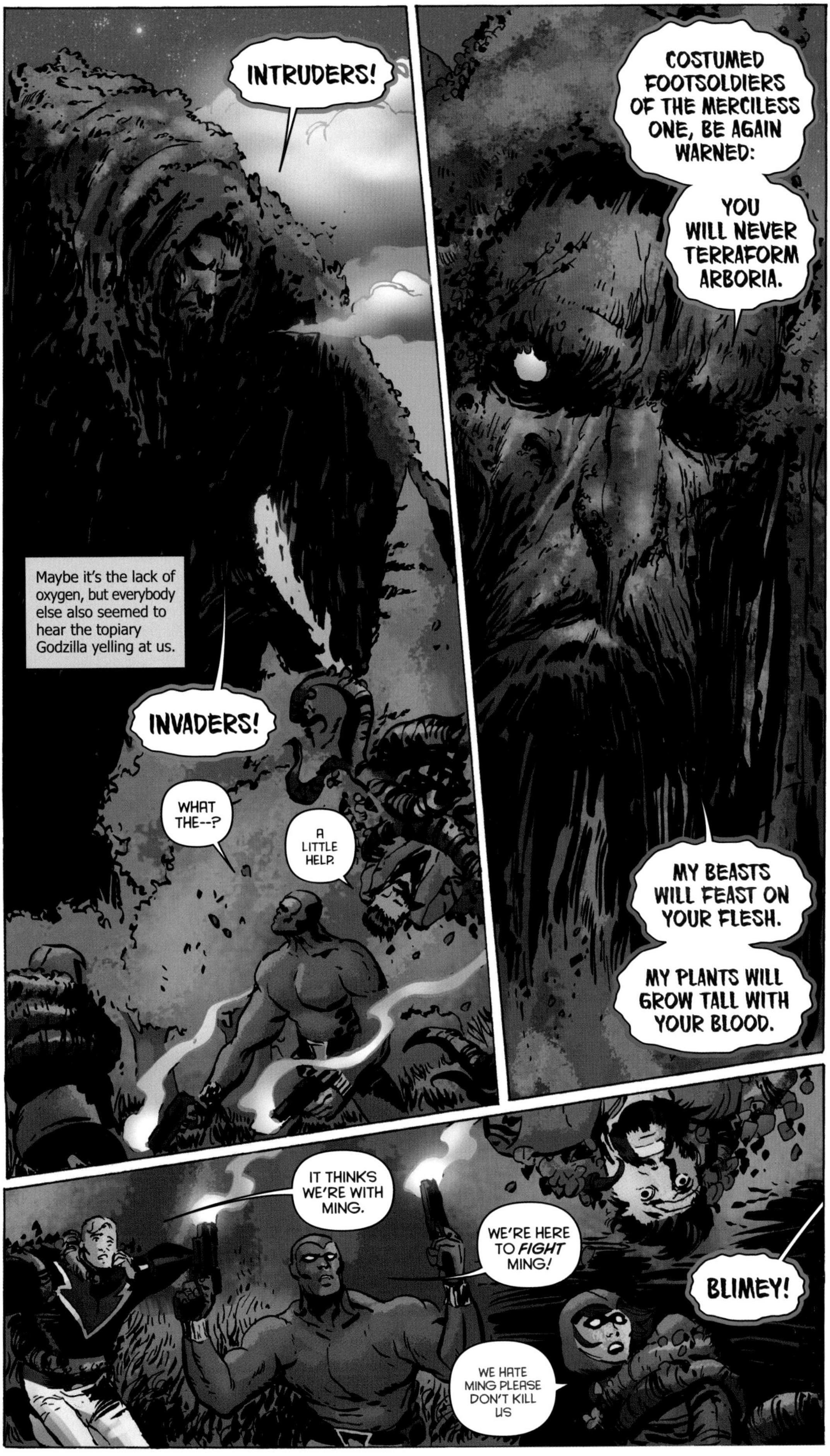
INTRUDERS!
Maybe it's the lack of oxygen, but everybody else also seemed to hear the topiary Godzilla yelling at us.
INVADERS!
WHAT THE--?
A LITTLE HELP.
COSTUMED FOOTSOLDIERS OF THE MERCILESS ONE, BE AGAIN WARNED:
YOU WILL NEVER TERRAFORM ARBORIA.
MY BEASTS WILL FEAST ON YOUR FLESH.
MY PLANTS WILL GROW TALL WITH YOUR BLOOD.
IT THINKS WE'RE WITH MING.
WE'RE HERE TO *FIGHT* MING!
WE HATE MING PLEASE DON'T KILL US
BLIMEY!

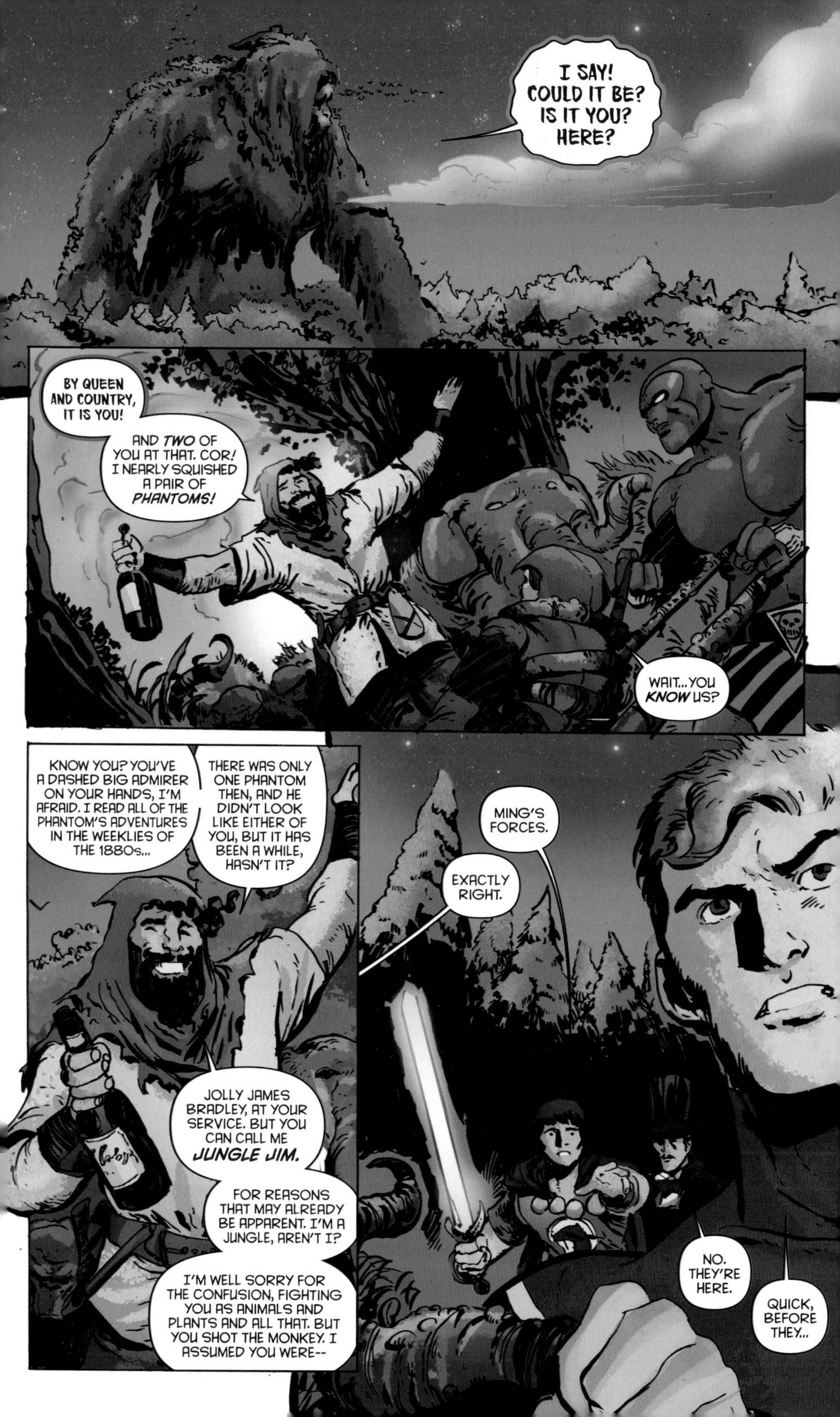
I SAY! COULD IT BE? IS IT YOU? HERE?
BY QUEEN AND COUNTRY, IT IS YOU!
AND TWO OF YOU AT THAT. COR! I NEARLY SQUISHED A PAIR OF PHANTOMS!
WAIT...YOU KNOW US?
KNOW YOU? YOU'VE A DASHED BIG ADMIRER ON YOUR HANDS, I'M AFRAID. I READ ALL OF THE PHANTOM'S ADVENTURES IN THE WEEKLIES OF THE 1880s...
THERE WAS ONLY ONE PHANTOM THEN, AND HE DIDN'T LOOK LIKE EITHER OF YOU, BUT IT HAS BEEN A WHILE, HASN'T IT?
JOLLY JAMES BRADLEY, AT YOUR SERVICE. BUT YOU CAN CALL ME JUNGLE JIM.
FOR REASONS THAT MAY ALREADY BE APPARENT. I'M A JUNGLE, AREN'T I?
I'M WELL SORRY FOR THE CONFUSION, FIGHTING YOU AS ANIMALS AND PLANTS AND ALL THAT. BUT YOU SHOT THE MONKEY. I ASSUMED YOU WERE--
MING'S FORCES.
EXACTLY RIGHT.
NO. THEY'RE HERE.
QUICK, BEFORE THEY...

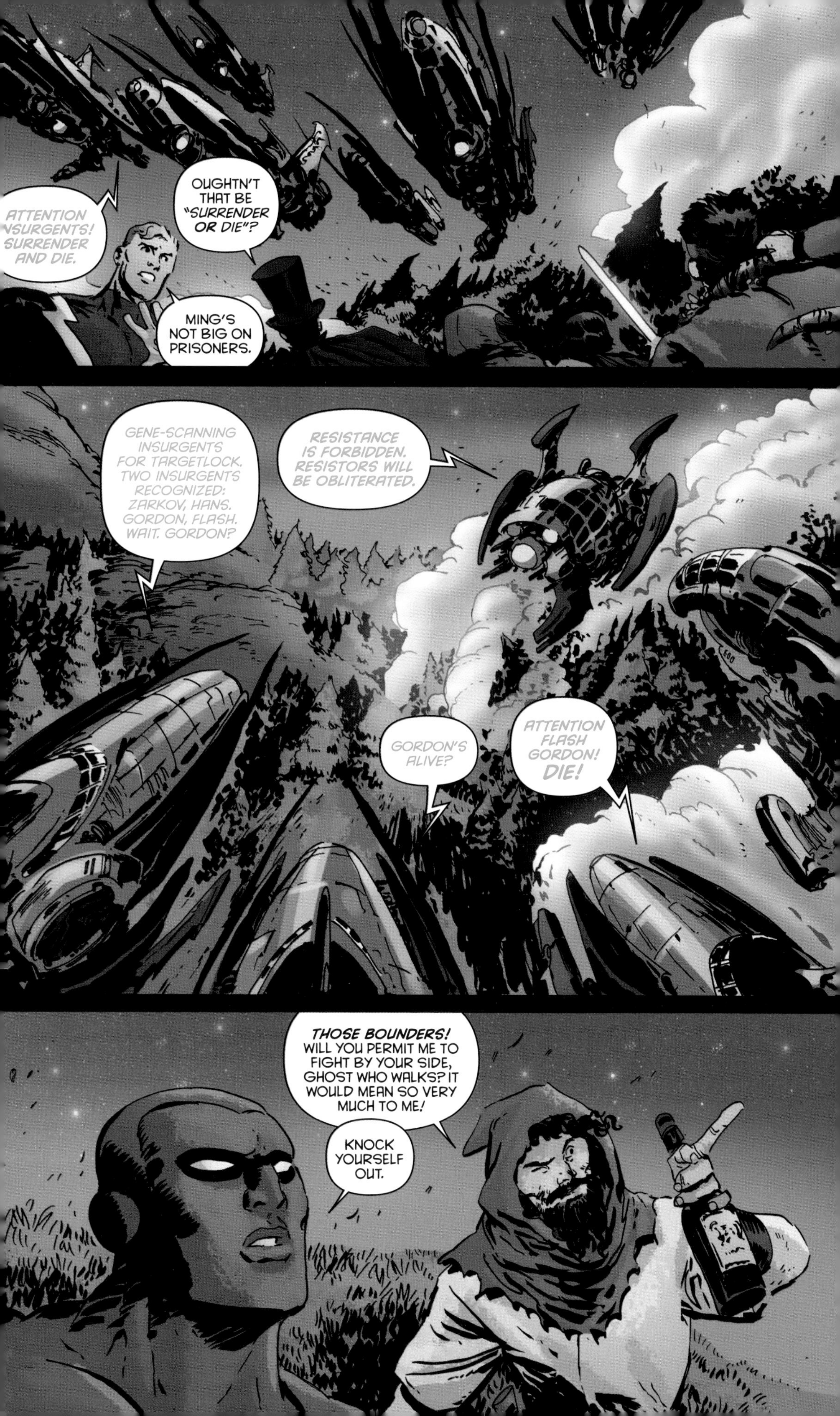
ATTENTION NSURGENTS! SURRENDER AND DIE.
OUGHTN'T THAT BE "SURRENDER OR DIE"?
MING'S NOT BIG ON PRISONERS.
GENE-SCANNING INSURGENTS FOR TARGETLOCK. TWO INSURGENTS RECOGNIZED: ZARKOV, HANS. GORDON, FLASH. WAIT. GORDON?
RESISTANCE IS FORBIDDEN. RESISTORS WILL BE OBLITERATED.
GORDON'S ALIVE?
ATTENTION FLASH GORDON! DIE!
THOSE BOUNDERS! WILL YOU PERMIT ME TO FIGHT BY YOUR SIDE, GHOST WHO WALKS? IT WOULD MEAN SO VERY MUCH TO ME!
KNOCK YOURSELF OUT.

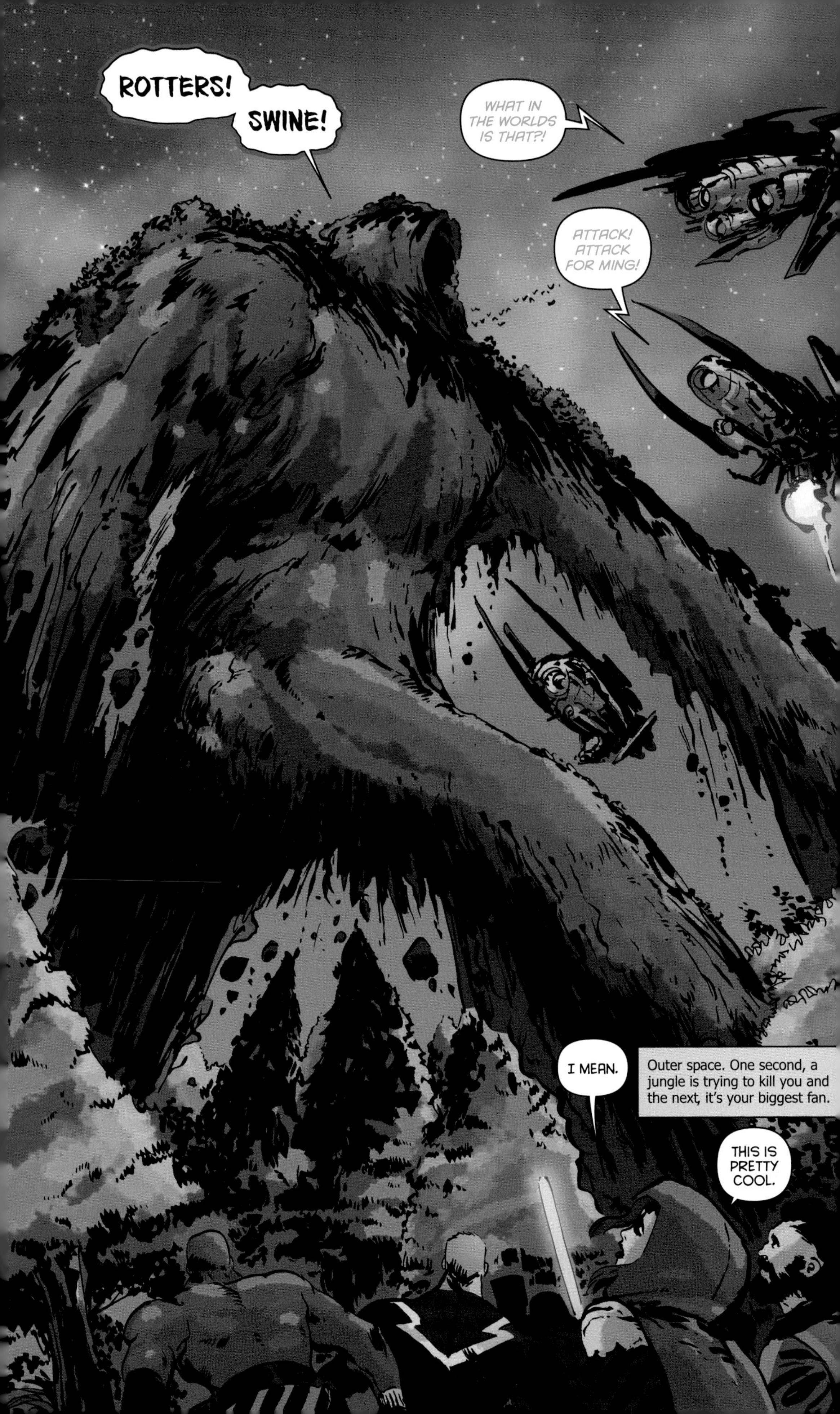
ROTTERS!
SWINE!
WHAT IN THE WORLDS IS THAT?!
ATTACK! ATTACK FOR MING!
I MEAN.
Outer space. One second, a jungle is trying to kill you and the next, it's your biggest fan.
THIS IS PRETTY COOL.

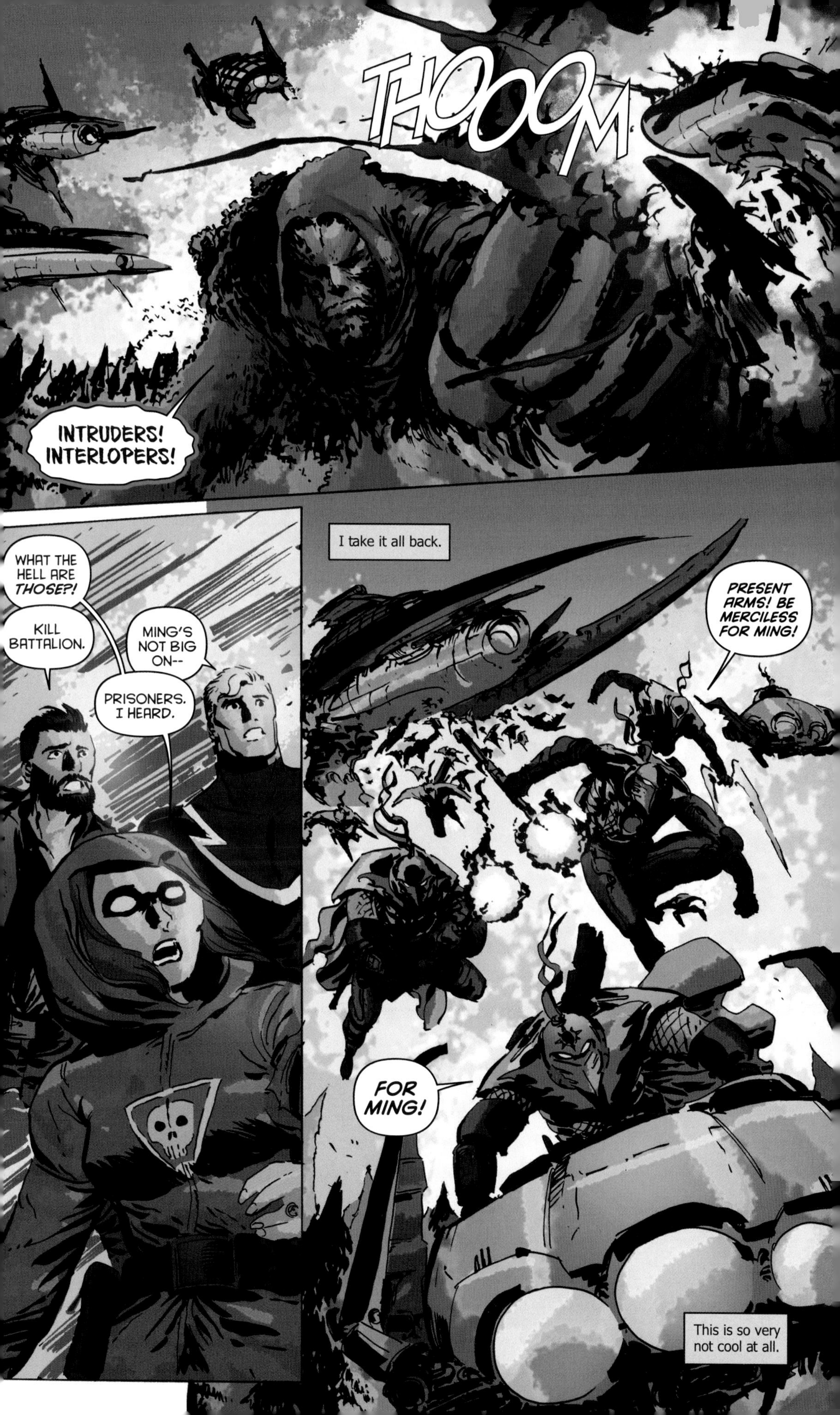
THOOOM
INTRUDERS! INTERLOPERS!
WHAT THE HELL ARE *THOSE?!*
KILL BATTALION.
MING'S NOT BIG ON--
PRISONERS. I HEARD.
I take it all back.
PRESENT ARMS! BE MERCILESS FOR MING!
FOR MING!
This is so very not cool at all.

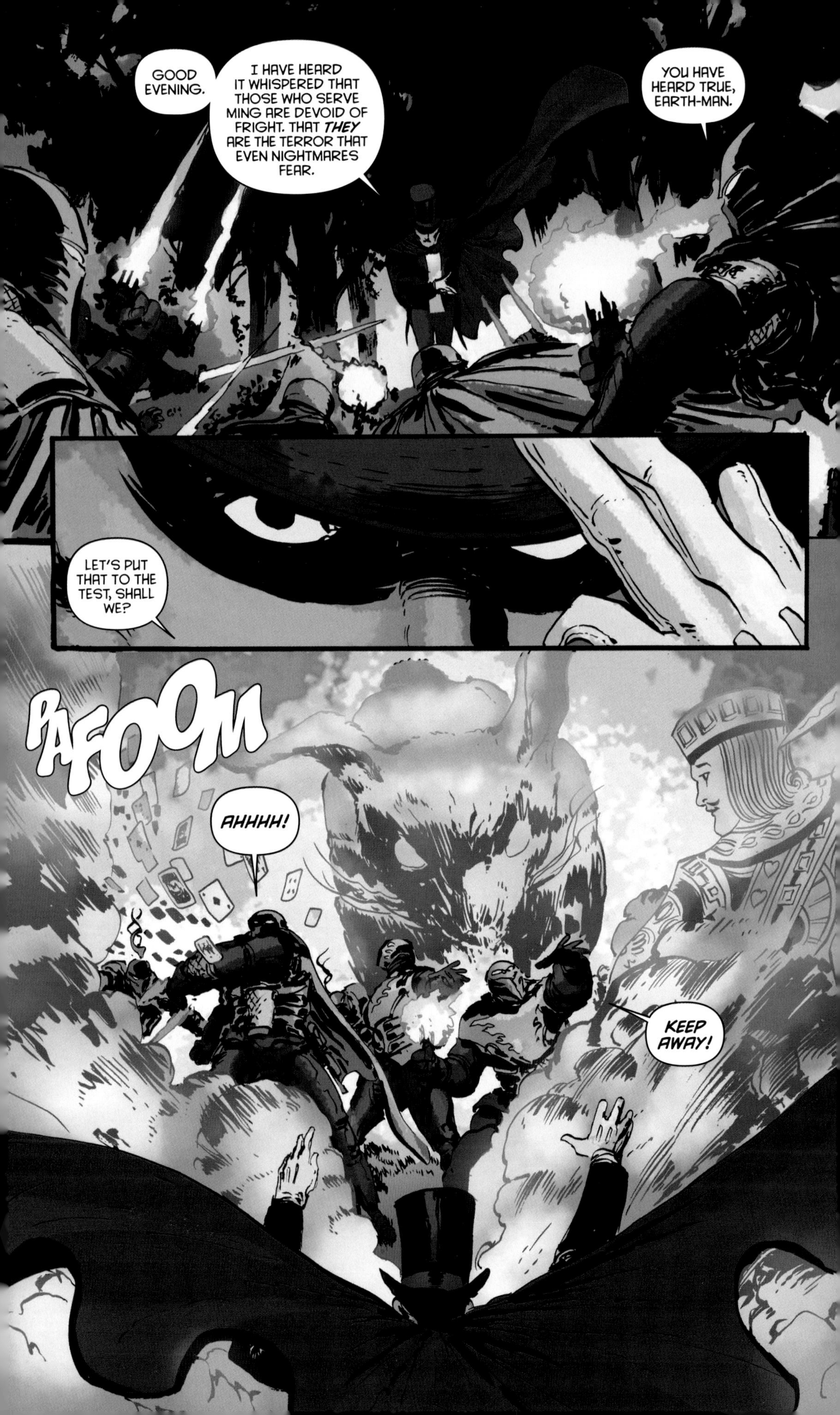
GOOD EVENING.
I HAVE HEARD IT WHISPERED THAT THOSE WHO SERVE MING ARE DEVOID OF FRIGHT. THAT *THEY* ARE THE TERROR THAT EVEN NIGHTMARES FEAR.
YOU HAVE HEARD TRUE, EARTH-MAN.
LET'S PUT THAT TO THE TEST, SHALL WE?
PAFOOM
AHHHH!
KEEP AWAY!

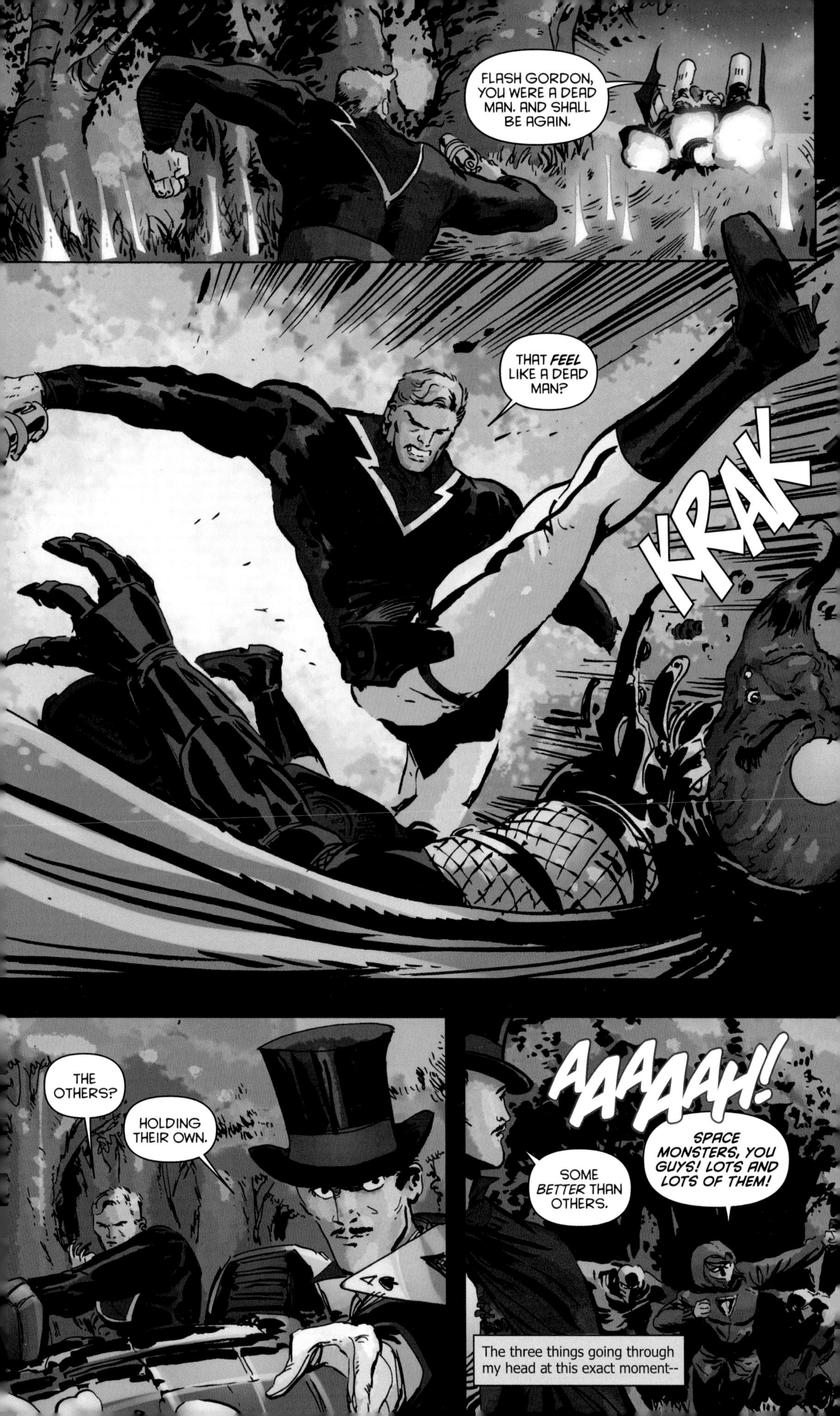
FLASH GORDON, YOU WERE A DEAD MAN. AND SHALL BE AGAIN.
THAT *FEEL* LIKE A DEAD MAN?
KRAK
THE OTHERS?
HOLDING THEIR OWN.
AAAAAAH!
SOME *BETTER* THAN OTHERS.
SPACE MONSTERS, YOU GUYS! LOTS AND LOTS OF THEM!
The three things going through my head at this exact moment--

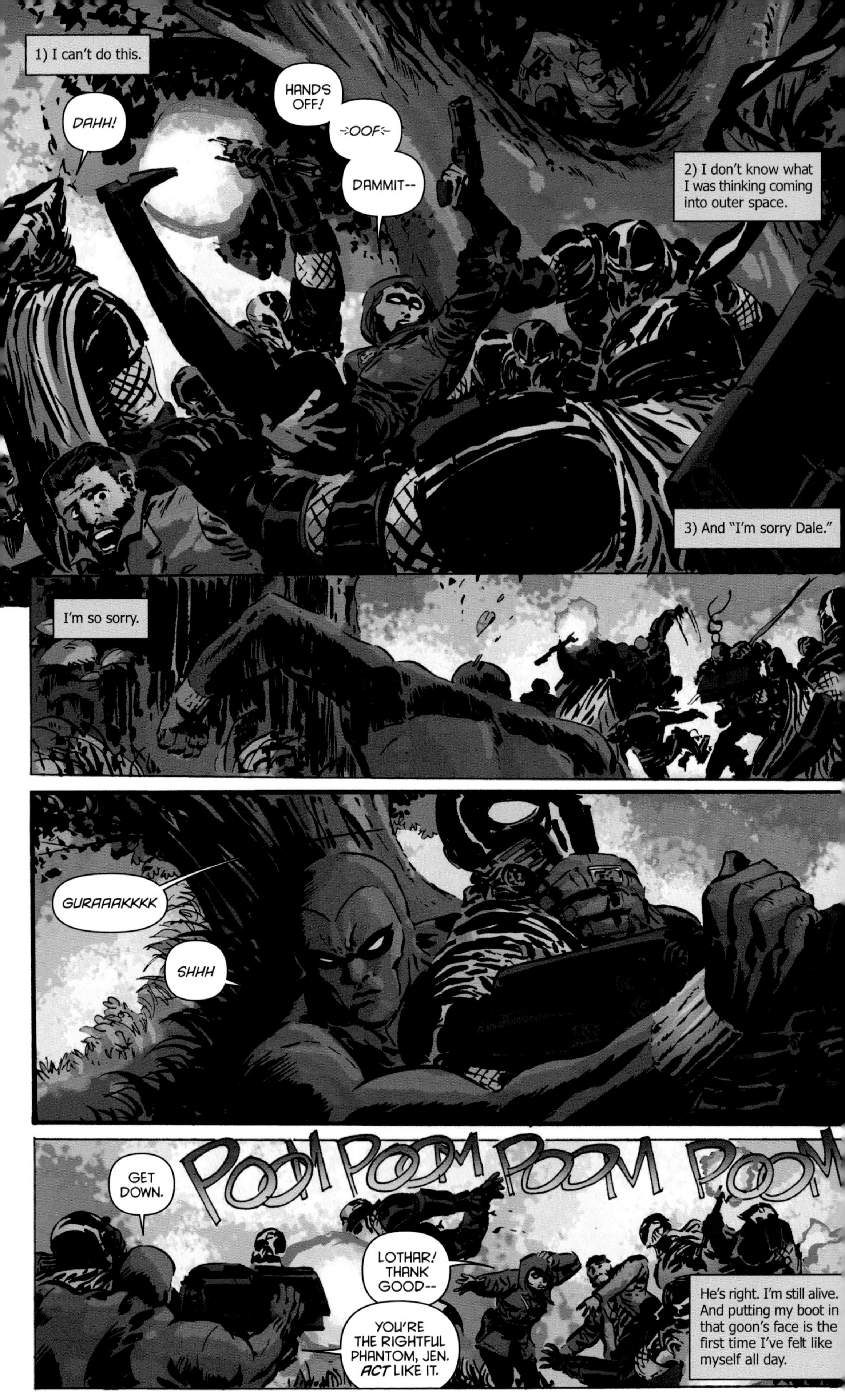
1) I can't do this.
DAHH!
HANDS OFF!
OOF
DAMMIT--
2) I don't know what I was thinking coming into outer space.
3) And "I'm sorry Dale."
I'm so sorry.
GURAAAKKKK
SHHH
GET DOWN.
POOM POOM POOM POOM
LOTHAR! THANK GOOD--
YOU'RE THE RIGHTFUL PHANTOM, JEN. ACT LIKE IT.
He's right. I'm still alive. And putting my boot in that goon's face is the first time I've felt like myself all day.

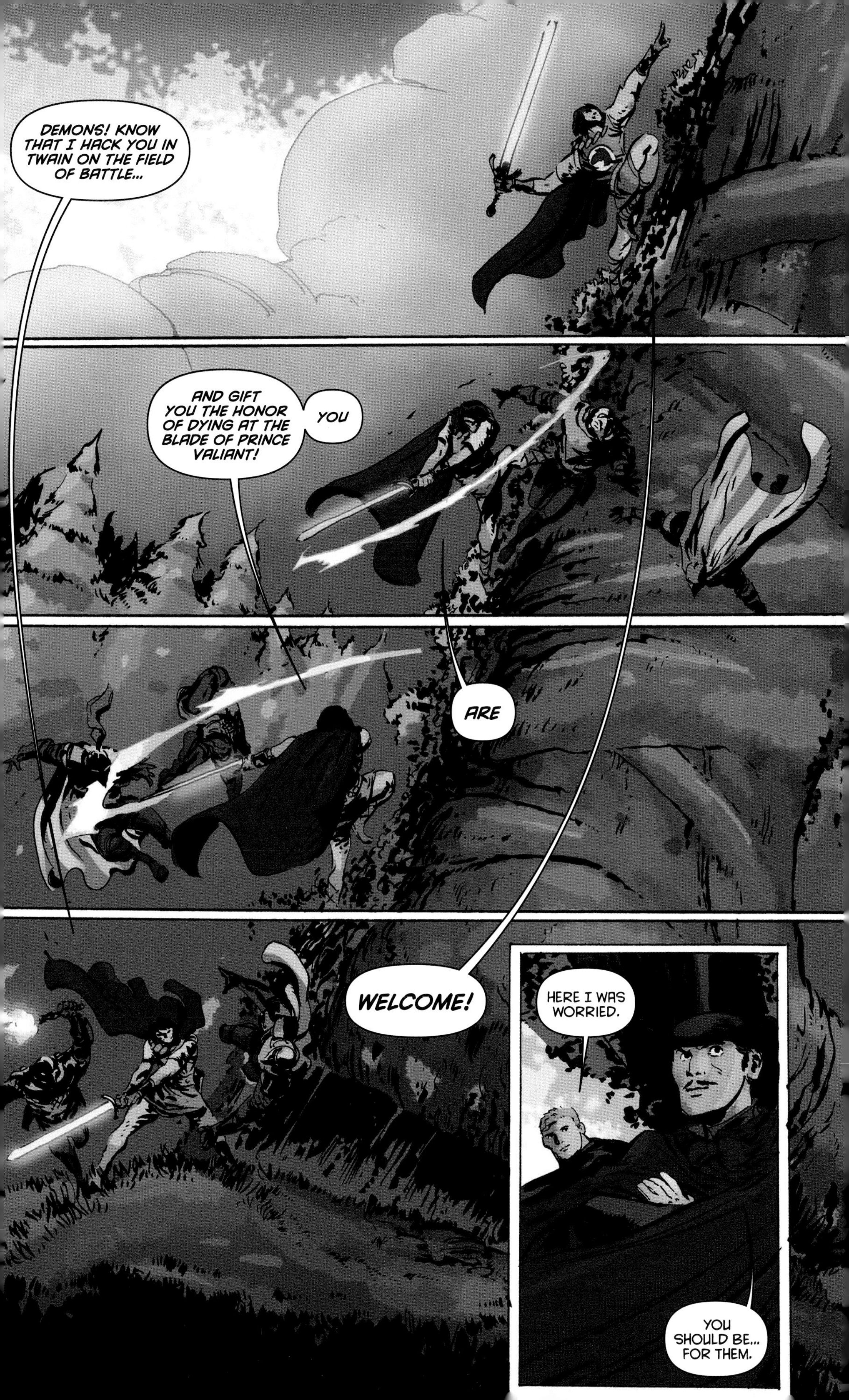
DEMONS! KNOW THAT I HACK YOU IN TWAIN ON THE FIELD OF BATTLE...
AND GIFT YOU THE HONOR OF DYING AT THE BLADE OF PRINCE VALIANT!
YOU
ARE
WELCOME!
HERE I WAS WORRIED.
YOU SHOULD BE... FOR THEM.

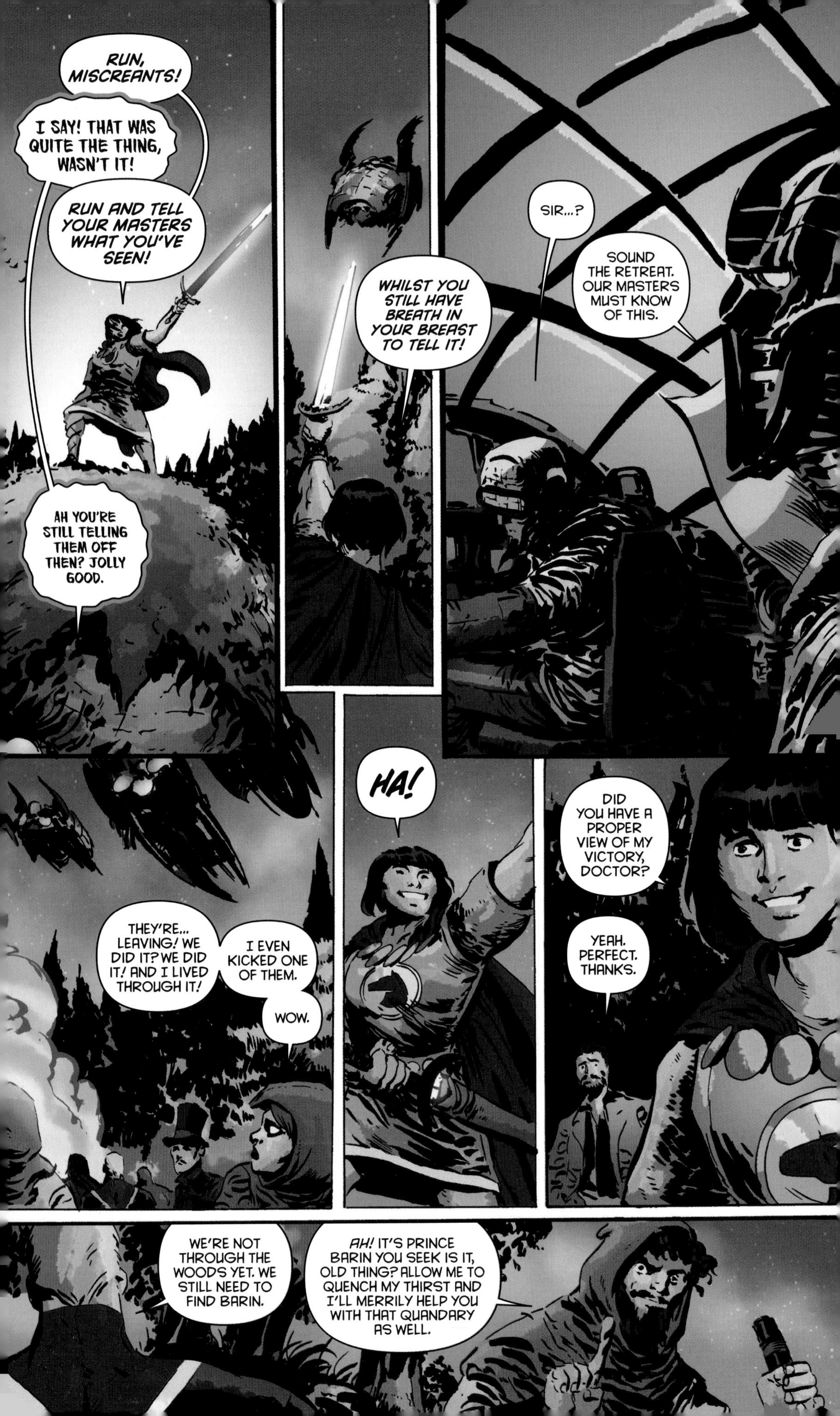
RUN, MISCREANTS!
I SAY! THAT WAS QUITE THE THING, WASN'T IT!
RUN AND TELL YOUR MASTERS WHAT YOU'VE SEEN!
AH YOU'RE STILL TELLING THEM OFF THEN? JOLLY GOOD.
WHILST YOU STILL HAVE BREATH IN YOUR BREAST TO TELL IT!
SIR...?
SOUND THE RETREAT. OUR MASTERS MUST KNOW OF THIS.
THEY'RE... LEAVING! WE DID IT? WE DID IT! AND I LIVED THROUGH IT!
I EVEN KICKED ONE OF THEM.
WOW.
HA!
DID YOU HAVE A PROPER VIEW OF MY VICTORY, DOCTOR?
YEAH. PERFECT. THANKS.
WE'RE NOT THROUGH THE WOODS YET. WE STILL NEED TO FIND BARIN.
AH! IT'S PRINCE BARIN YOU SEEK IS IT, OLD THING? ALLOW ME TO QUENCH MY THIRST AND I'LL MERRILY HELP YOU WITH THAT QUANDARY AS WELL.

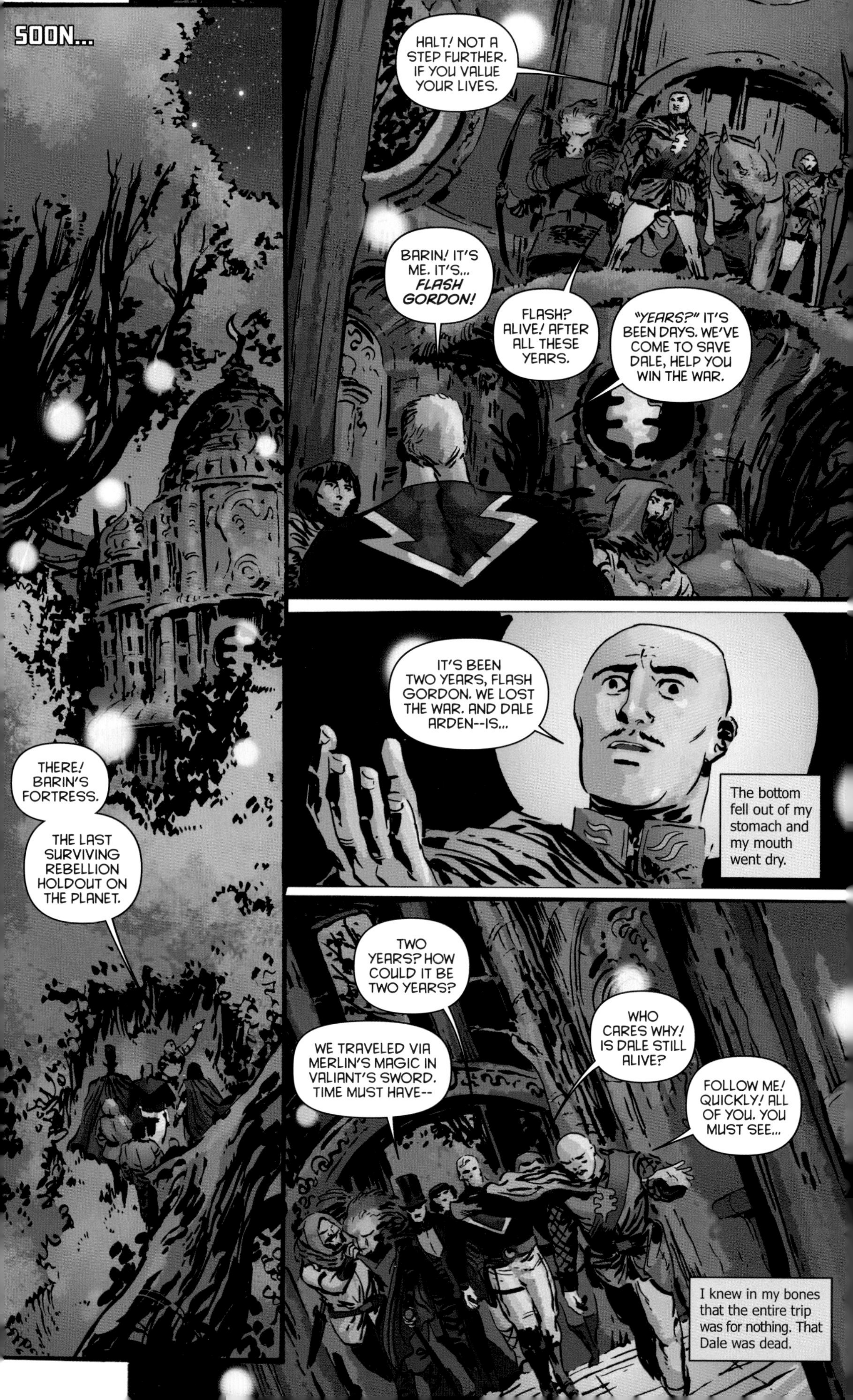
SOON...
THERE! BARIN'S FORTRESS.
THE LAST SURVIVING REBELLION HOLDOUT ON THE PLANET.
HALT! NOT A STEP FURTHER. IF YOU VALUE YOUR LIVES.
BARIN! IT'S ME. IT'S... FLASH GORDON!
FLASH? ALIVE! AFTER ALL THESE YEARS.
"YEARS?" IT'S BEEN DAYS. WE'VE COME TO SAVE DALE, HELP YOU WIN THE WAR.
IT'S BEEN TWO YEARS, FLASH GORDON. WE LOST THE WAR. AND DALE ARDEN--IS...
The bottom fell out of my stomach and my mouth went dry.
TWO YEARS? HOW COULD IT BE TWO YEARS?
WE TRAVELED VIA MERLIN'S MAGIC IN VALIANT'S SWORD. TIME MUST HAVE--
WHO CARES WHY! IS DALE STILL ALIVE?
FOLLOW ME! QUICKLY! ALL OF YOU. YOU MUST SEE...
I knew in my bones that the entire trip was for nothing. That Dale was dead.

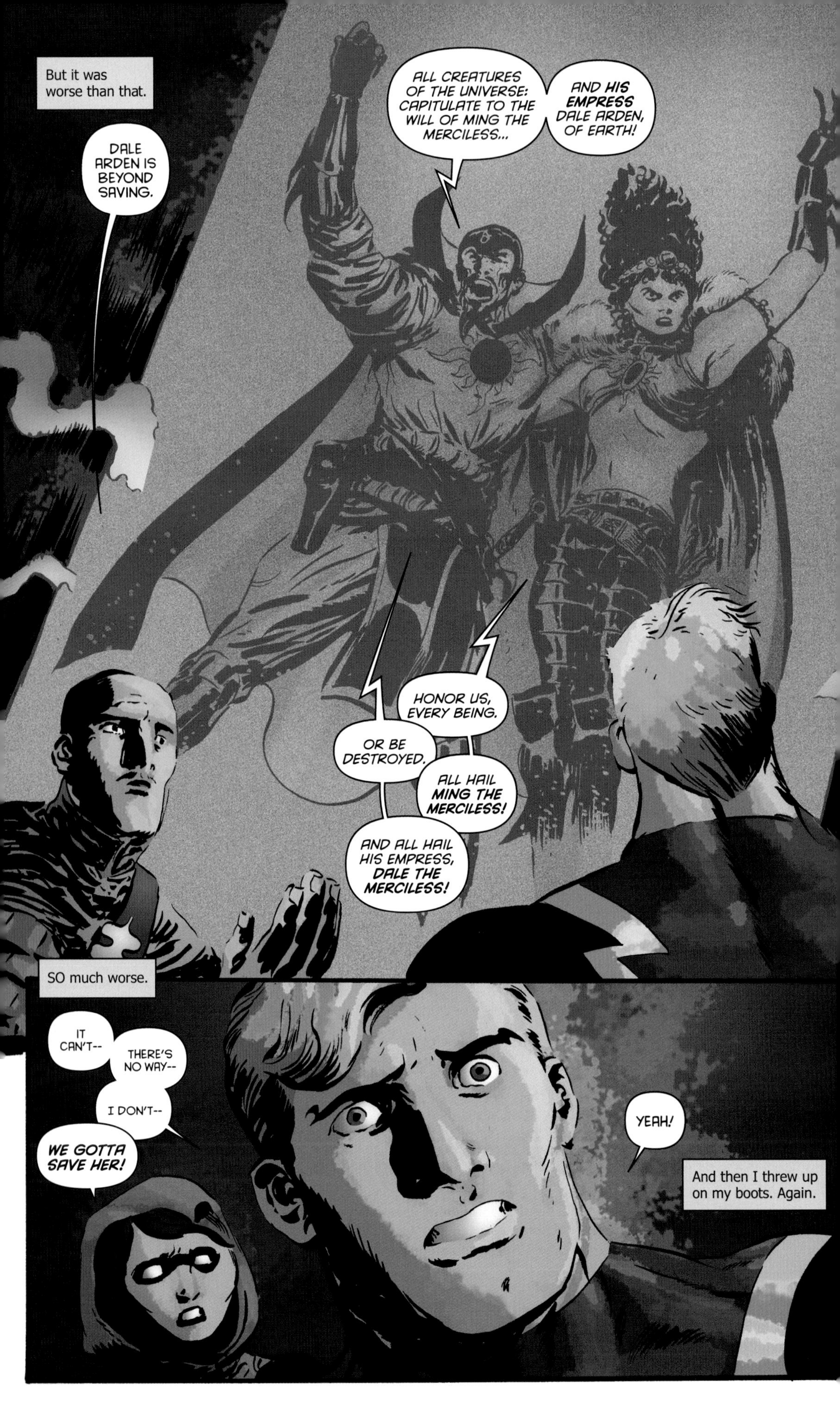
But it was worse than that.
DALE ARDEN IS BEYOND SAVING.
ALL CREATURES OF THE UNIVERSE: CAPITULATE TO THE WILL OF MING THE MERCILESS...
AND HIS EMPRESS DALE ARDEN, OF EARTH!
HONOR US, EVERY BEING.
OR BE DESTROYED.
ALL HAIL MING THE MERCILESS!
AND ALL HAIL HIS EMPRESS, DALE THE MERCILESS!
SO much worse.
IT CAN'T--
THERE'S NO WAY--
I DON'T--
WE GOTTA SAVE HER!
YEAH!
And then I threw up on my boots. Again.

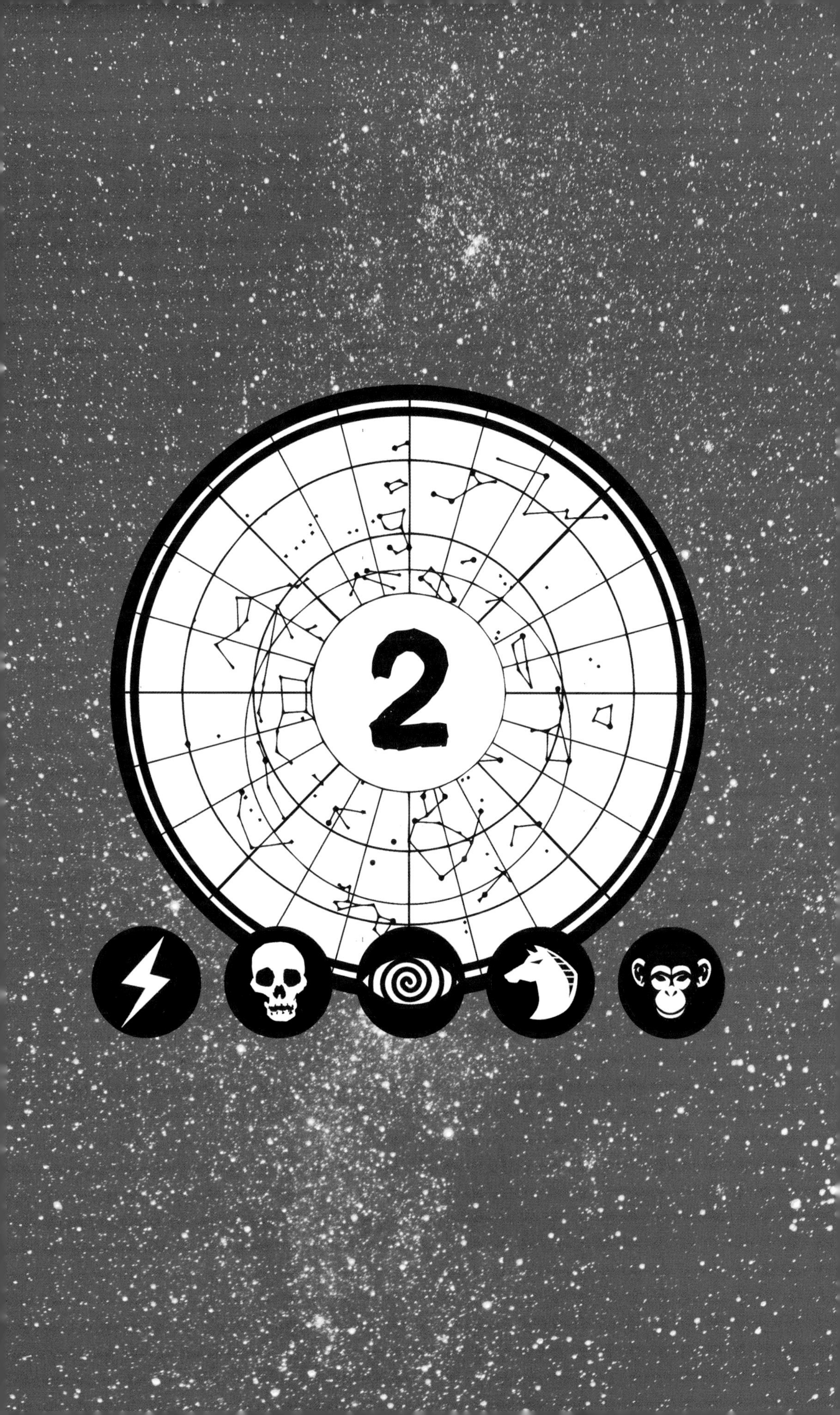
2

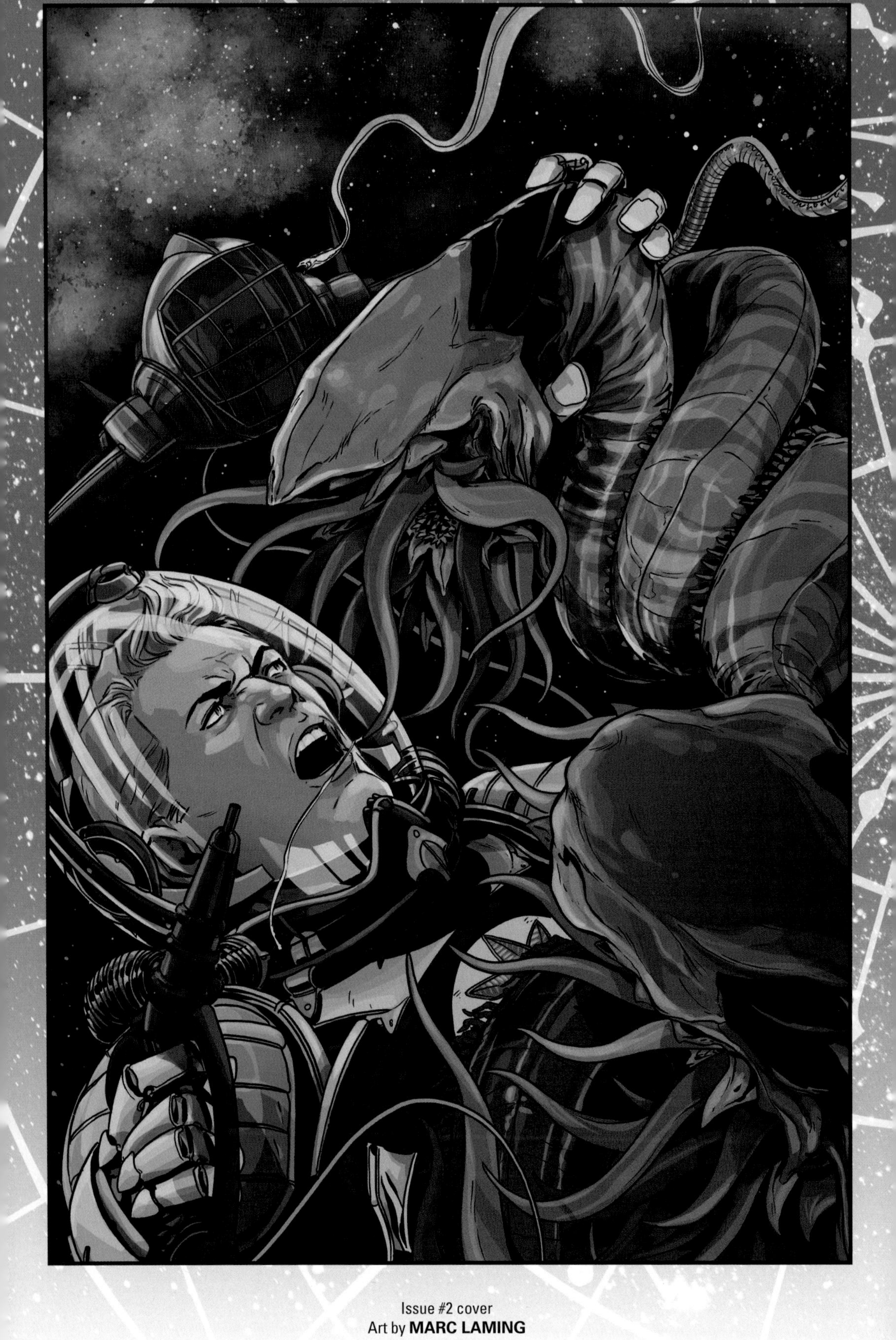

Issue #2 cover
Art by **MARC LAMING**

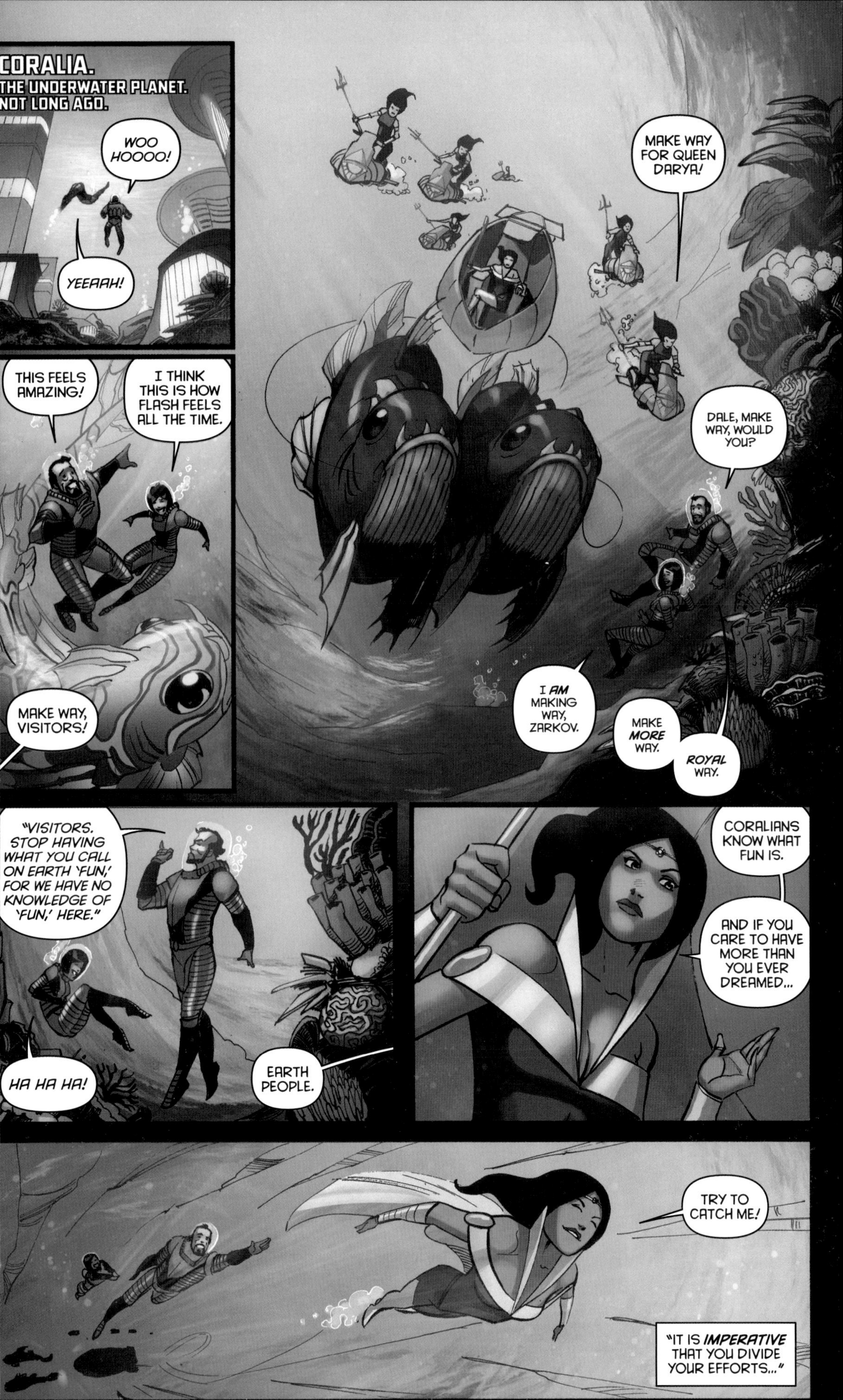

CORALIA.
THE UNDERWATER PLANET.
NOT LONG AGO.
WOO HOOOO!
YEEAAH!
MAKE WAY FOR QUEEN DARYA!
THIS FEELS AMAZING!
I THINK THIS IS HOW FLASH FEELS ALL THE TIME.
DALE, MAKE WAY, WOULD YOU?
MAKE WAY, VISITORS!
I AM MAKING WAY, ZARKOV.
MAKE MORE WAY.
ROYAL WAY.
"VISITORS. STOP HAVING WHAT YOU CALL ON EARTH 'FUN,' FOR WE HAVE NO KNOWLEDGE OF 'FUN,' HERE."
HA HA HA!
EARTH PEOPLE.
CORALIANS KNOW WHAT FUN IS.
AND IF YOU CARE TO HAVE MORE THAN YOU EVER DREAMED...
TRY TO CATCH ME!
"IT IS IMPERATIVE THAT YOU DIVIDE YOUR EFFORTS..."

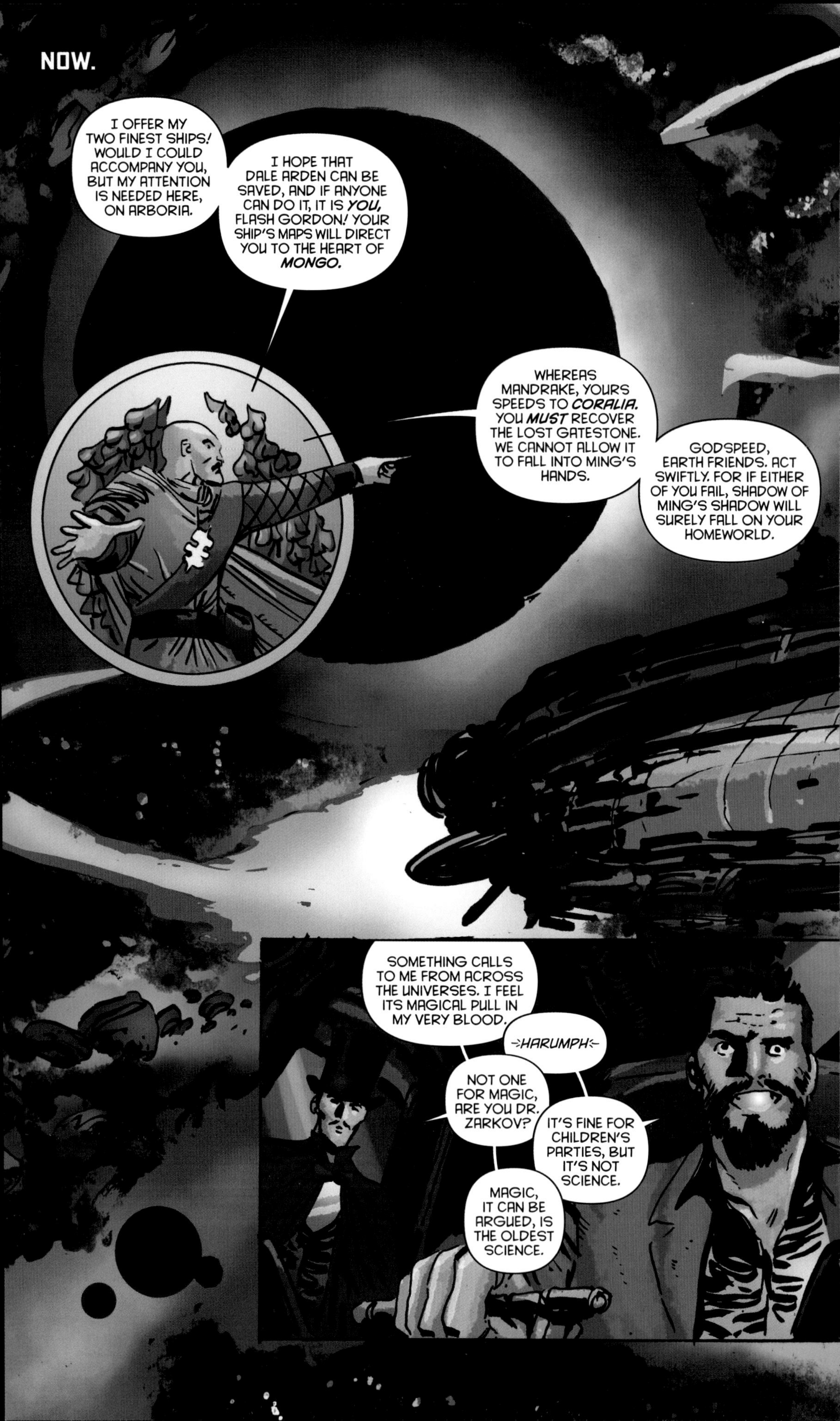
NOW.
I OFFER MY TWO FINEST SHIPS! WOULD I COULD ACCOMPANY YOU, BUT MY ATTENTION IS NEEDED HERE, ON ARBORIA.
I HOPE THAT DALE ARDEN CAN BE SAVED, AND IF ANYONE CAN DO IT, IT IS YOU, FLASH GORDON! YOUR SHIP'S MAPS WILL DIRECT YOU TO THE HEART OF MONGO.
WHEREAS MANDRAKE, YOURS SPEEDS TO CORALIA. YOU MUST RECOVER THE LOST GATESTONE. WE CANNOT ALLOW IT TO FALL INTO MING'S HANDS.
GODSPEED, EARTH FRIENDS. ACT SWIFTLY. FOR IF EITHER OF YOU FAIL, SHADOW OF MING'S SHADOW WILL SURELY FALL ON YOUR HOMEWORLD.
SOMETHING CALLS TO ME FROM ACROSS THE UNIVERSES. I FEEL ITS MAGICAL PULL IN MY VERY BLOOD.
HARUMPH
NOT ONE FOR MAGIC, ARE YOU DR. ZARKOV?
IT'S FINE FOR CHILDREN'S PARTIES, BUT IT'S NOT SCIENCE.
MAGIC, IT CAN BE ARGUED, IS THE OLDEST SCIENCE.

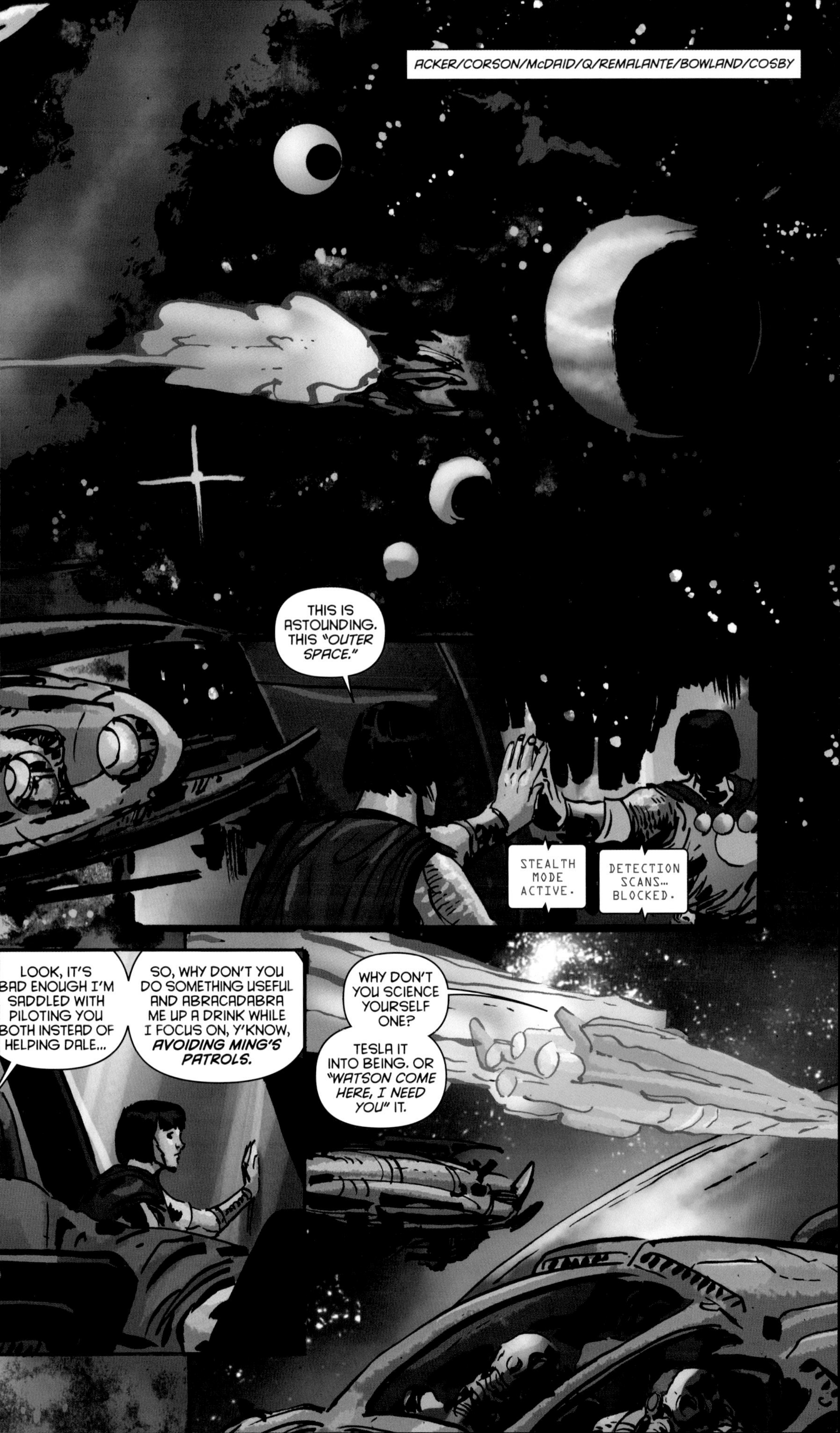
ACKER/CORSON/McDAID/Q/REMALANTE/BOWLAND/COSBY
THIS IS ASTOUNDING. THIS "OUTER SPACE."
STEALTH MODE ACTIVE.
DETECTION SCANS... BLOCKED.
LOOK, IT'S BAD ENOUGH I'M SADDLED WITH PILOTING YOU BOTH INSTEAD OF HELPING DALE...
SO, WHY DON'T YOU DO SOMETHING USEFUL AND ABRACADABRA ME UP A DRINK WHILE I FOCUS ON, Y'KNOW, AVOIDING MING'S PATROLS.
WHY DON'T YOU SCIENCE YOURSELF ONE?
TESLA IT INTO BEING. OR "WATSON COME HERE, I NEED YOU" IT.

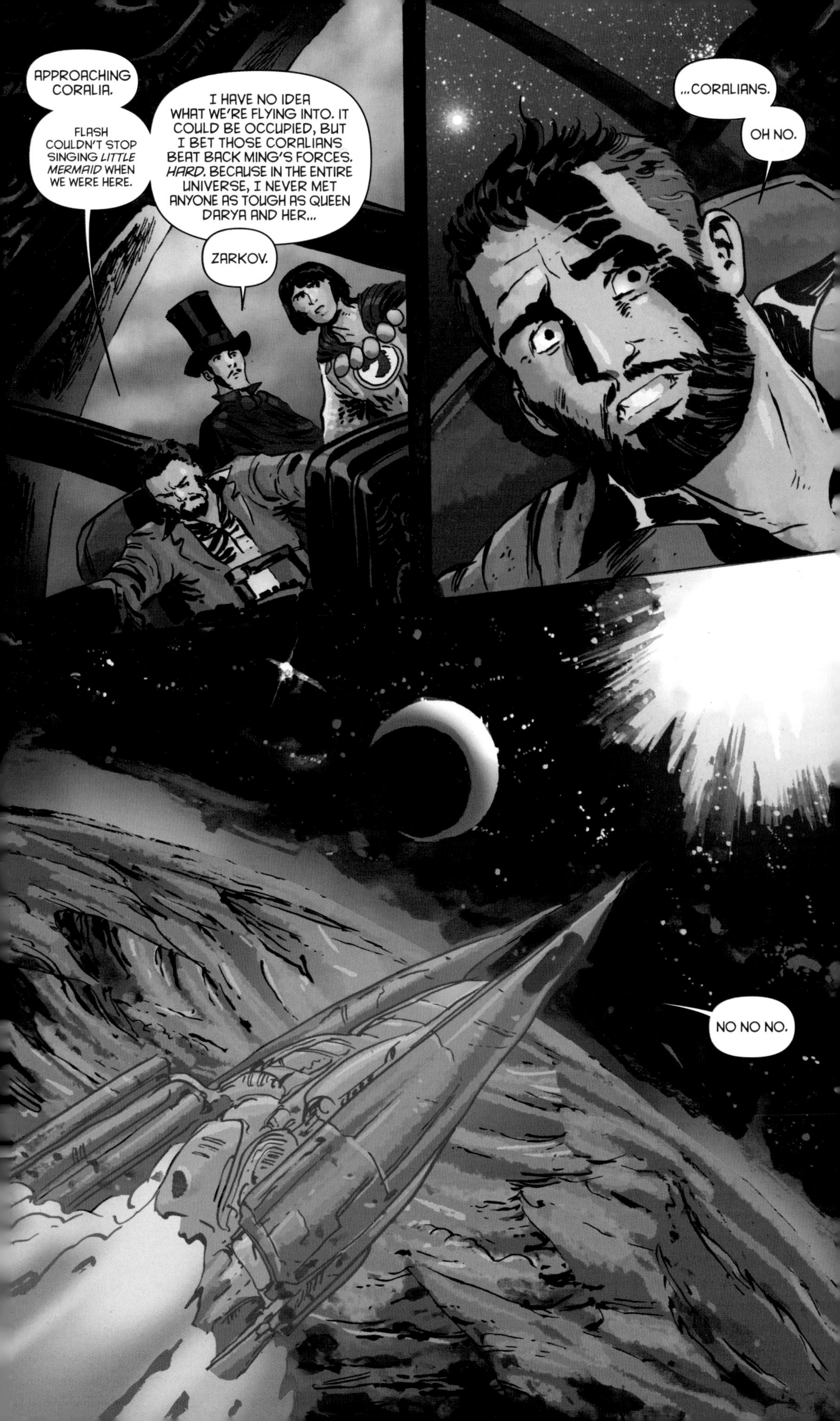
APPROACHING CORALIA.
FLASH COULDN'T STOP SINGING *LITTLE MERMAID* WHEN WE WERE HERE.
I HAVE NO IDEA WHAT WE'RE FLYING INTO. IT COULD BE OCCUPIED, BUT I BET THOSE CORALIANS BEAT BACK MING'S FORCES. *HARD.* BECAUSE IN THE ENTIRE UNIVERSE, I NEVER MET ANYONE AS TOUGH AS QUEEN DARYA AND HER...
ZARKOV.
...CORALIANS.
OH NO.
NO NO NO.

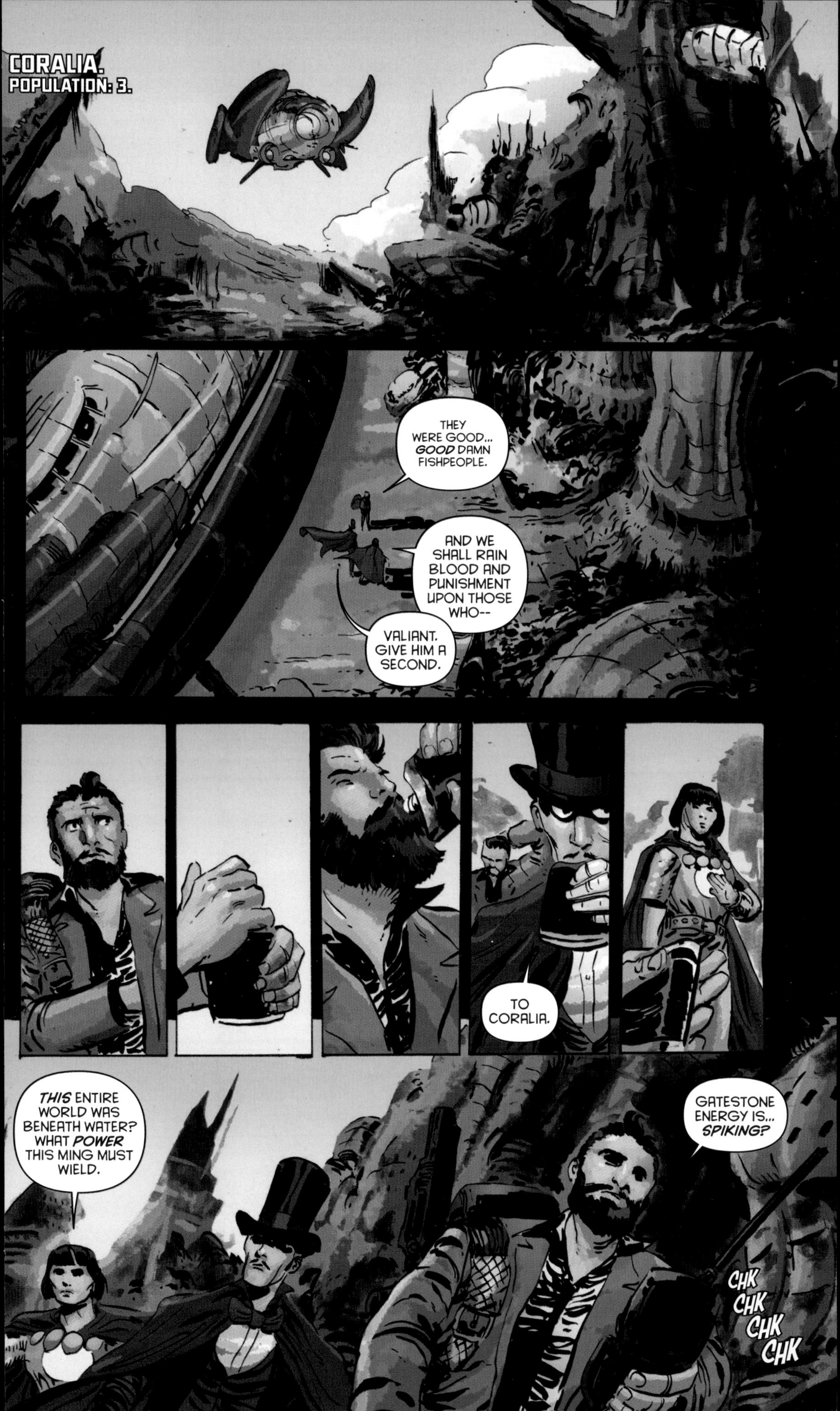

CORALIA.
POPULATION: 3.
THEY WERE GOOD... *GOOD* DAMN FISHPEOPLE.
AND WE SHALL RAIN BLOOD AND PUNISHMENT UPON THOSE WHO--
VALIANT. GIVE HIM A SECOND.
TO CORALIA.
THIS ENTIRE WORLD WAS BENEATH WATER? WHAT *POWER* THIS MING MUST WIELD.
GATESTONE ENERGY IS... *SPIKING?*
CHK CHK CHK CHK

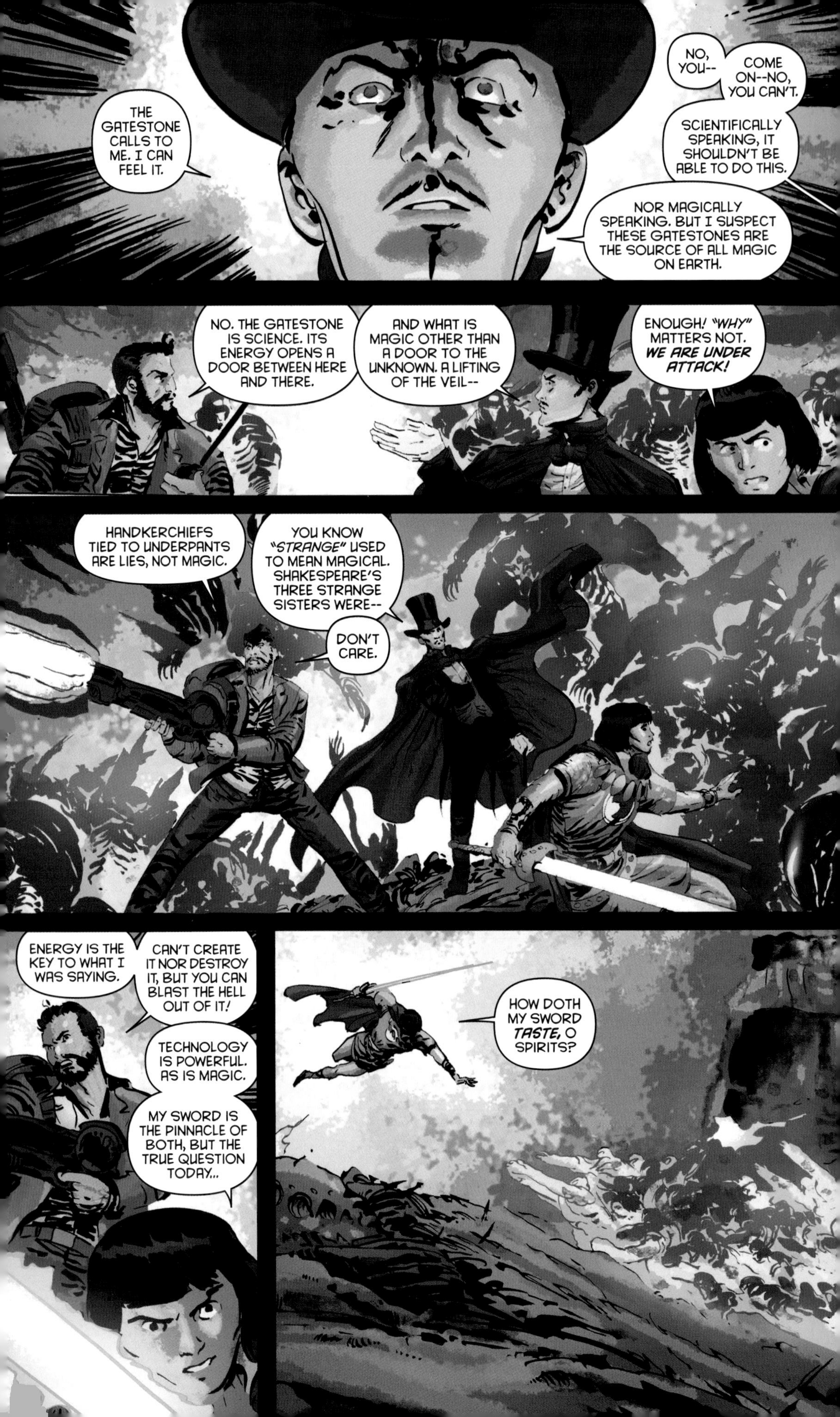

THE GATESTONE CALLS TO ME. I CAN FEEL IT.
NO, YOU--
COME ON--NO, YOU CAN'T.
SCIENTIFICALLY SPEAKING, IT SHOULDN'T BE ABLE TO DO THIS.
NOR MAGICALLY SPEAKING. BUT I SUSPECT THESE GATESTONES ARE THE SOURCE OF ALL MAGIC ON EARTH.
NO. THE GATESTONE IS SCIENCE. ITS ENERGY OPENS A DOOR BETWEEN HERE AND THERE.
AND WHAT IS MAGIC OTHER THAN A DOOR TO THE UNKNOWN. A LIFTING OF THE VEIL--
ENOUGH! *"WHY"* MATTERS NOT. ***WE ARE UNDER ATTACK!***
HANDKERCHIEFS TIED TO UNDERPANTS ARE LIES, NOT MAGIC.
YOU KNOW *"STRANGE"* USED TO MEAN MAGICAL. SHAKESPEARE'S THREE STRANGE SISTERS WERE--
DON'T CARE.
ENERGY IS THE KEY TO WHAT I WAS SAYING.
CAN'T CREATE IT NOR DESTROY IT, BUT YOU CAN BLAST THE HELL OUT OF IT!
TECHNOLOGY IS POWERFUL. AS IS MAGIC.
MY SWORD IS THE PINNACLE OF BOTH, BUT THE TRUE QUESTION TODAY...
HOW DOTH MY SWORD *TASTE,* O SPIRITS?

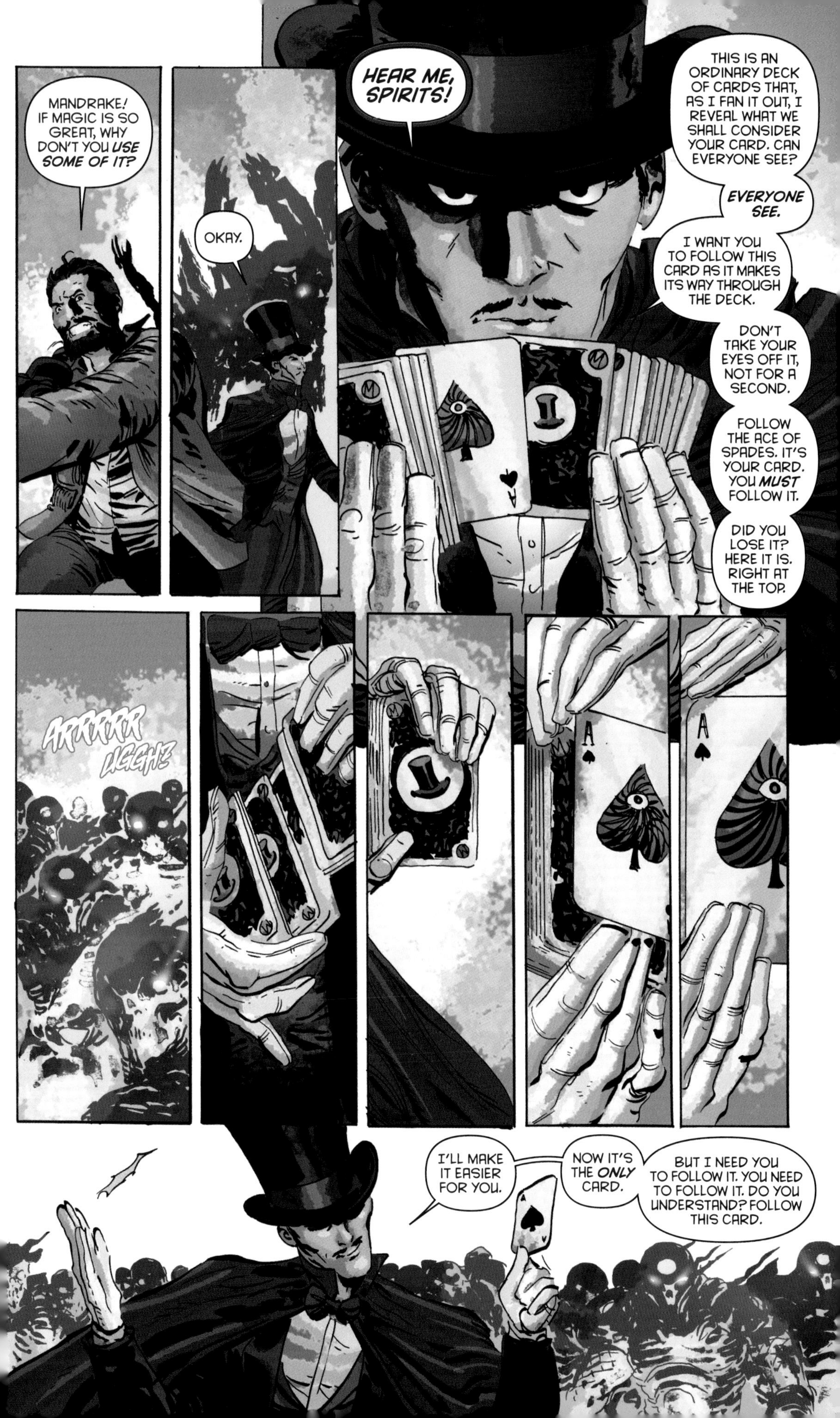
MANDRAKE! IF MAGIC IS SO GREAT, WHY DON'T YOU *USE SOME OF IT?*
OKAY.
HEAR ME, SPIRITS!
THIS IS AN ORDINARY DECK OF CARDS THAT, AS I FAN IT OUT, I REVEAL WHAT WE SHALL CONSIDER YOUR CARD. CAN EVERYONE SEE?
EVERYONE SEE.
I WANT YOU TO FOLLOW THIS CARD AS IT MAKES ITS WAY THROUGH THE DECK.
DON'T TAKE YOUR EYES OFF IT, NOT FOR A SECOND.
FOLLOW THE ACE OF SPADES. IT'S YOUR CARD. YOU *MUST* FOLLOW IT.
DID YOU LOSE IT? HERE IT IS. RIGHT AT THE TOP.
ARRRRR UGGH!
I'LL MAKE IT EASIER FOR YOU.
NOW IT'S THE *ONLY* CARD.
BUT I NEED YOU TO FOLLOW IT. YOU NEED TO FOLLOW IT. DO YOU UNDERSTAND? FOLLOW THIS CARD.

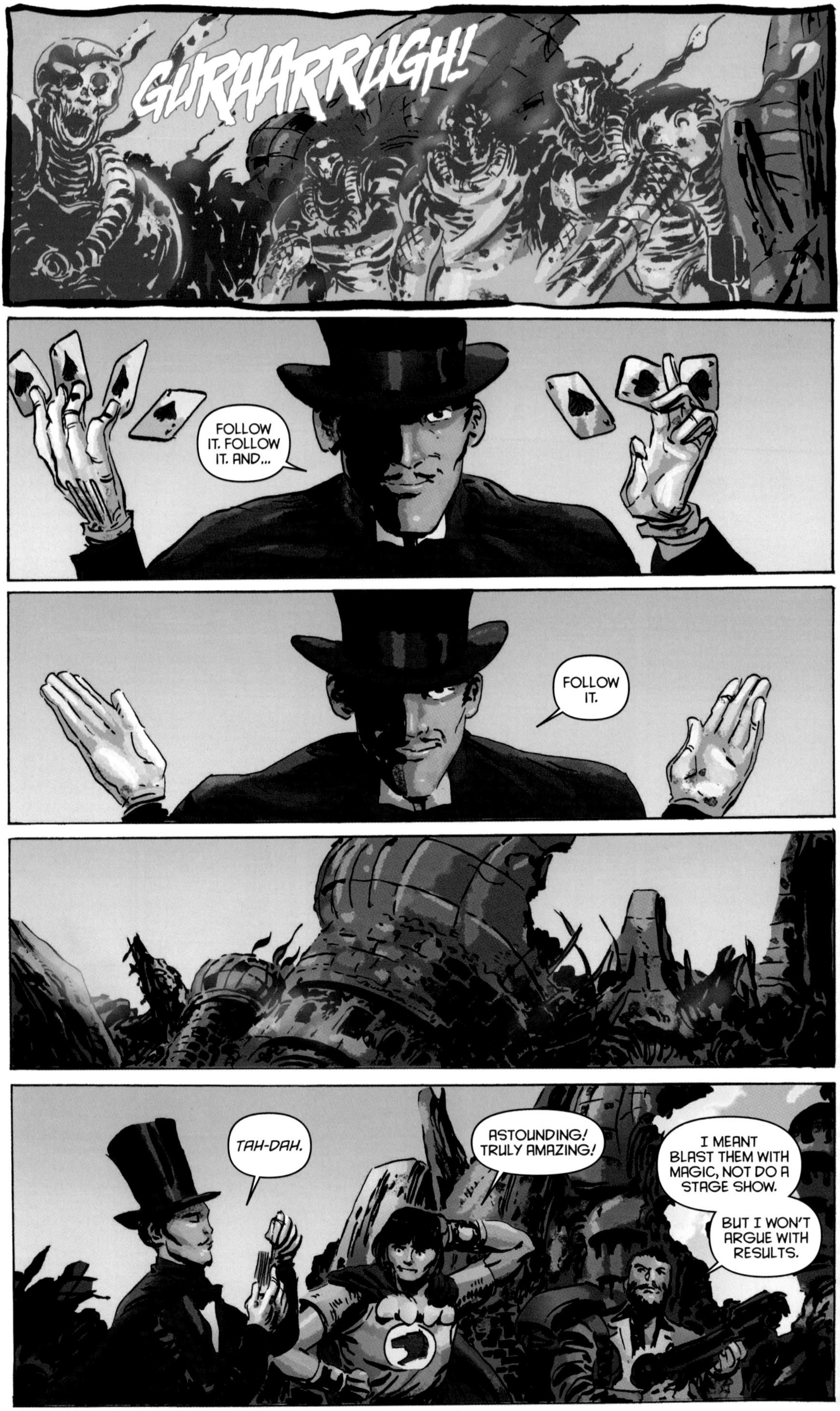
GURAARRUGH!
FOLLOW IT. FOLLOW IT. AND...
FOLLOW IT.
TAH-DAH.
ASTOUNDING! TRULY AMAZING!
I MEANT BLAST THEM WITH MAGIC, NOT DO A STAGE SHOW.
BUT I WON'T ARGUE WITH RESULTS.

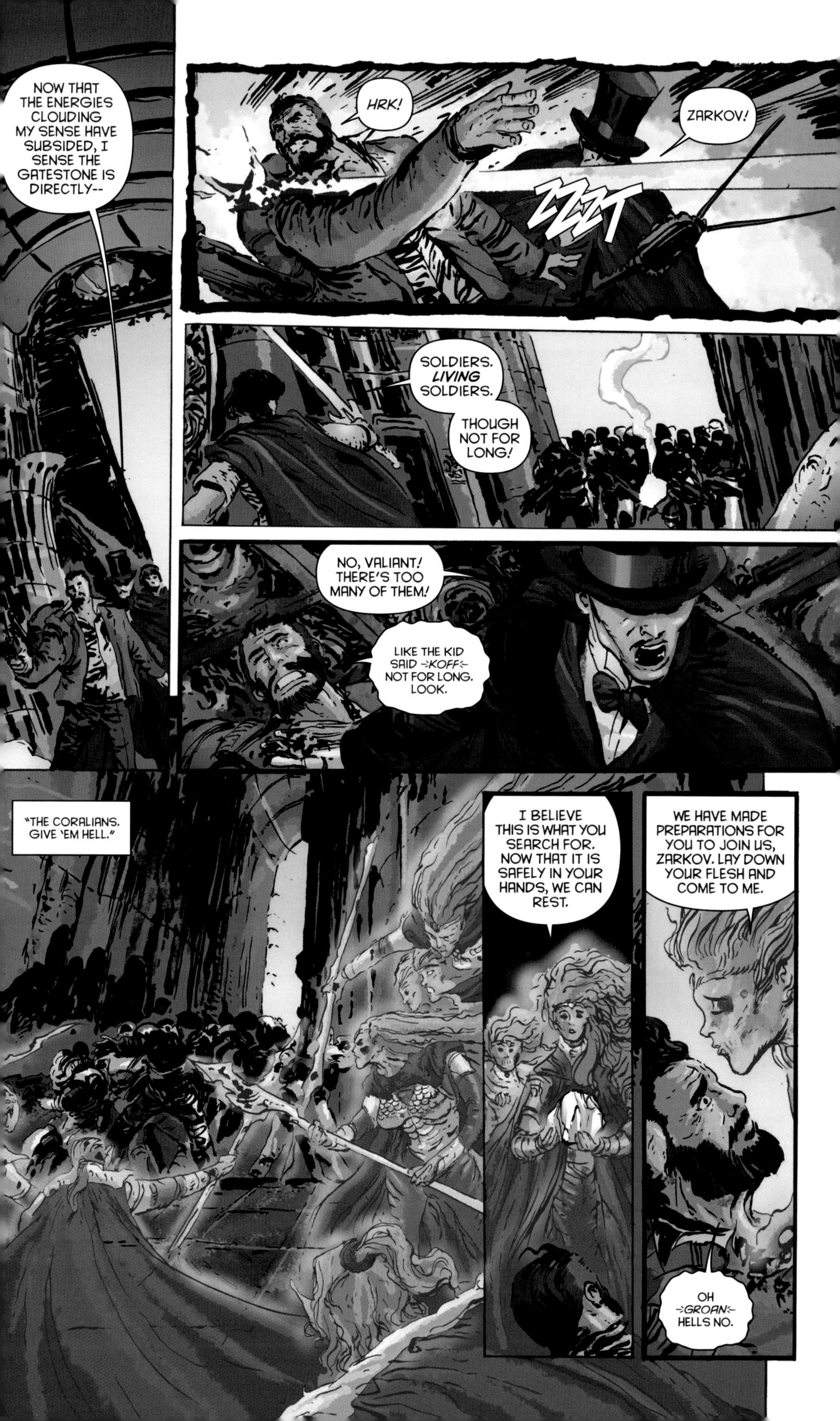
NOW THAT THE ENERGIES CLOUDING MY SENSE HAVE SUBSIDED, I SENSE THE GATESTONE IS DIRECTLY--
HRK!
ZARKOV!
ZZZT
SOLDIERS. *LIVING* SOLDIERS.
THOUGH NOT FOR LONG!
NO, VALIANT! THERE'S TOO MANY OF THEM!
LIKE THE KID SAID -KOFF- NOT FOR LONG. LOOK.
"THE CORALIANS. GIVE 'EM HELL."
I BELIEVE THIS IS WHAT YOU SEARCH FOR. NOW THAT IT IS SAFELY IN YOUR HANDS, WE CAN REST.
WE HAVE MADE PREPARATIONS FOR YOU TO JOIN US, ZARKOV. LAY DOWN YOUR FLESH AND COME TO ME.
OH -GROAN- HELLS NO.

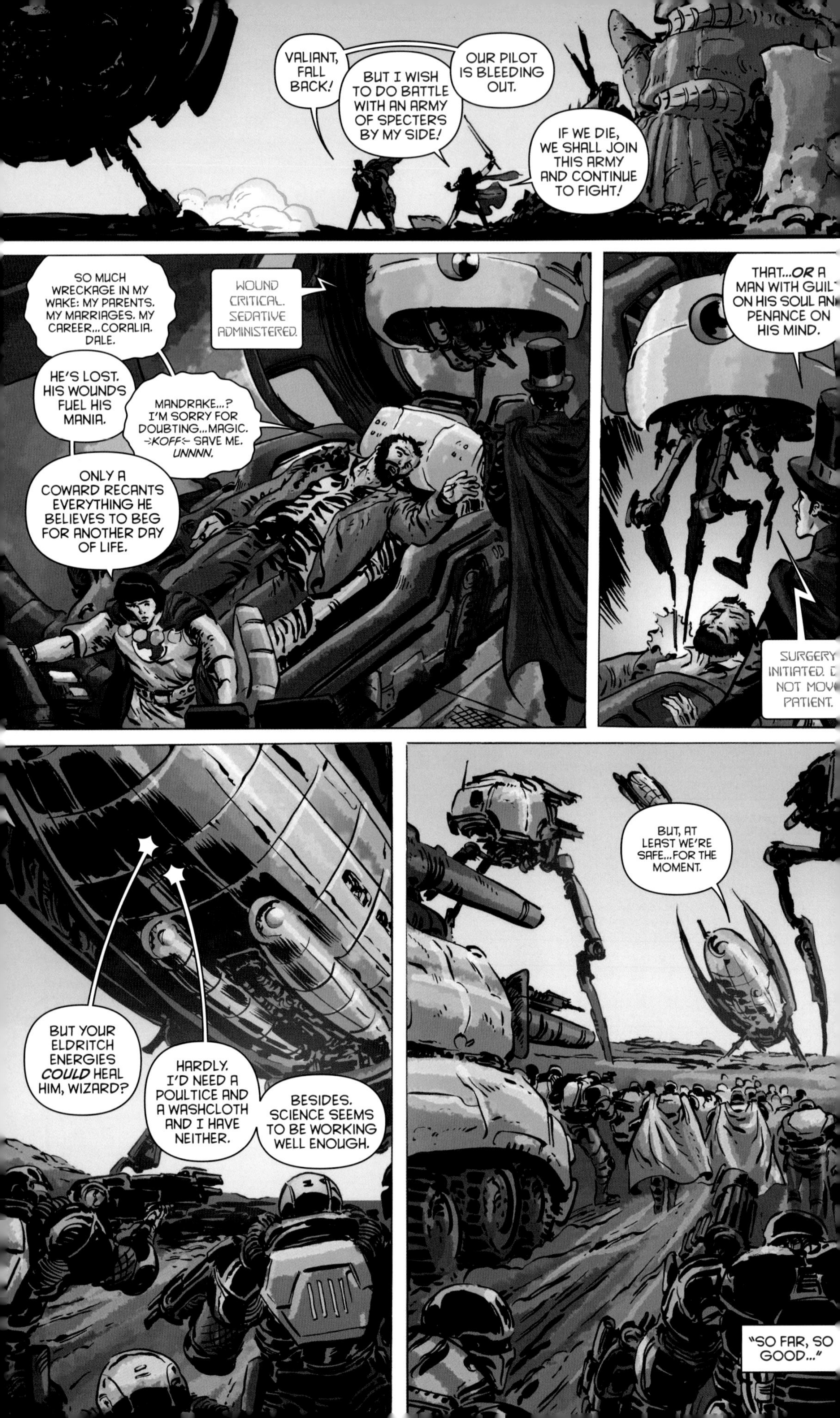
VALIANT, FALL BACK!
BUT I WISH TO DO BATTLE WITH AN ARMY OF SPECTERS BY MY SIDE!
OUR PILOT IS BLEEDING OUT.
IF WE DIE, WE SHALL JOIN THIS ARMY AND CONTINUE TO FIGHT!
SO MUCH WRECKAGE IN MY WAKE: MY PARENTS. MY MARRIAGES. MY CAREER...CORALIA. DALE.
WOUND CRITICAL. SEDATIVE ADMINISTERED.
HE'S LOST. HIS WOUNDS FUEL HIS MANIA.
MANDRAKE...? I'M SORRY FOR DOUBTING...MAGIC. -KOFF- SAVE ME. UNNNN.
ONLY A COWARD RECANTS EVERYTHING HE BELIEVES TO BEG FOR ANOTHER DAY OF LIFE.
THAT...OR A MAN WITH GUIL ON HIS SOUL AN PENANCE ON HIS MIND.
SURGERY INITIATED. D NOT MOV PATIENT.
BUT YOUR ELDRITCH ENERGIES COULD HEAL HIM, WIZARD?
HARDLY. I'D NEED A POULTICE AND A WASHCLOTH AND I HAVE NEITHER.
BESIDES. SCIENCE SEEMS TO BE WORKING WELL ENOUGH.
BUT, AT LEAST WE'RE SAFE...FOR THE MOMENT.
"SO FAR, SO GOOD..."

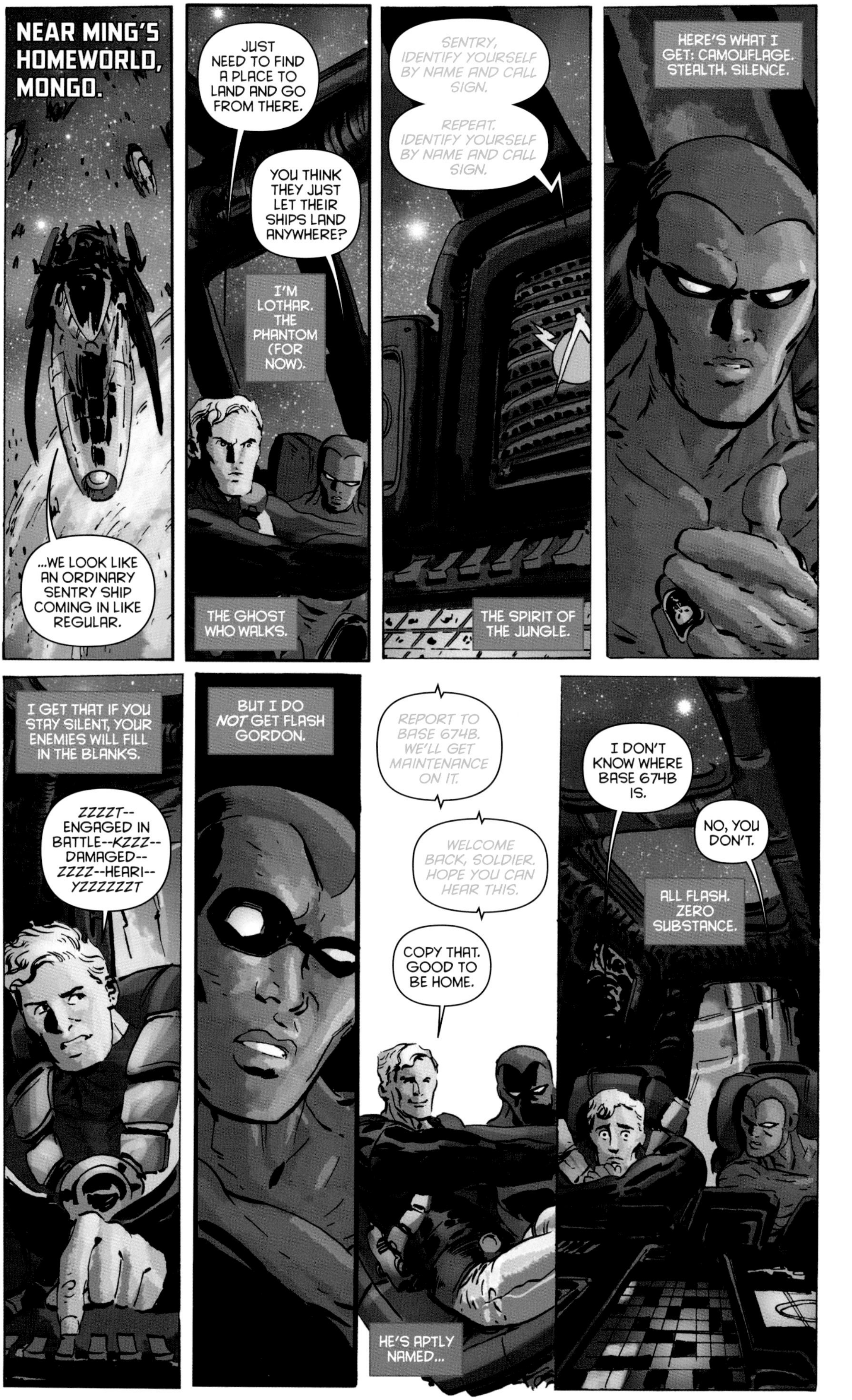

NEAR MING'S HOMEWORLD, MONGO.
...WE LOOK LIKE AN ORDINARY SENTRY SHIP COMING IN LIKE REGULAR.
JUST NEED TO FIND A PLACE TO LAND AND GO FROM THERE.
YOU THINK THEY JUST LET THEIR SHIPS LAND ANYWHERE?
I'M LOTHAR. THE PHANTOM (FOR NOW).
THE GHOST WHO WALKS.
SENTRY, IDENTIFY YOURSELF BY NAME AND CALL SIGN.
REPEAT. IDENTIFY YOURSELF BY NAME AND CALL SIGN.
THE SPIRIT OF THE JUNGLE.
HERE'S WHAT I GET: CAMOUFLAGE. STEALTH. SILENCE.
I GET THAT IF YOU STAY SILENT, YOUR ENEMIES WILL FILL IN THE BLANKS.
ZZZZT--ENGAGED IN BATTLE--KZZZ--DAMAGED--ZZZZ--HEARI--YZZZZZZT
BUT I DO NOT GET FLASH GORDON.
REPORT TO BASE 674B. WE'LL GET MAINTENANCE ON IT.
WELCOME BACK, SOLDIER. HOPE YOU CAN HEAR THIS.
COPY THAT. GOOD TO BE HOME.
HE'S APTLY NAMED...
I DON'T KNOW WHERE BASE 674B IS.
NO, YOU DON'T.
ALL FLASH. ZERO SUBSTANCE.

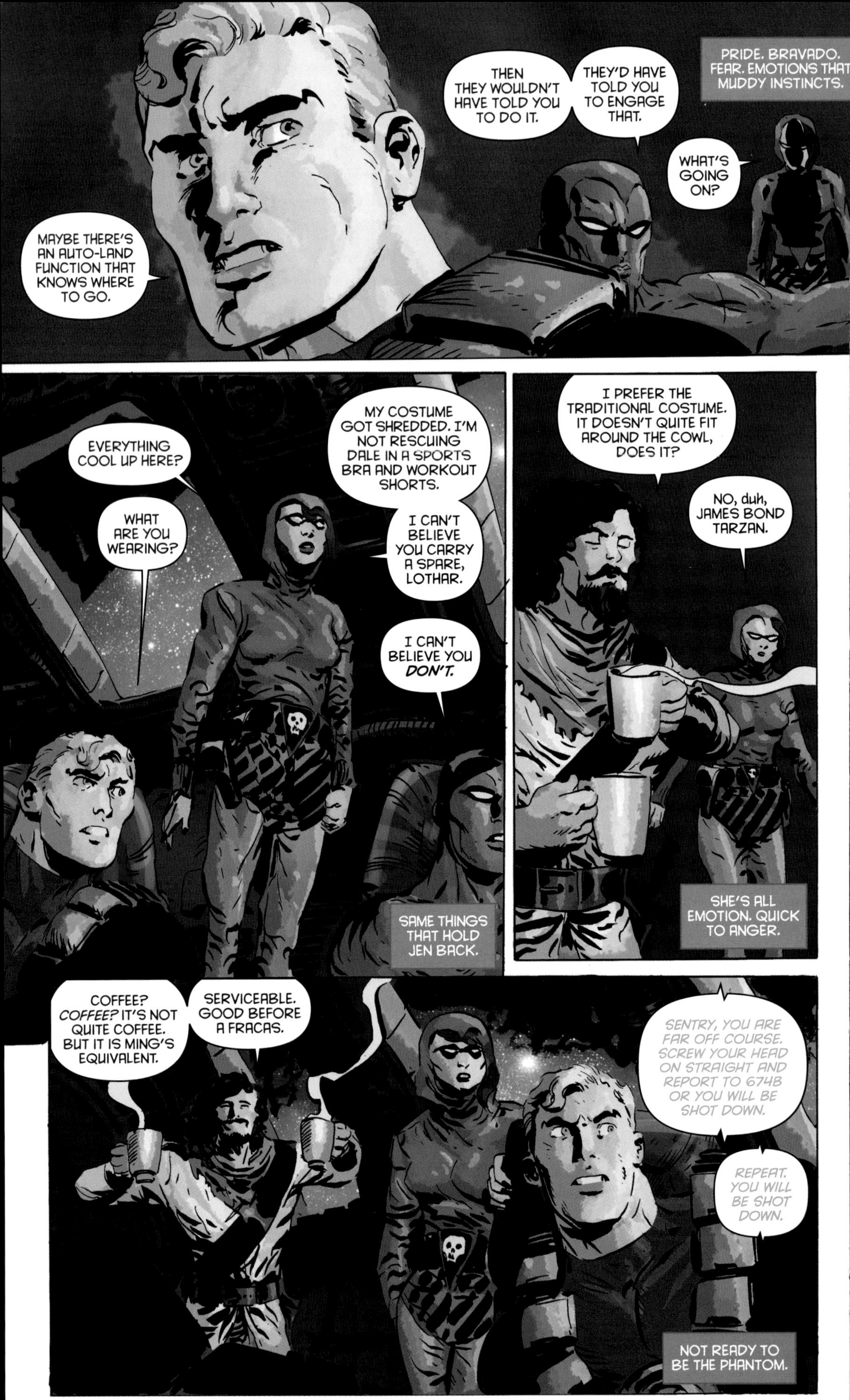
PRIDE. BRAVADO. FEAR. EMOTIONS THAT MUDDY INSTINCTS.
THEN THEY WOULDN'T HAVE TOLD YOU TO DO IT.
THEY'D HAVE TOLD YOU TO ENGAGE THAT.
WHAT'S GOING ON?
MAYBE THERE'S AN AUTO-LAND FUNCTION THAT KNOWS WHERE TO GO.
EVERYTHING COOL UP HERE?
WHAT ARE YOU WEARING?
MY COSTUME GOT SHREDDED. I'M NOT RESCUING DALE IN A SPORTS BRA AND WORKOUT SHORTS.
I CAN'T BELIEVE YOU CARRY A SPARE, LOTHAR.
I CAN'T BELIEVE YOU *DON'T.*
SAME THINGS THAT HOLD JEN BACK.
I PREFER THE TRADITIONAL COSTUME. IT DOESN'T QUITE FIT AROUND THE COWL, DOES IT?
NO, duh, JAMES BOND TARZAN.
SHE'S ALL EMOTION. QUICK TO ANGER.
COFFEE? *COFFEE?* IT'S NOT QUITE COFFEE. BUT IT IS MING'S EQUIVALENT.
SERVICEABLE. GOOD BEFORE A FRACAS.
SENTRY, YOU ARE FAR OFF COURSE. SCREW YOUR HEAD ON STRAIGHT AND REPORT TO 674B OR YOU WILL BE SHOT DOWN.
REPEAT. YOU WILL BE SHOT DOWN.
NOT READY TO BE THE PHANTOM.

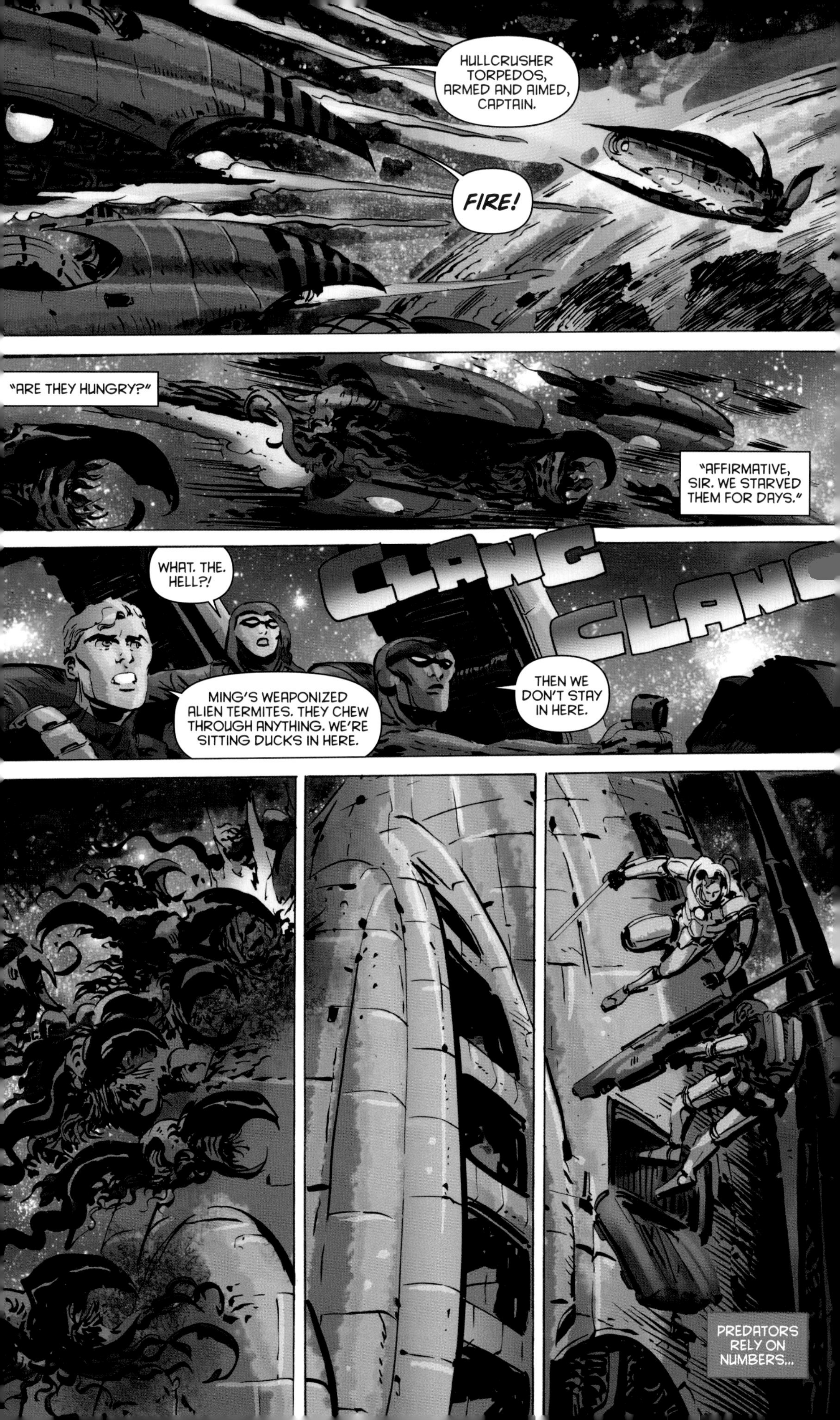
HULLCRUSHER TORPEDOS, ARMED AND AIMED, CAPTAIN.
FIRE!
"ARE THEY HUNGRY?"
"AFFIRMATIVE, SIR. WE STARVED THEM FOR DAYS."
WHAT. THE. HELL?!
CLANG
CLANG
MING'S WEAPONIZED ALIEN TERMITES. THEY CHEW THROUGH ANYTHING. WE'RE SITTING DUCKS IN HERE.
THEN WE DON'T STAY IN HERE.
PREDATORS RELY ON NUMBERS...

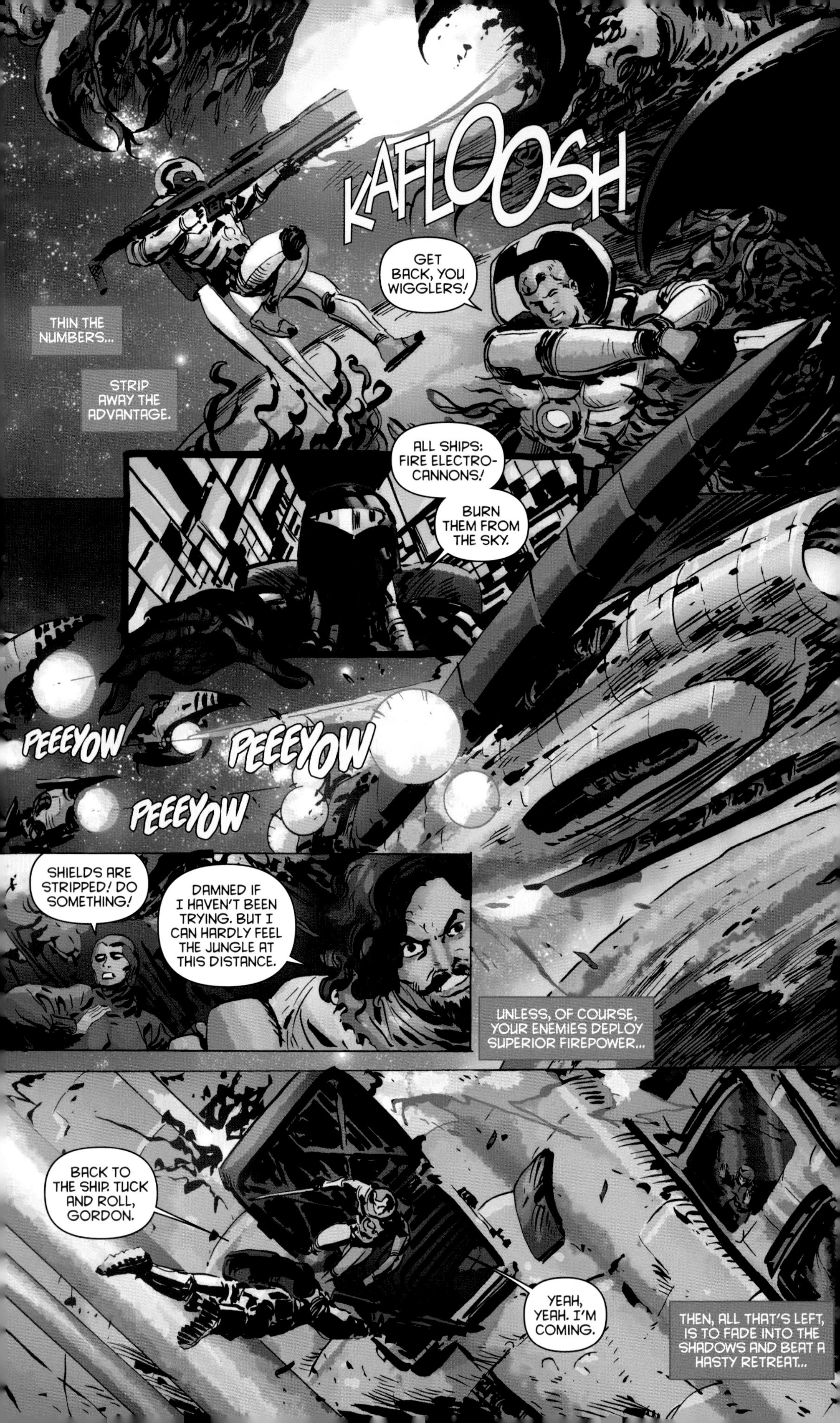
KAFLOOSH
GET BACK, YOU WIGGLERS!
THIN THE NUMBERS...
STRIP AWAY THE ADVANTAGE.
ALL SHIPS: FIRE ELECTRO-CANNONS!
BURN THEM FROM THE SKY.
PEEEYOW
PEEEYOW
PEEEYOW
SHIELDS ARE STRIPPED! DO SOMETHING!
DAMNED IF I HAVEN'T BEEN TRYING. BUT I CAN HARDLY FEEL THE JUNGLE AT THIS DISTANCE.
UNLESS, OF COURSE, YOUR ENEMIES DEPLOY SUPERIOR FIREPOWER...
BACK TO THE SHIP. TUCK AND ROLL, GORDON.
YEAH, YEAH. I'M COMING.
THEN, ALL THAT'S LEFT, IS TO FADE INTO THE SHADOWS AND BEAT A HASTY RETREAT...

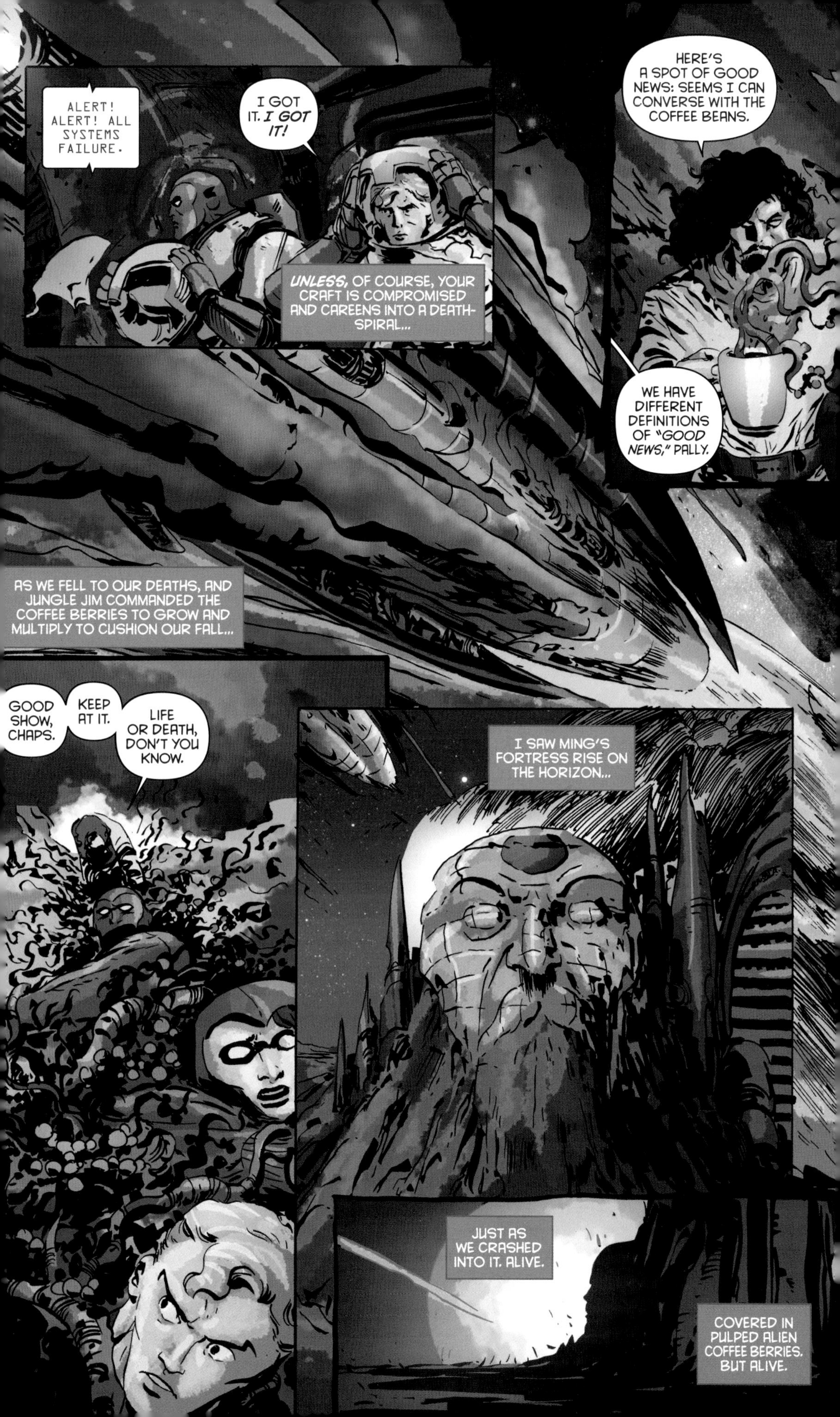
ALERT! ALERT! ALL SYSTEMS FAILURE.
I GOT IT. I GOT IT!
UNLESS, OF COURSE, YOUR CRAFT IS COMPROMISED AND CAREENS INTO A DEATH-SPIRAL...
HERE'S A SPOT OF GOOD NEWS: SEEMS I CAN CONVERSE WITH THE COFFEE BEANS.
WE HAVE DIFFERENT DEFINITIONS OF "GOOD NEWS," PALLY.
AS WE FELL TO OUR DEATHS, AND JUNGLE JIM COMMANDED THE COFFEE BERRIES TO GROW AND MULTIPLY TO CUSHION OUR FALL...
GOOD SHOW, CHAPS.
KEEP AT IT.
LIFE OR DEATH, DON'T YOU KNOW.
I SAW MING'S FORTRESS RISE ON THE HORIZON...
JUST AS WE CRASHED INTO IT. ALIVE.
COVERED IN PULPED ALIEN COFFEE BERRIES. BUT ALIVE.

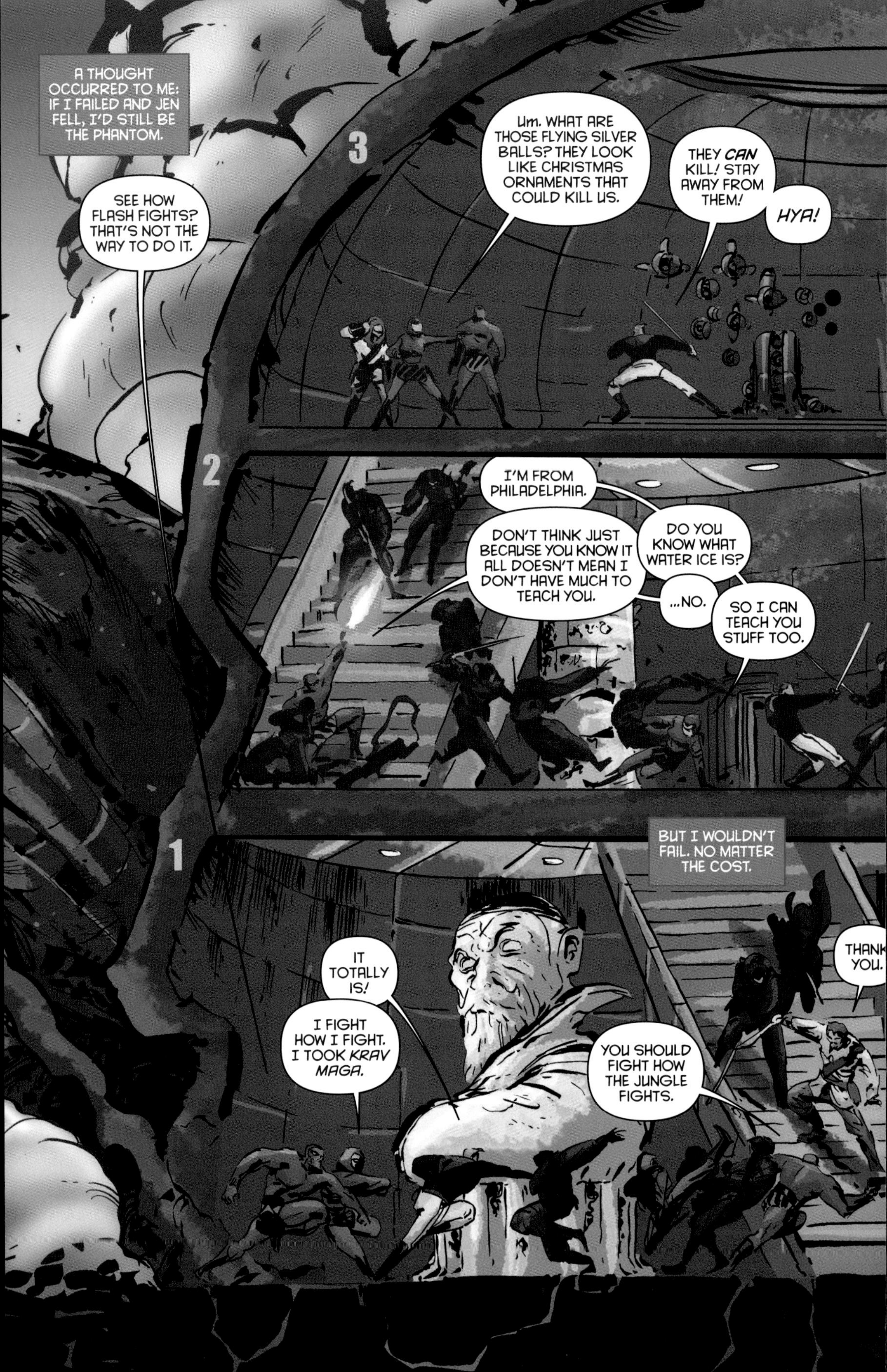

A THOUGHT OCCURRED TO ME: IF I FAILED AND JEN FELL, I'D STILL BE THE PHANTOM.
3
Um. WHAT ARE THOSE FLYING SILVER BALLS? THEY LOOK LIKE CHRISTMAS ORNAMENTS THAT COULD KILL US.
THEY *CAN* KILL! STAY AWAY FROM THEM!
HYA!
SEE HOW FLASH FIGHTS? THAT'S NOT THE WAY TO DO IT.
2
I'M FROM PHILADELPHIA.
DON'T THINK JUST BECAUSE YOU KNOW IT ALL DOESN'T MEAN I DON'T HAVE MUCH TO TEACH YOU.
DO YOU KNOW WHAT WATER ICE IS?
...NO.
SO I CAN TEACH YOU STUFF TOO.
1
BUT I WOULDN'T FAIL. NO MATTER THE COST.
IT TOTALLY IS!
I FIGHT HOW I FIGHT. I TOOK *KRAV MAGA*.
YOU SHOULD FIGHT HOW THE JUNGLE FIGHTS.
THANK YOU.

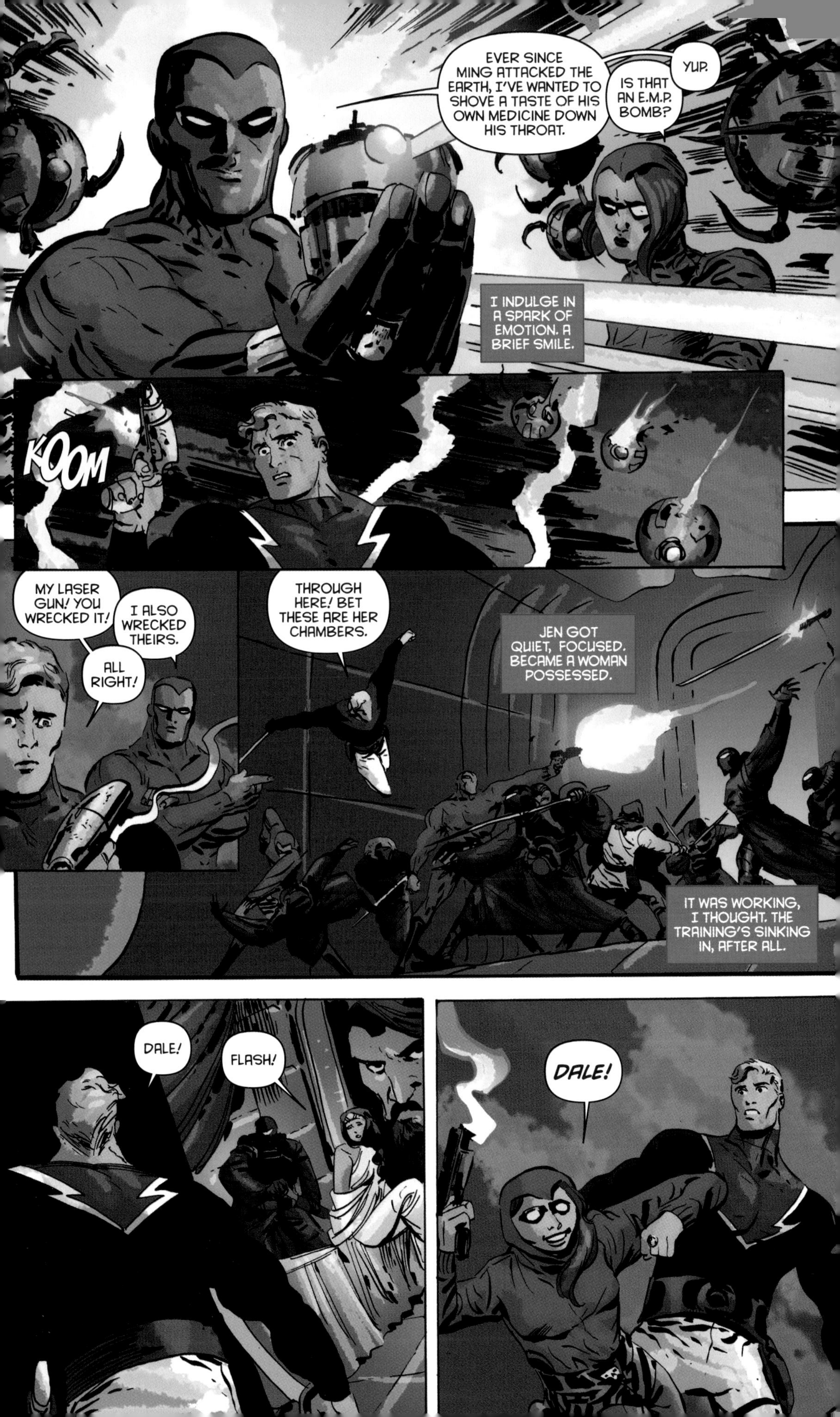
EVER SINCE MING ATTACKED THE EARTH, I'VE WANTED TO SHOVE A TASTE OF HIS OWN MEDICINE DOWN HIS THROAT.
IS THAT AN E.M.P. BOMB?
YUP.
I INDULGE IN A SPARK OF EMOTION. A BRIEF SMILE.
KOOM
MY LASER GUN! YOU WRECKED IT!
I ALSO WRECKED THEIRS.
ALL RIGHT!
THROUGH HERE! BET THESE ARE HER CHAMBERS.
JEN GOT QUIET, FOCUSED. BECAME A WOMAN POSSESSED.
IT WAS WORKING, I THOUGHT. THE TRAINING'S SINKING IN, AFTER ALL.
DALE!
FLASH!
DALE!

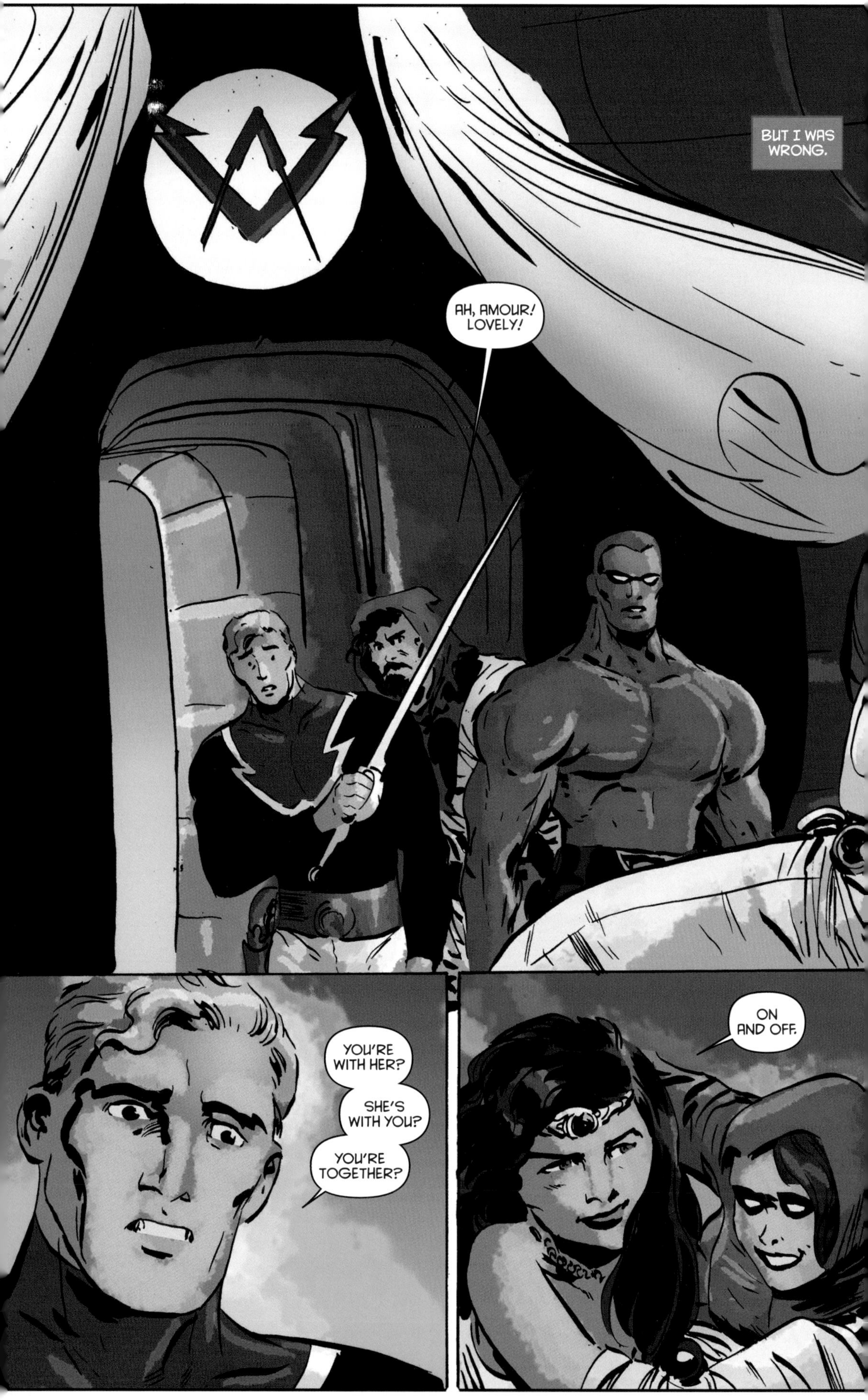
BUT I WAS WRONG.
AH, AMOUR! LOVELY!
YOU'RE WITH HER?
SHE'S WITH YOU?
YOU'RE TOGETHER?
ON AND OFF.

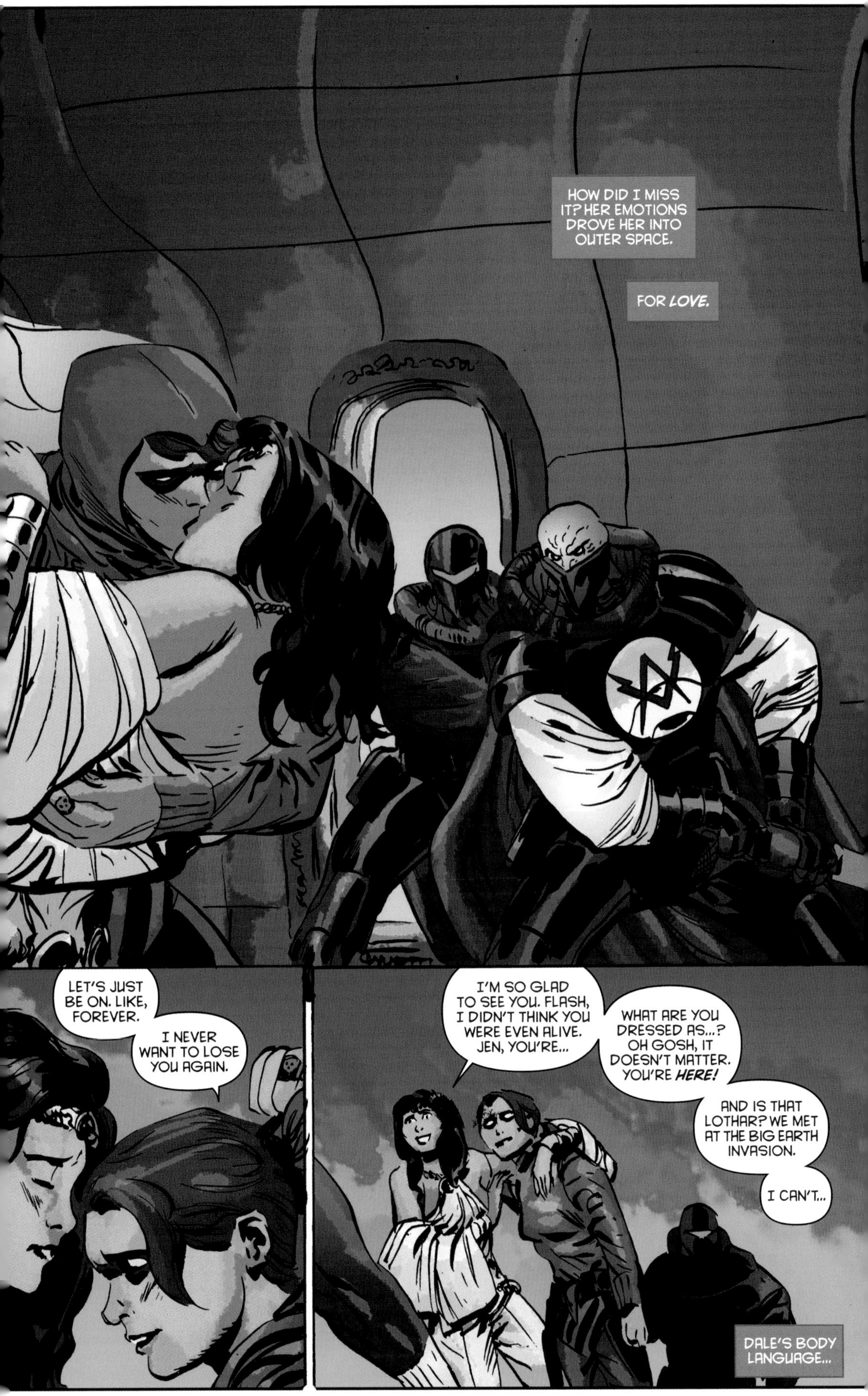
HOW DID I MISS IT? HER EMOTIONS DROVE HER INTO OUTER SPACE.
FOR *LOVE.*
LET'S JUST BE ON. LIKE, FOREVER.
I NEVER WANT TO LOSE YOU AGAIN.
I'M SO GLAD TO SEE YOU. FLASH, I DIDN'T THINK YOU WERE EVEN ALIVE. JEN, YOU'RE...
WHAT ARE YOU DRESSED AS...? OH GOSH, IT DOESN'T MATTER. YOU'RE *HERE!*
AND IS THAT LOTHAR? WE MET AT THE BIG EARTH INVASION.
I CAN'T...
DALE'S BODY LANGUAGE...

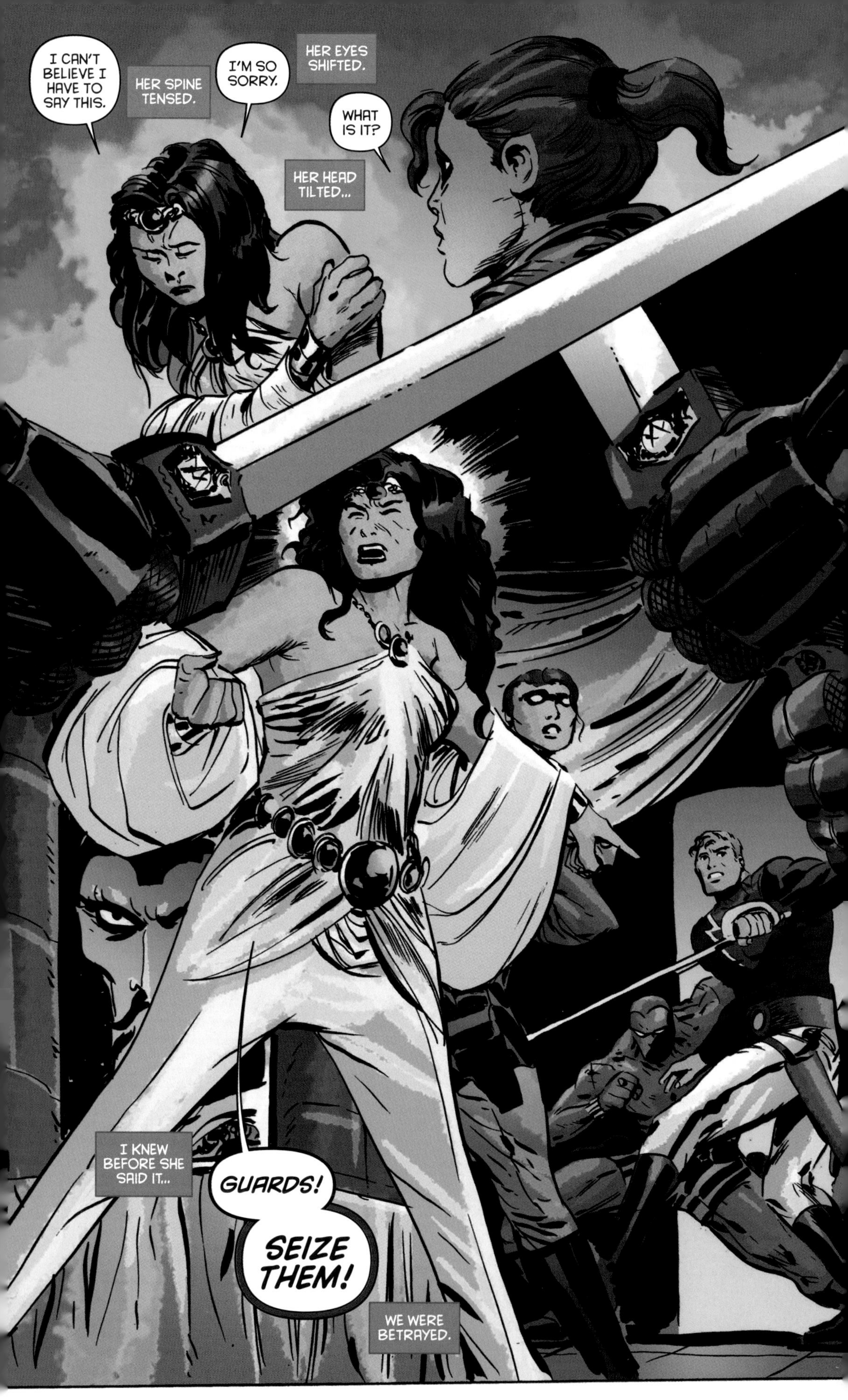
I CAN'T BELIEVE I HAVE TO SAY THIS.
HER SPINE TENSED.
I'M SO SORRY.
HER EYES SHIFTED.
WHAT IS IT?
HER HEAD TILTED...
I KNEW BEFORE SHE SAID IT...
GUARDS!
SEIZE THEM!
WE WERE BETRAYED.

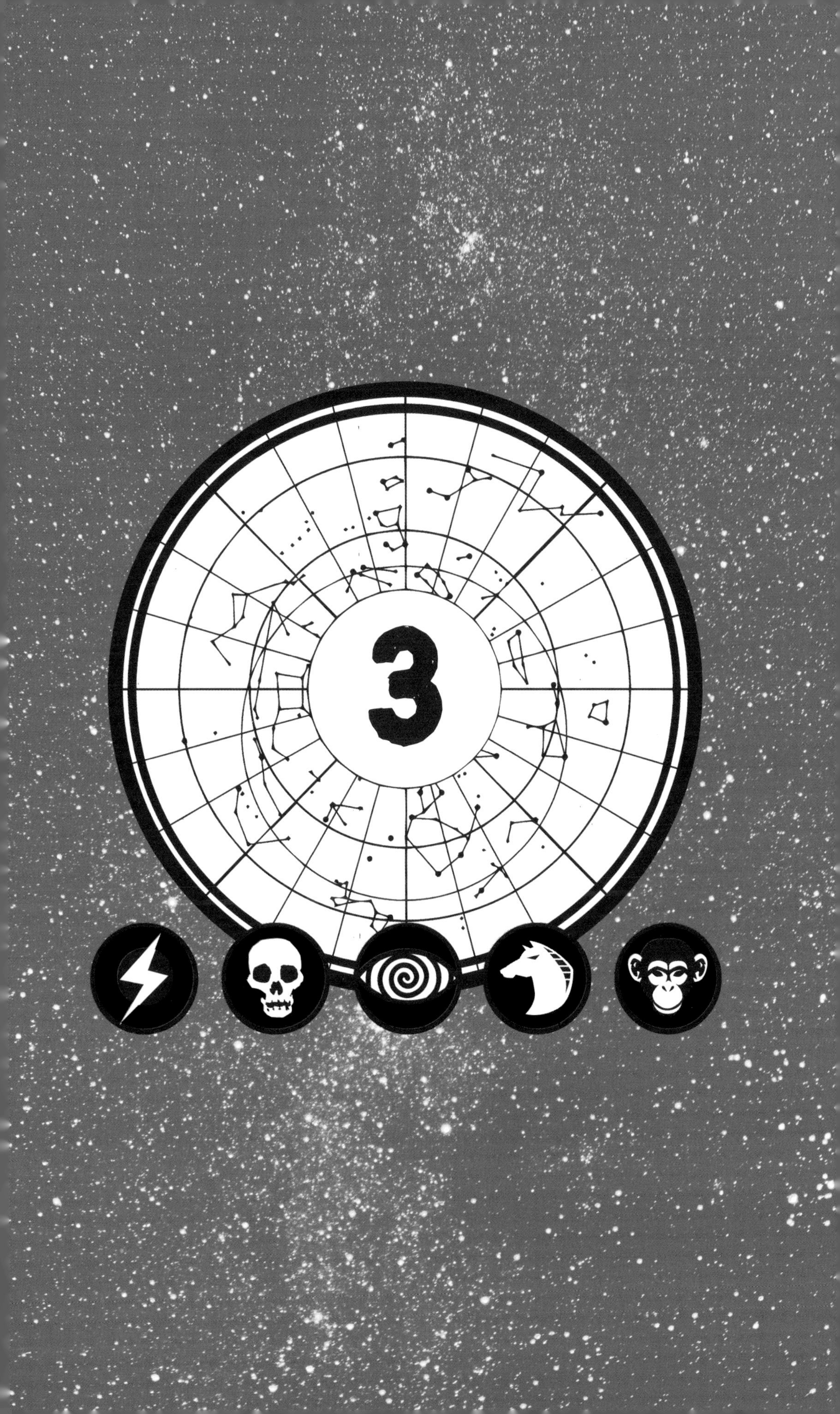
3

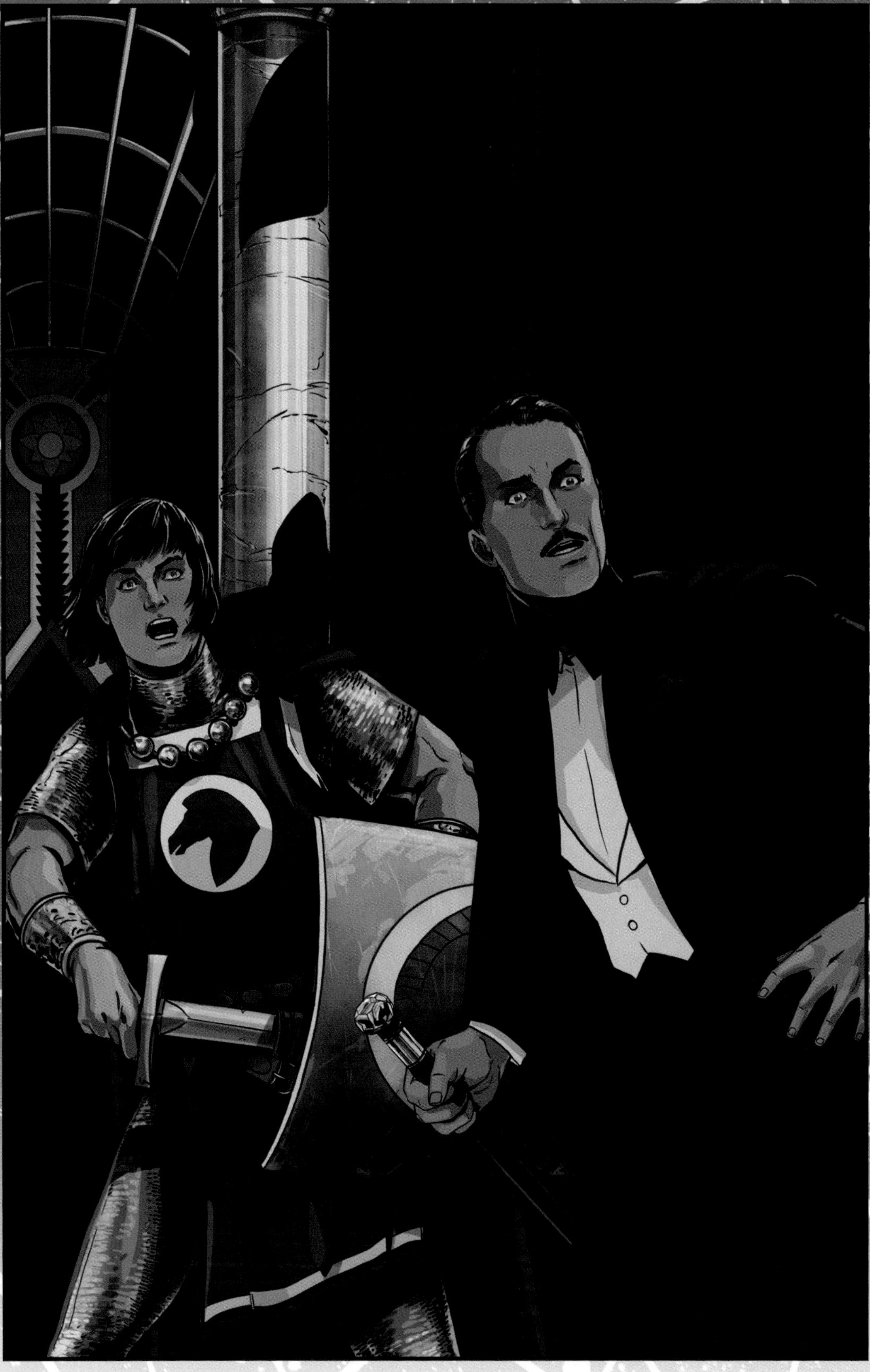

Issue #3 cover
Art by **MARC LAMING**

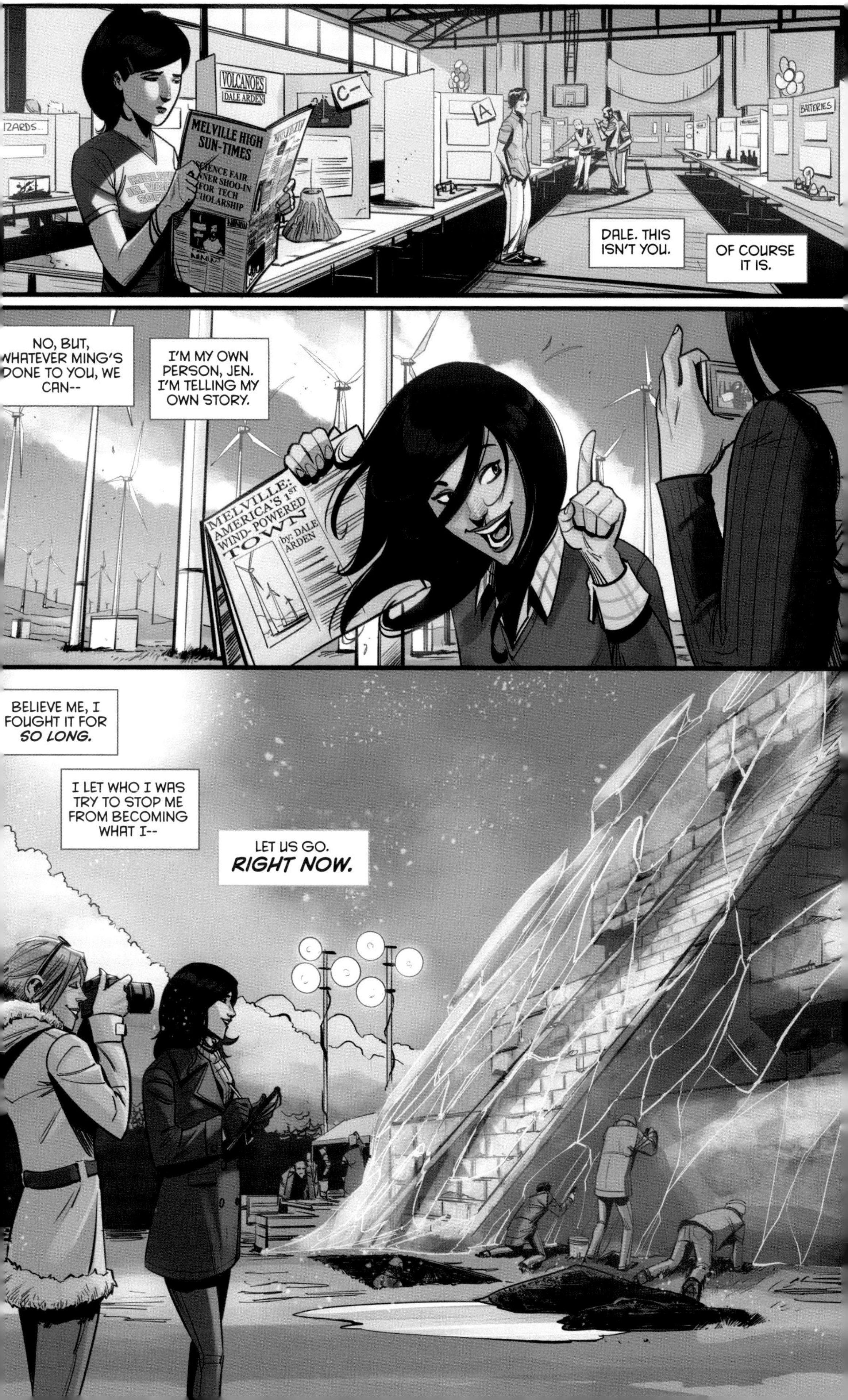
VOLCANOES
DALE ARDEN
C-
A
BATTERIES
MELVILLE HIGH SUN-TIMES
DALE. THIS ISN'T YOU.
OF COURSE IT IS.
NO, BUT, WHATEVER MING'S DONE TO YOU, WE CAN--
I'M MY OWN PERSON, JEN. I'M TELLING MY OWN STORY.
MELVILLE: AMERICA'S 1st WIND-POWERED TOWN
by: DALE ARDEN
BELIEVE ME, I FOUGHT IT FOR *SO LONG.*
I LET WHO I WAS TRY TO STOP ME FROM BECOMING WHAT I--
LET US GO. ***RIGHT NOW.***

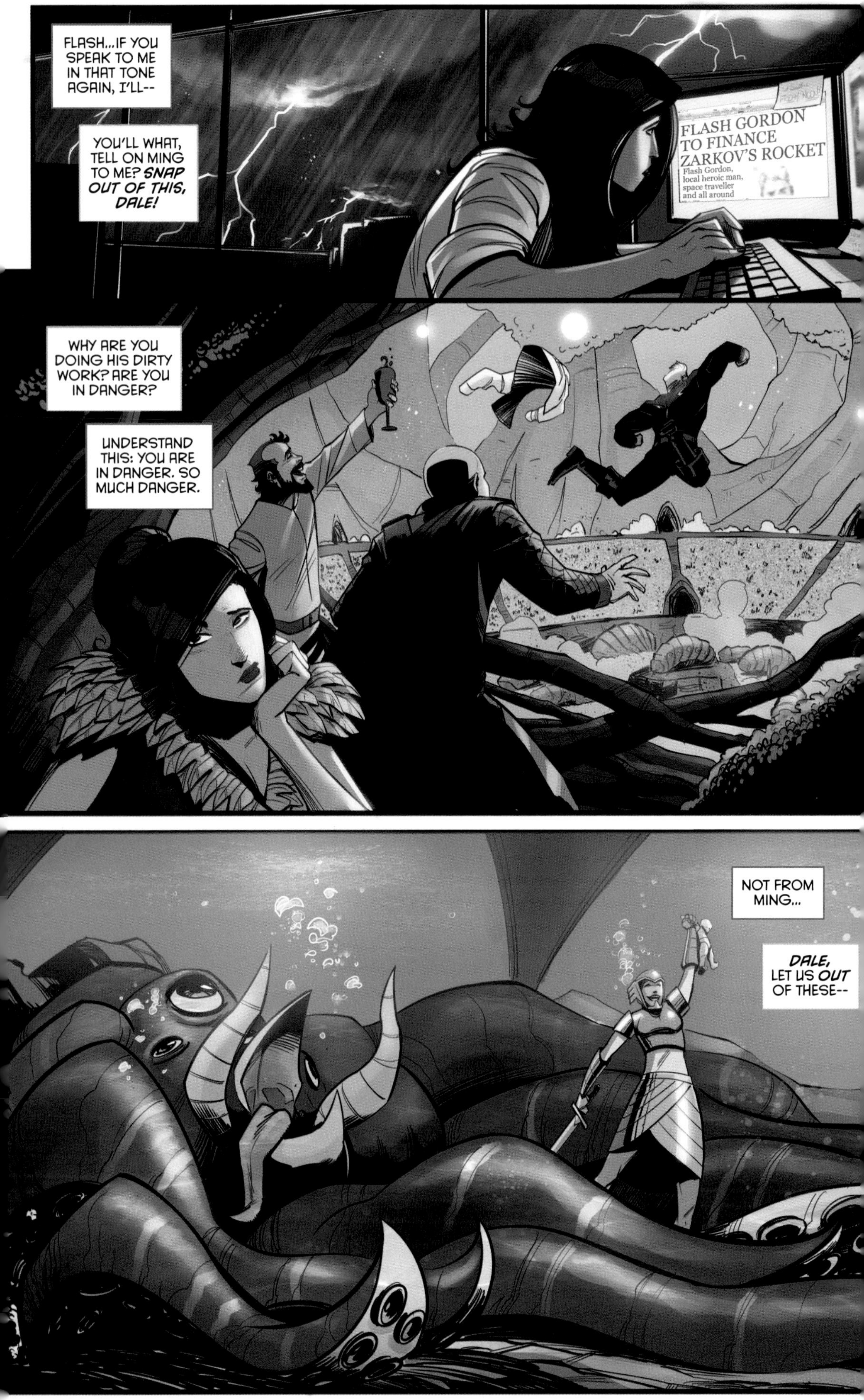
FLASH...IF YOU SPEAK TO ME IN THAT TONE AGAIN, I'LL--
YOU'LL WHAT, TELL ON MING TO ME? *SNAP OUT OF THIS, DALE!*
FLASH GORDON TO FINANCE ZARKOV'S ROCKET
Flash Gordon, local heroic man, space traveller and all around
WHY ARE YOU DOING HIS DIRTY WORK? ARE YOU IN DANGER?
UNDERSTAND THIS: YOU ARE IN DANGER. SO MUCH DANGER.
NOT FROM MING...
DALE, LET US *OUT* OF THESE--

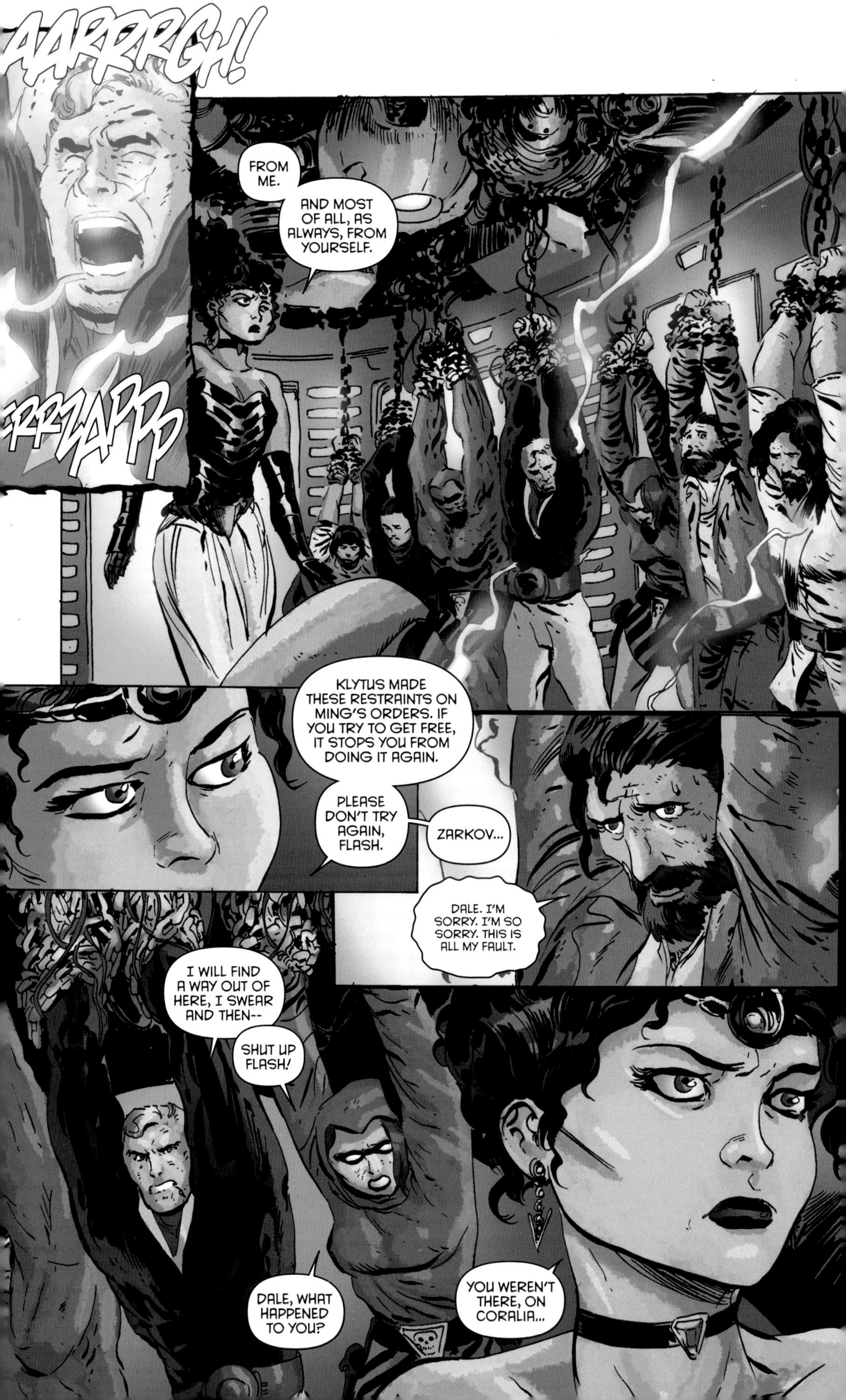
AARRRGH!
FROM ME.
AND MOST OF ALL, AS ALWAYS, FROM YOURSELF.
ERRZAPPP
KLYTUS MADE THESE RESTRAINTS ON MING'S ORDERS. IF YOU TRY TO GET FREE, IT STOPS YOU FROM DOING IT AGAIN.
PLEASE DON'T TRY AGAIN, FLASH.
ZARKOV...
DALE. I'M SORRY. I'M SO SORRY. THIS IS ALL MY FAULT.
I WILL FIND A WAY OUT OF HERE, I SWEAR AND THEN--
SHUT UP FLASH!
DALE, WHAT HAPPENED TO YOU?
YOU WEREN'T THERE, ON CORALIA...

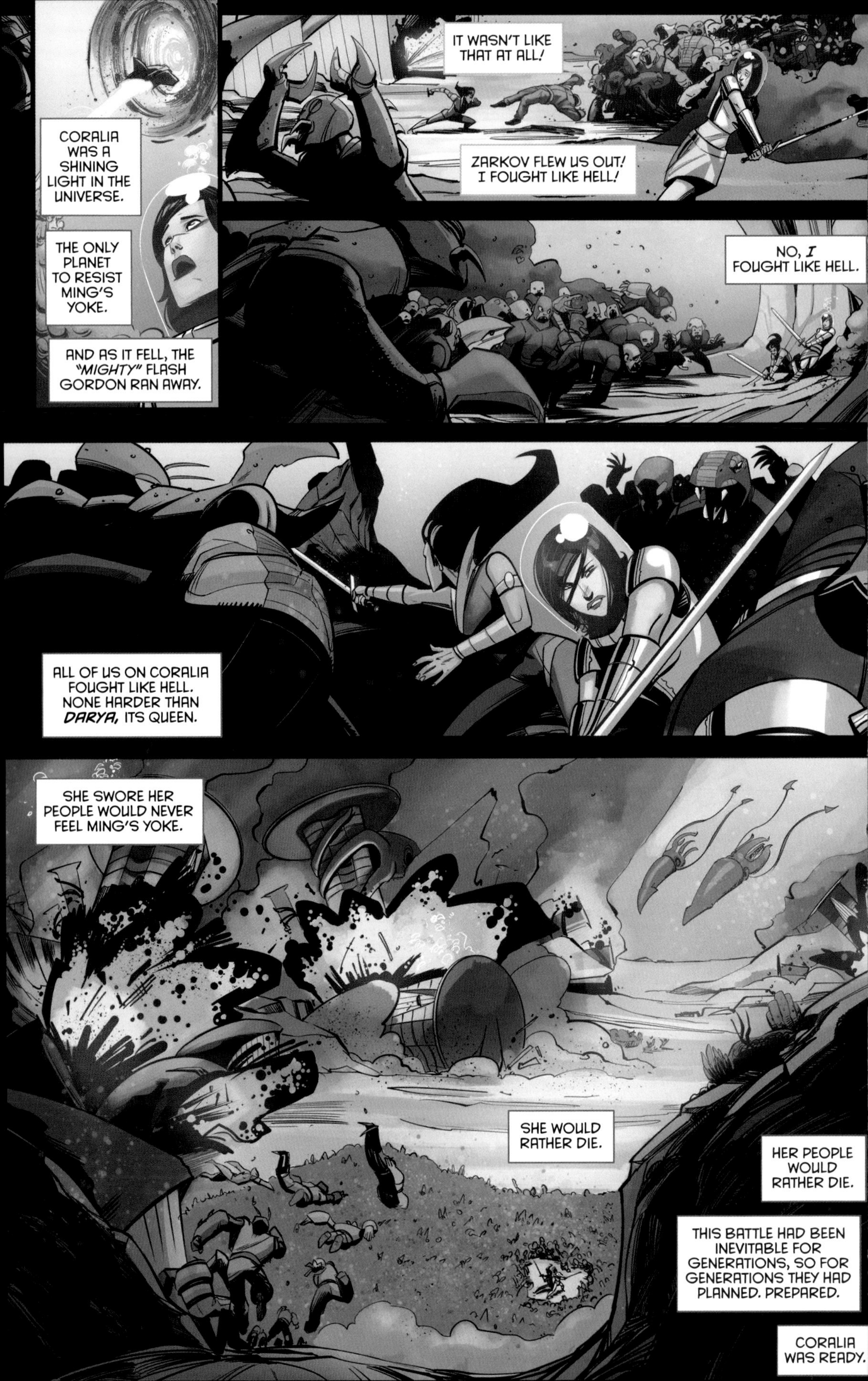
CORALIA WAS A SHINING LIGHT IN THE UNIVERSE.
THE ONLY PLANET TO RESIST MING'S YOKE.
AND AS IT FELL, THE "MIGHTY" FLASH GORDON RAN AWAY.
IT WASN'T LIKE THAT AT ALL!
ZARKOV FLEW US OUT! I FOUGHT LIKE HELL!
NO, *I* FOUGHT LIKE HELL.
ALL OF US ON CORALIA FOUGHT LIKE HELL. NONE HARDER THAN *DARYA,* ITS QUEEN.
SHE SWORE HER PEOPLE WOULD NEVER FEEL MING'S YOKE.
SHE WOULD RATHER DIE.
HER PEOPLE WOULD RATHER DIE.
THIS BATTLE HAD BEEN INEVITABLE FOR GENERATIONS, SO FOR GENERATIONS THEY HAD PLANNED. PREPARED.
CORALIA WAS READY.

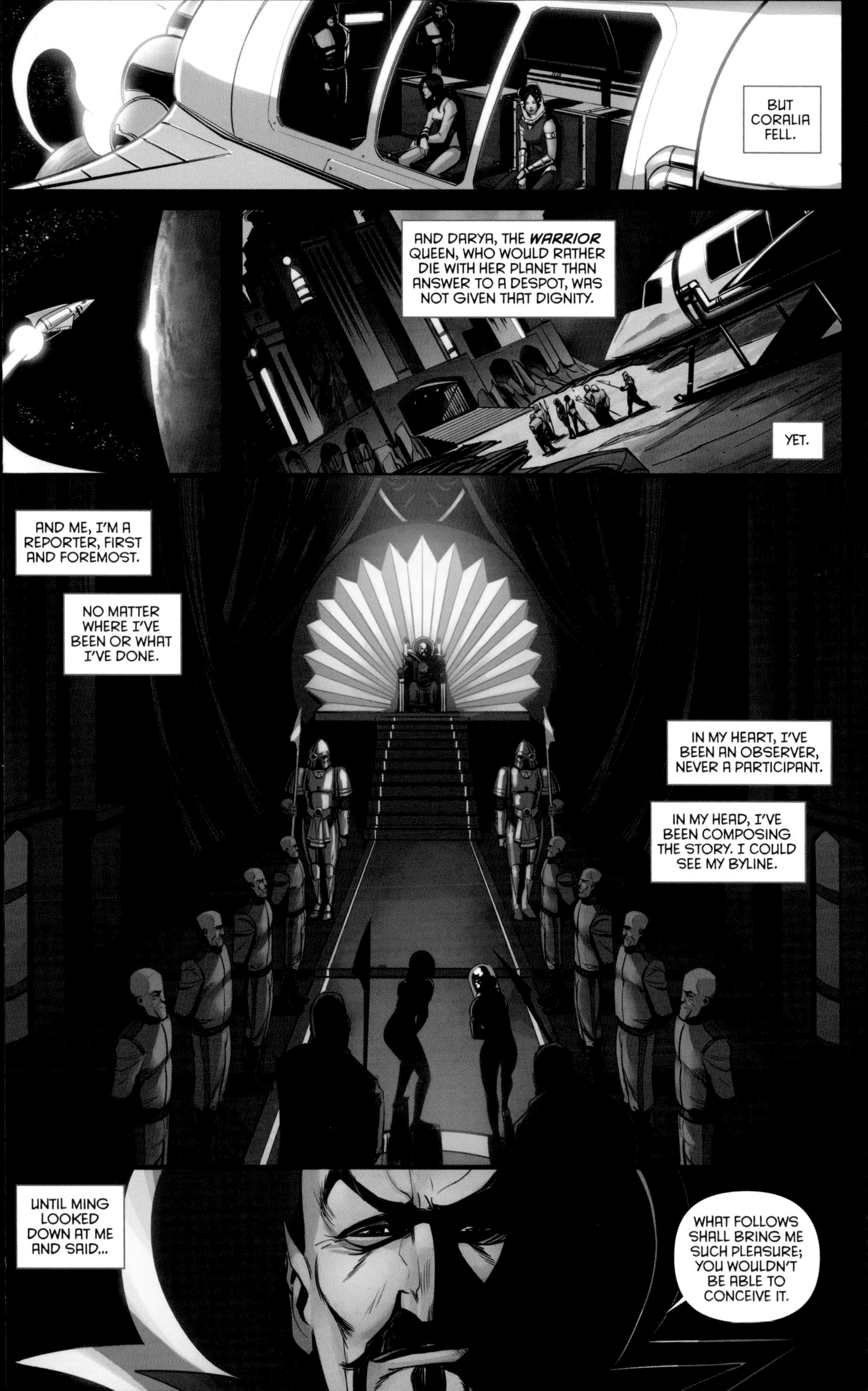
BUT CORALIA FELL.
AND DARYA, THE WARRIOR QUEEN, WHO WOULD RATHER DIE WITH HER PLANET THAN ANSWER TO A DESPOT, WAS NOT GIVEN THAT DIGNITY.
YET.
AND ME, I'M A REPORTER, FIRST AND FOREMOST.
NO MATTER WHERE I'VE BEEN OR WHAT I'VE DONE.
IN MY HEART, I'VE BEEN AN OBSERVER, NEVER A PARTICIPANT.
IN MY HEAD, I'VE BEEN COMPOSING THE STORY. I COULD SEE MY BYLINE.
UNTIL MING LOOKED DOWN AT ME AND SAID...
WHAT FOLLOWS SHALL BRING ME SUCH PLEASURE; YOU WOULDN'T BE ABLE TO CONCEIVE IT.

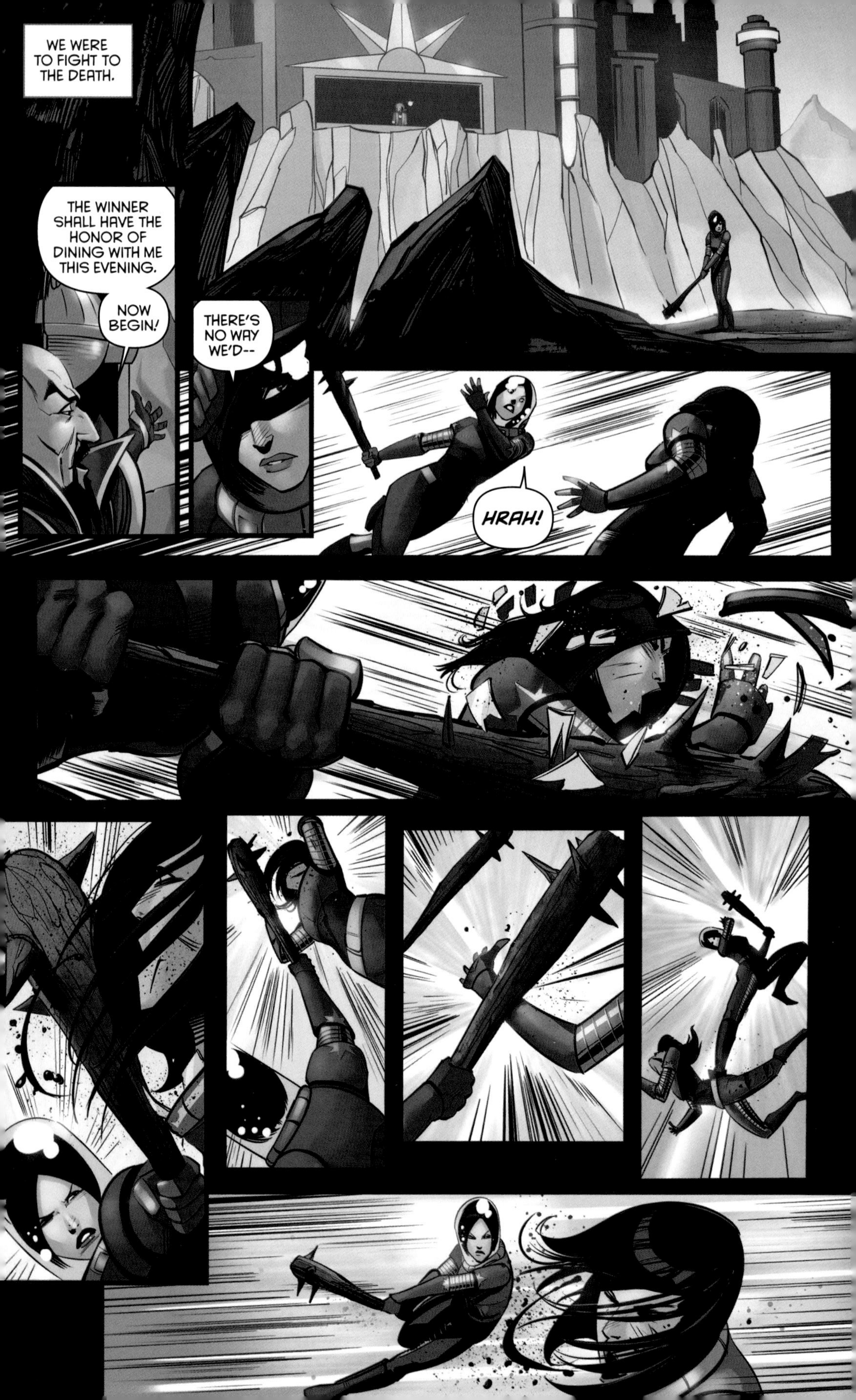

WE WERE TO FIGHT TO THE DEATH.
THE WINNER SHALL HAVE THE HONOR OF DINING WITH ME THIS EVENING.
NOW BEGIN!
THERE'S NO WAY WE'D--
HRAH!

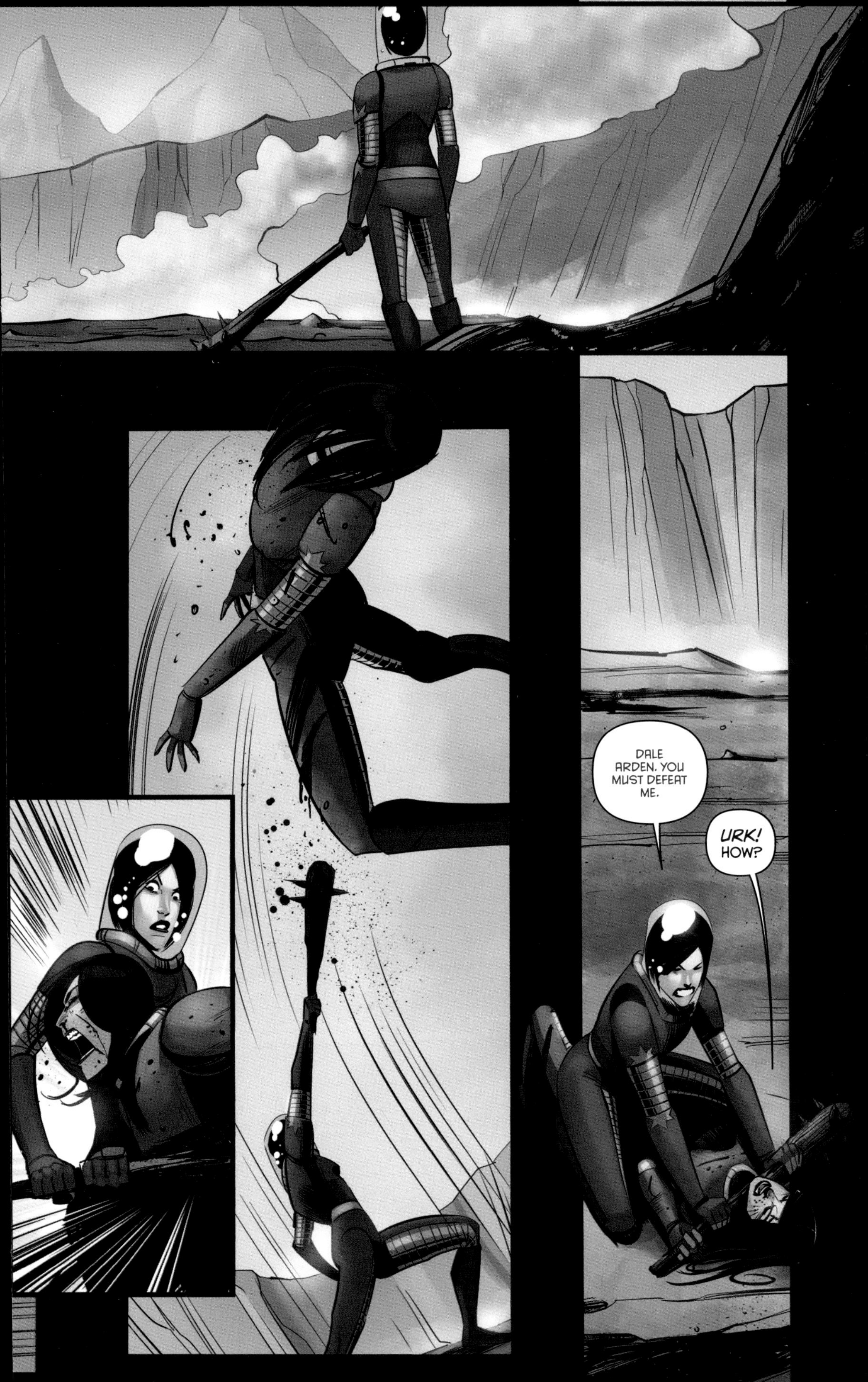
DALE ARDEN. YOU MUST DEFEAT ME.
URK! HOW?

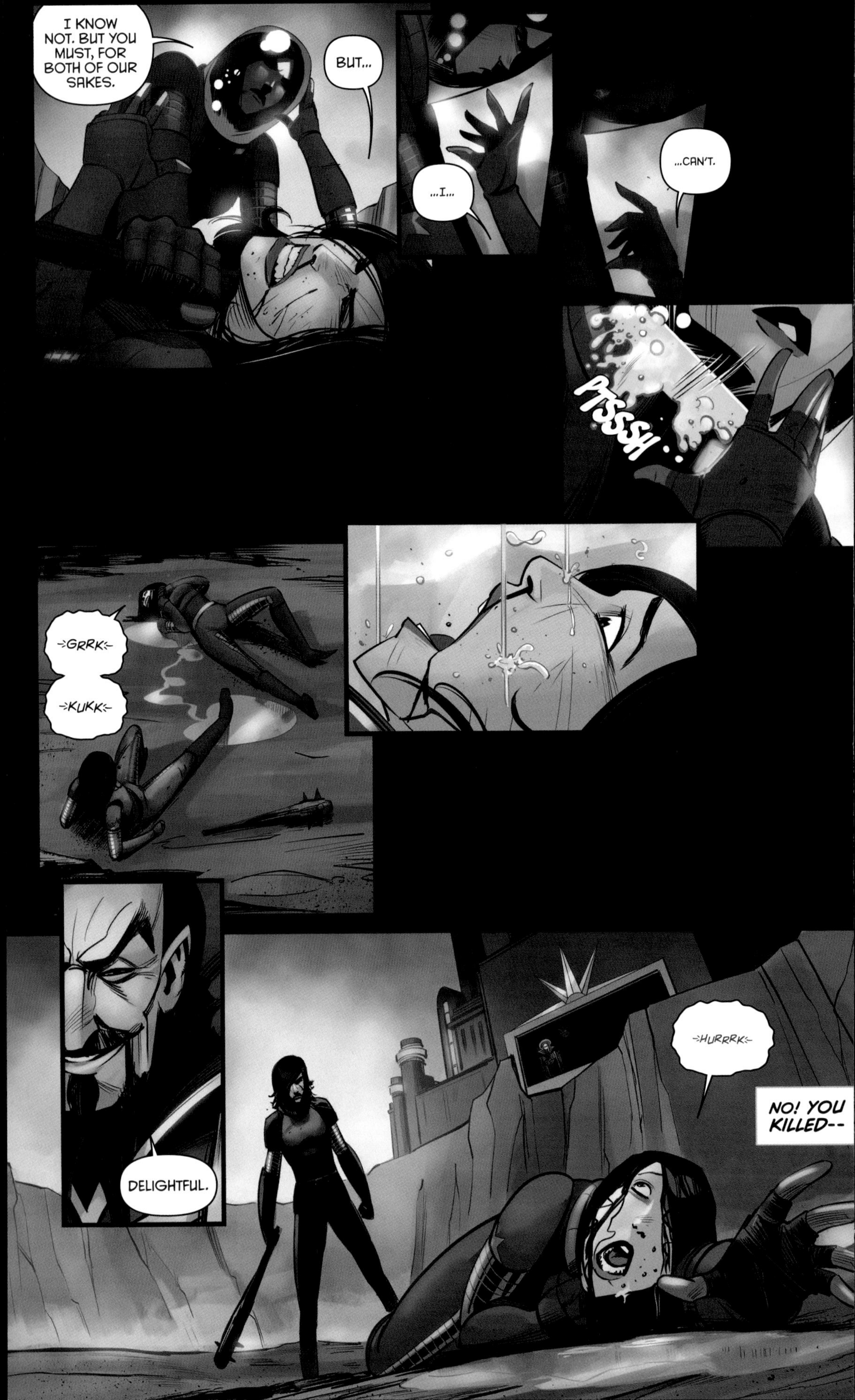
I KNOW NOT. BUT YOU MUST, FOR BOTH OF OUR SAKES.
BUT...
...I...
...CAN'T.
PSSSH
-GRRK-
-KUKK-
DELIGHTFUL.
-HURRRK-
NO! YOU KILLED--

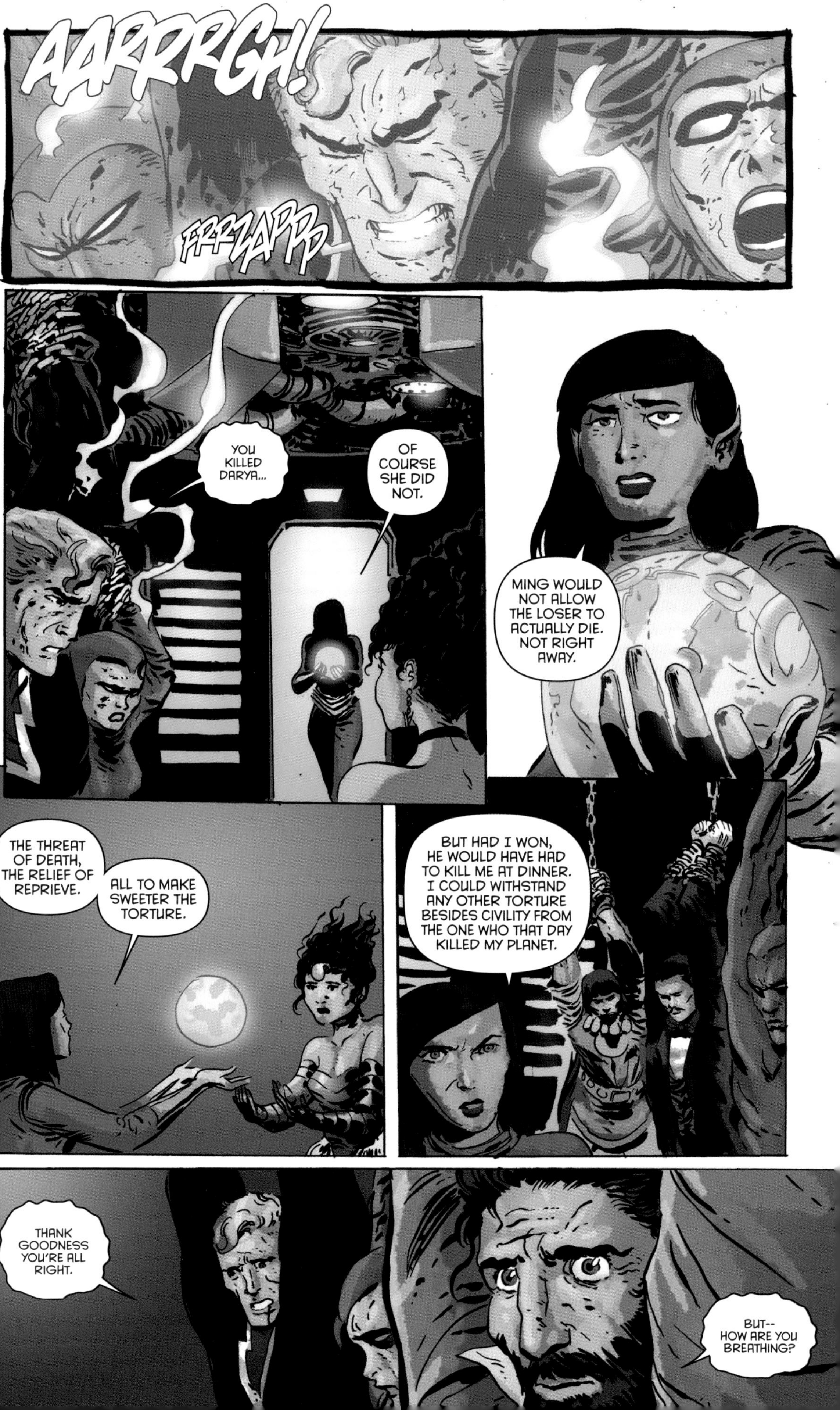
AARRRGH!
FRRZAPPP
YOU KILLED DARYA...
OF COURSE SHE DID NOT.
MING WOULD NOT ALLOW THE LOSER TO ACTUALLY DIE. NOT RIGHT AWAY.
THE THREAT OF DEATH, THE RELIEF OF REPRIEVE.
ALL TO MAKE SWEETER THE TORTURE.
BUT HAD I WON, HE WOULD HAVE HAD TO KILL ME AT DINNER. I COULD WITHSTAND ANY OTHER TORTURE BESIDES CIVILITY FROM THE ONE WHO THAT DAY KILLED MY PLANET.
THANK GOODNESS YOU'RE ALL RIGHT.
BUT-- HOW ARE YOU BREATHING?

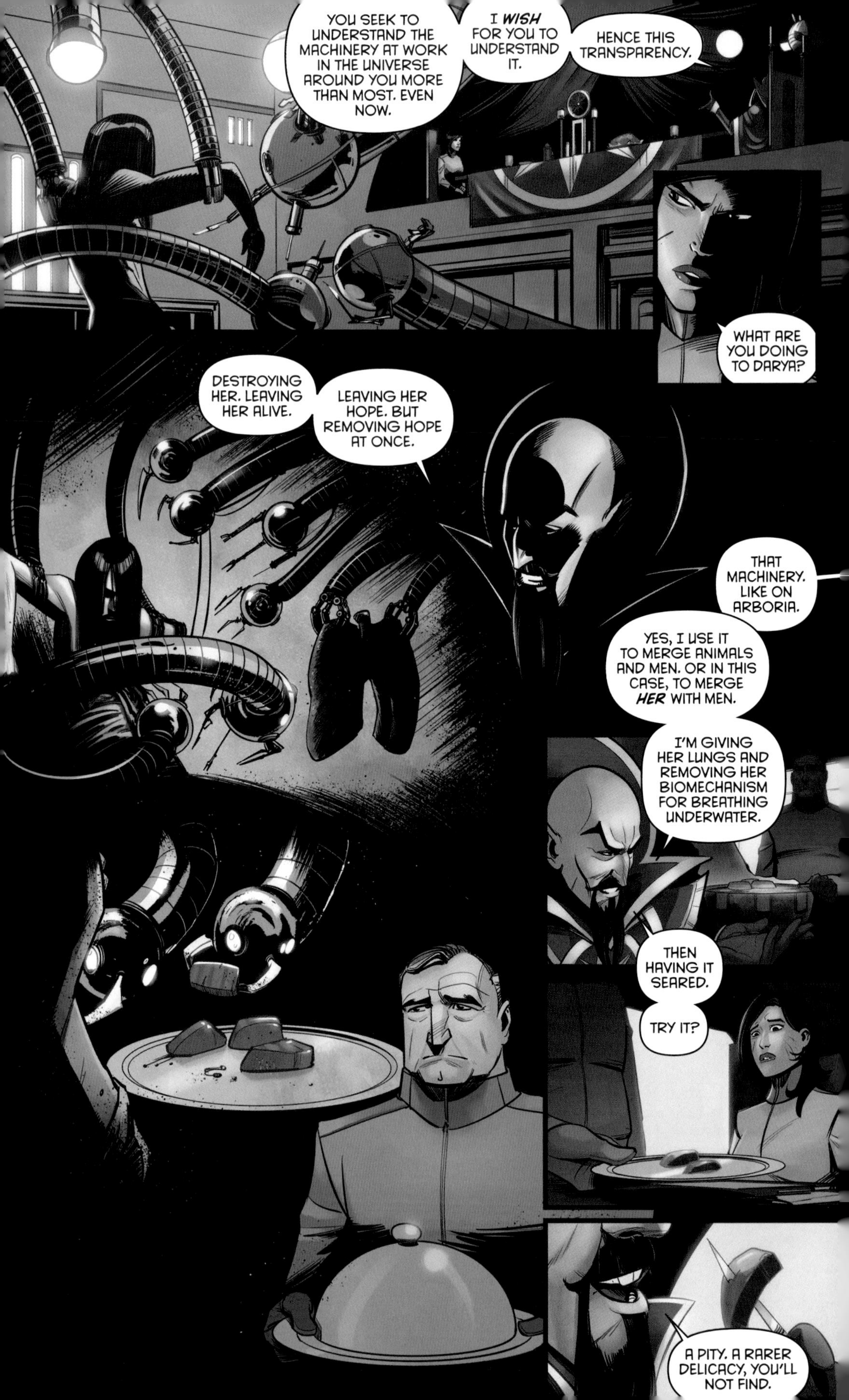
YOU SEEK TO UNDERSTAND THE MACHINERY AT WORK IN THE UNIVERSE AROUND YOU MORE THAN MOST. EVEN NOW.
I **WISH** FOR YOU TO UNDERSTAND IT.
HENCE THIS TRANSPARENCY.
WHAT ARE YOU DOING TO DARYA?
DESTROYING HER. LEAVING HER ALIVE.
LEAVING HER HOPE. BUT REMOVING HOPE AT ONCE.
THAT MACHINERY. LIKE ON ARBORIA.
YES, I USE IT TO MERGE ANIMALS AND MEN. OR IN THIS CASE, TO MERGE **HER** WITH MEN.
I'M GIVING HER LUNGS AND REMOVING HER BIOMECHANISM FOR BREATHING UNDERWATER.
THEN HAVING IT SEARED.
TRY IT?
A PITY. A RARER DELICACY, YOU'LL NOT FIND.

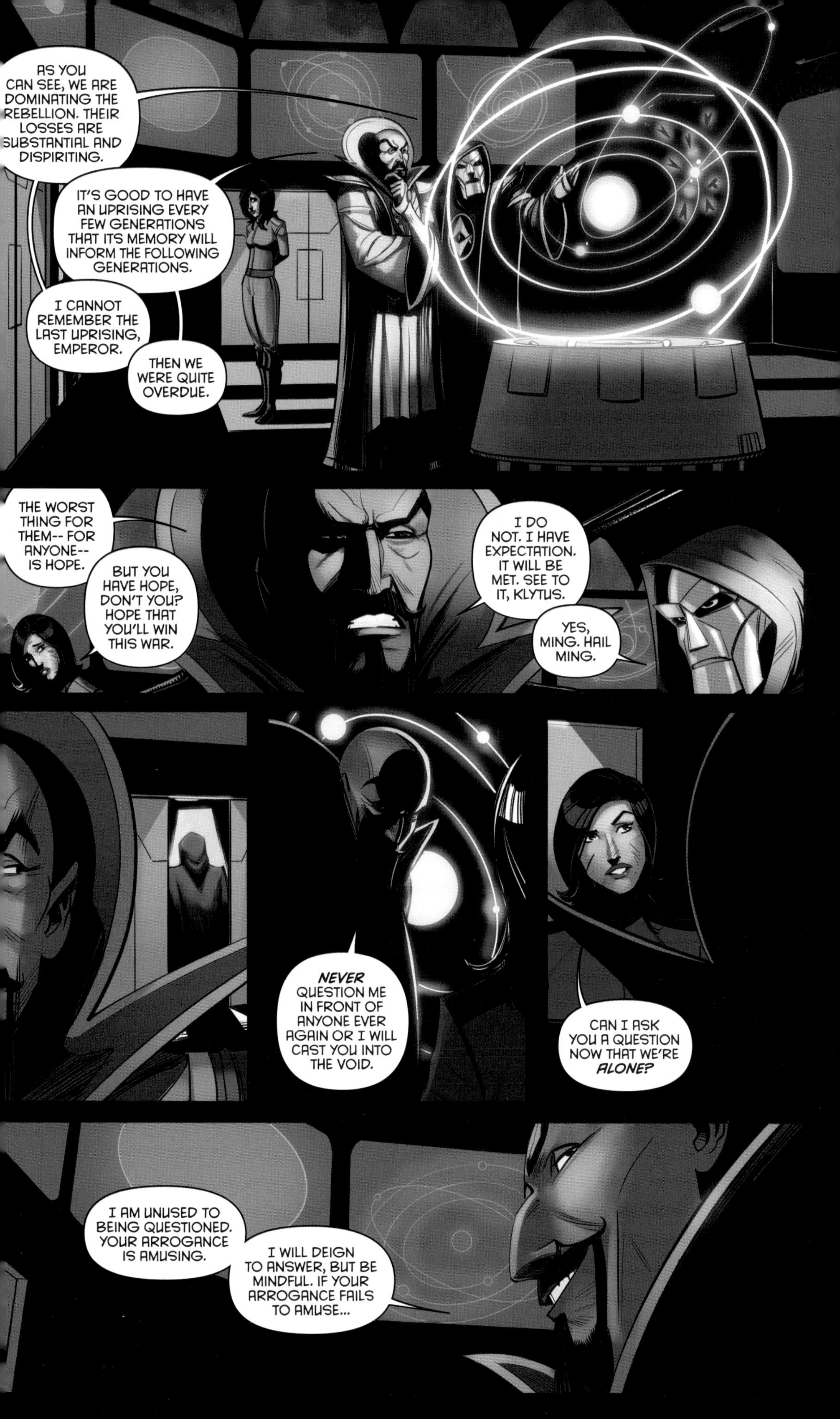
AS YOU CAN SEE, WE ARE DOMINATING THE REBELLION. THEIR LOSSES ARE SUBSTANTIAL AND DISPIRITING.
IT'S GOOD TO HAVE AN UPRISING EVERY FEW GENERATIONS THAT ITS MEMORY WILL INFORM THE FOLLOWING GENERATIONS.
I CANNOT REMEMBER THE LAST UPRISING, EMPEROR.
THEN WE WERE QUITE OVERDUE.
THE WORST THING FOR THEM-- FOR ANYONE-- IS HOPE.
BUT YOU HAVE HOPE, DON'T YOU? HOPE THAT YOU'LL WIN THIS WAR.
I DO NOT. I HAVE EXPECTATION. IT WILL BE MET. SEE TO IT, KLYTUS.
YES, MING. HAIL MING.
NEVER QUESTION ME IN FRONT OF ANYONE EVER AGAIN OR I WILL CAST YOU INTO THE VOID.
CAN I ASK YOU A QUESTION NOW THAT WE'RE *ALONE?*
I AM UNUSED TO BEING QUESTIONED. YOUR ARROGANCE IS AMUSING.
I WILL DEIGN TO ANSWER, BUT BE MINDFUL. IF YOUR ARROGANCE FAILS TO AMUSE...

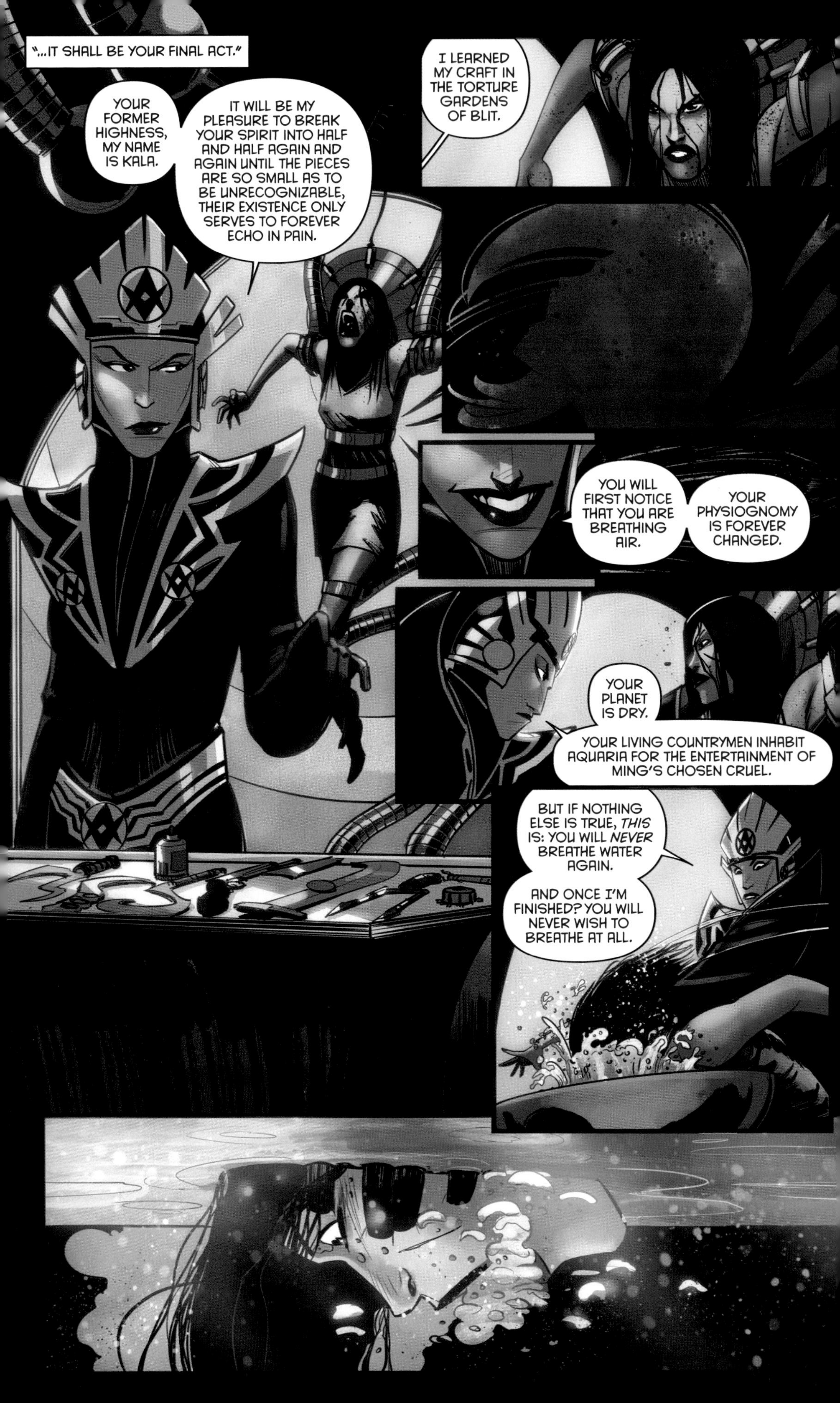
"...IT SHALL BE YOUR FINAL ACT."
YOUR FORMER HIGHNESS, MY NAME IS KALA.
IT WILL BE MY PLEASURE TO BREAK YOUR SPIRIT INTO HALF AND HALF AGAIN AND AGAIN UNTIL THE PIECES ARE SO SMALL AS TO BE UNRECOGNIZABLE, THEIR EXISTENCE ONLY SERVES TO FOREVER ECHO IN PAIN.
I LEARNED MY CRAFT IN THE TORTURE GARDENS OF BLIT.
YOU WILL FIRST NOTICE THAT YOU ARE BREATHING AIR.
YOUR PHYSIOGNOMY IS FOREVER CHANGED.
YOUR PLANET IS DRY.
YOUR LIVING COUNTRYMEN INHABIT AQUARIA FOR THE ENTERTAINMENT OF MING'S CHOSEN CRUEL.
BUT IF NOTHING ELSE IS TRUE, *THIS* IS: YOU WILL *NEVER* BREATHE WATER AGAIN.
AND ONCE I'M FINISHED? YOU WILL NEVER WISH TO BREATHE AT ALL.

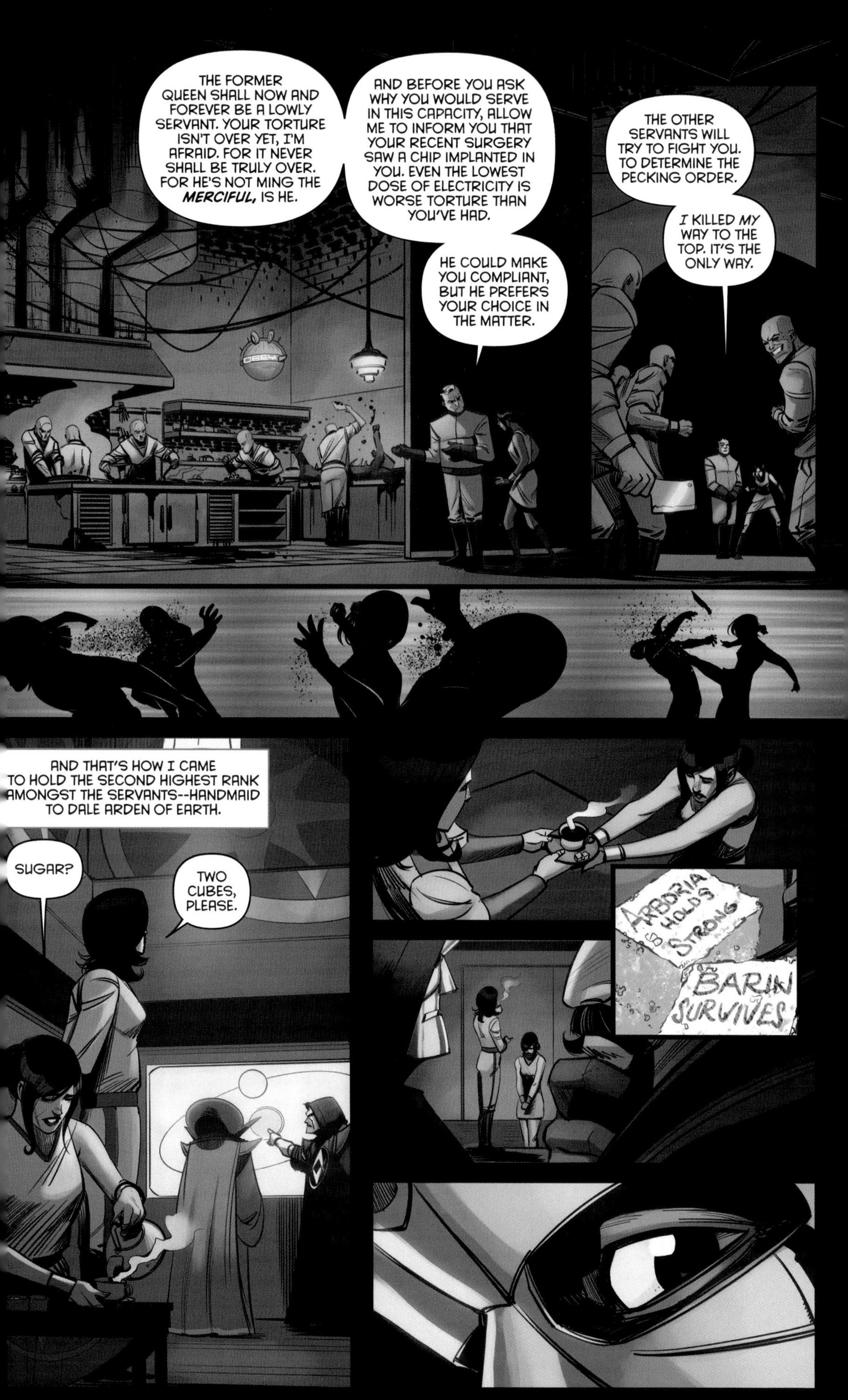

THE FORMER QUEEN SHALL NOW AND FOREVER BE A LOWLY SERVANT. YOUR TORTURE ISN'T OVER YET, I'M AFRAID. FOR IT NEVER SHALL BE TRULY OVER. FOR HE'S NOT MING THE *MERCIFUL*, IS HE.
AND BEFORE YOU ASK WHY YOU WOULD SERVE IN THIS CAPACITY, ALLOW ME TO INFORM YOU THAT YOUR RECENT SURGERY SAW A CHIP IMPLANTED IN YOU. EVEN THE LOWEST DOSE OF ELECTRICITY IS WORSE TORTURE THAN YOU'VE HAD.
HE COULD MAKE YOU COMPLIANT, BUT HE PREFERS YOUR CHOICE IN THE MATTER.
OBEY
THE OTHER SERVANTS WILL TRY TO FIGHT YOU. TO DETERMINE THE PECKING ORDER.
I KILLED *MY* WAY TO THE TOP. IT'S THE ONLY WAY.
AND THAT'S HOW I CAME TO HOLD THE SECOND HIGHEST RANK AMONGST THE SERVANTS--HANDMAID TO DALE ARDEN OF EARTH.
SUGAR?
TWO CUBES, PLEASE.
ARBORIA HOLDS STRONG
BARIN SURVIVES

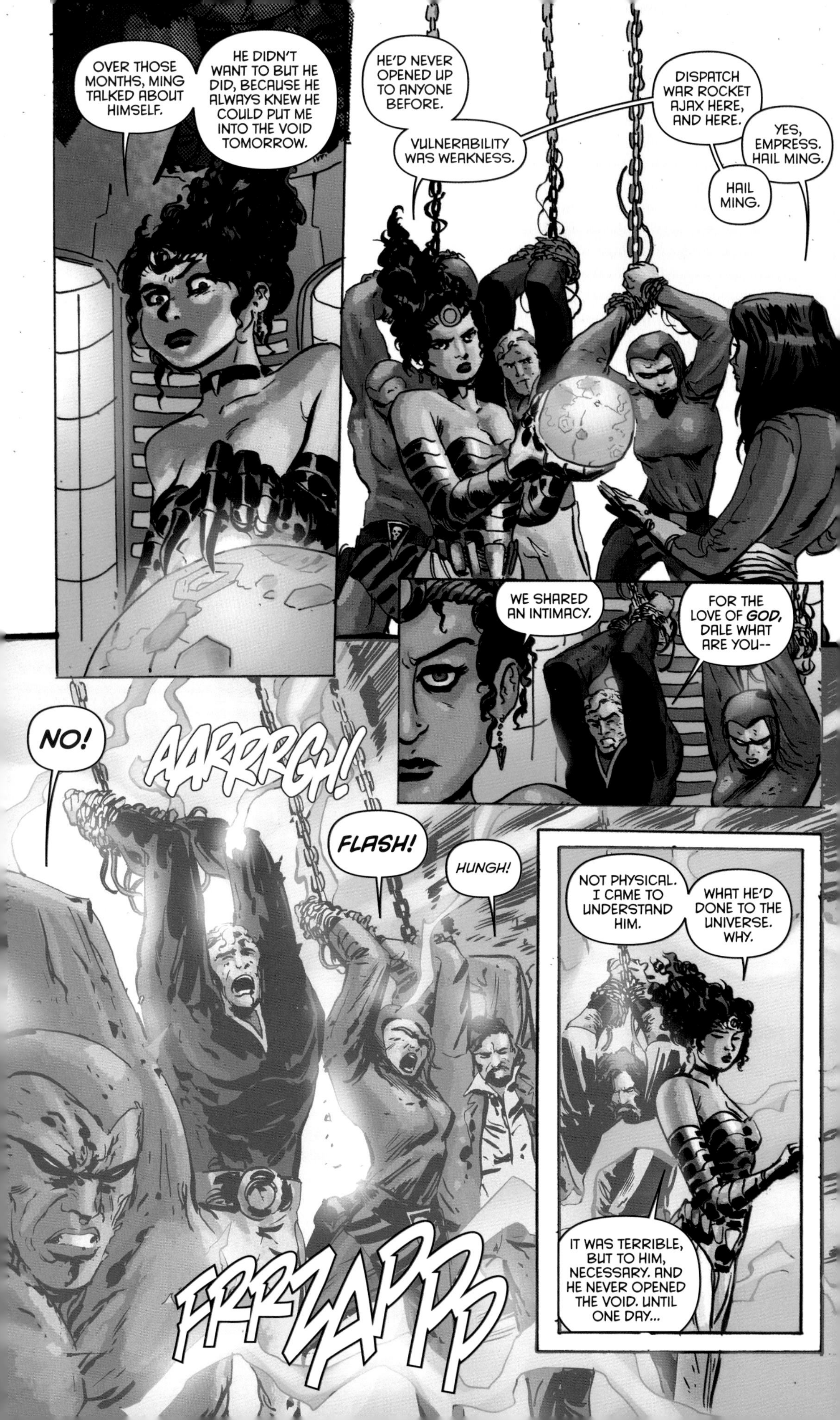

OVER THOSE MONTHS, MING TALKED ABOUT HIMSELF.
HE DIDN'T WANT TO BUT HE DID, BECAUSE HE ALWAYS KNEW HE COULD PUT ME INTO THE VOID TOMORROW.
HE'D NEVER OPENED UP TO ANYONE BEFORE.
VULNERABILITY WAS WEAKNESS.
DISPATCH WAR ROCKET AJAX HERE, AND HERE.
YES, EMPRESS. HAIL MING.
HAIL MING.
WE SHARED AN INTIMACY.
FOR THE LOVE OF *GOD,* DALE WHAT ARE YOU--
NO!
AARRRGH!
FLASH!
HUNGH!
FRRZAPPP
NOT PHYSICAL. I CAME TO UNDERSTAND HIM.
WHAT HE'D DONE TO THE UNIVERSE. WHY.
IT WAS TERRIBLE, BUT TO HIM, NECESSARY. AND HE NEVER OPENED THE VOID. UNTIL ONE DAY...

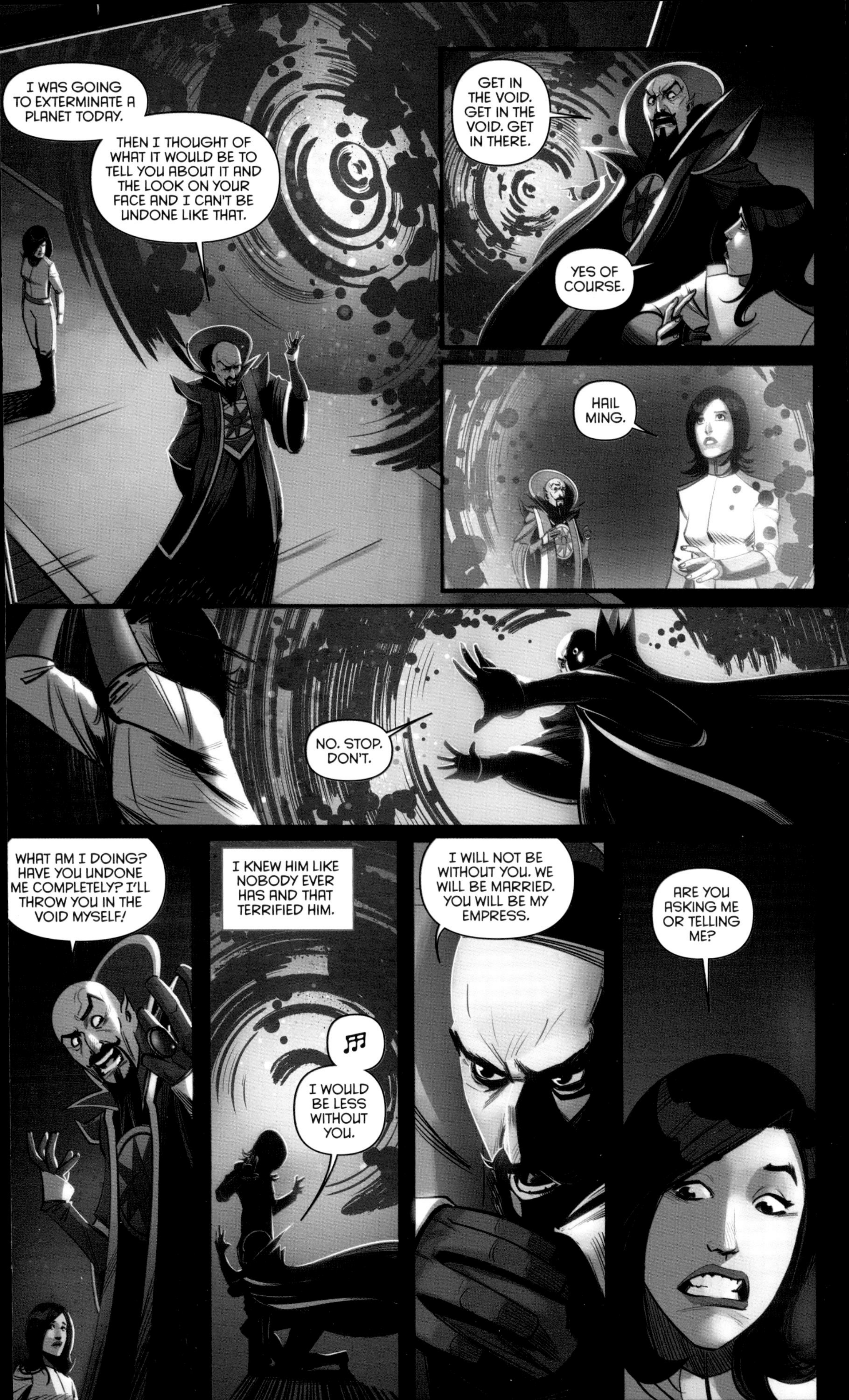
I WAS GOING TO EXTERMINATE A PLANET TODAY.
THEN I THOUGHT OF WHAT IT WOULD BE TO TELL YOU ABOUT IT AND THE LOOK ON YOUR FACE AND I CAN'T BE UNDONE LIKE THAT.
GET IN THE VOID. GET IN THE VOID. GET IN THERE.
YES OF COURSE.
HAIL MING.
NO. STOP. DON'T.
WHAT AM I DOING? HAVE YOU UNDONE ME COMPLETELY? I'LL THROW YOU IN THE VOID MYSELF!
I KNEW HIM LIKE NOBODY EVER HAS AND THAT TERRIFIED HIM.
I WOULD BE LESS WITHOUT YOU.
I WILL NOT BE WITHOUT YOU. WE WILL BE MARRIED. YOU WILL BE MY EMPRESS.
ARE YOU ASKING ME OR TELLING ME?

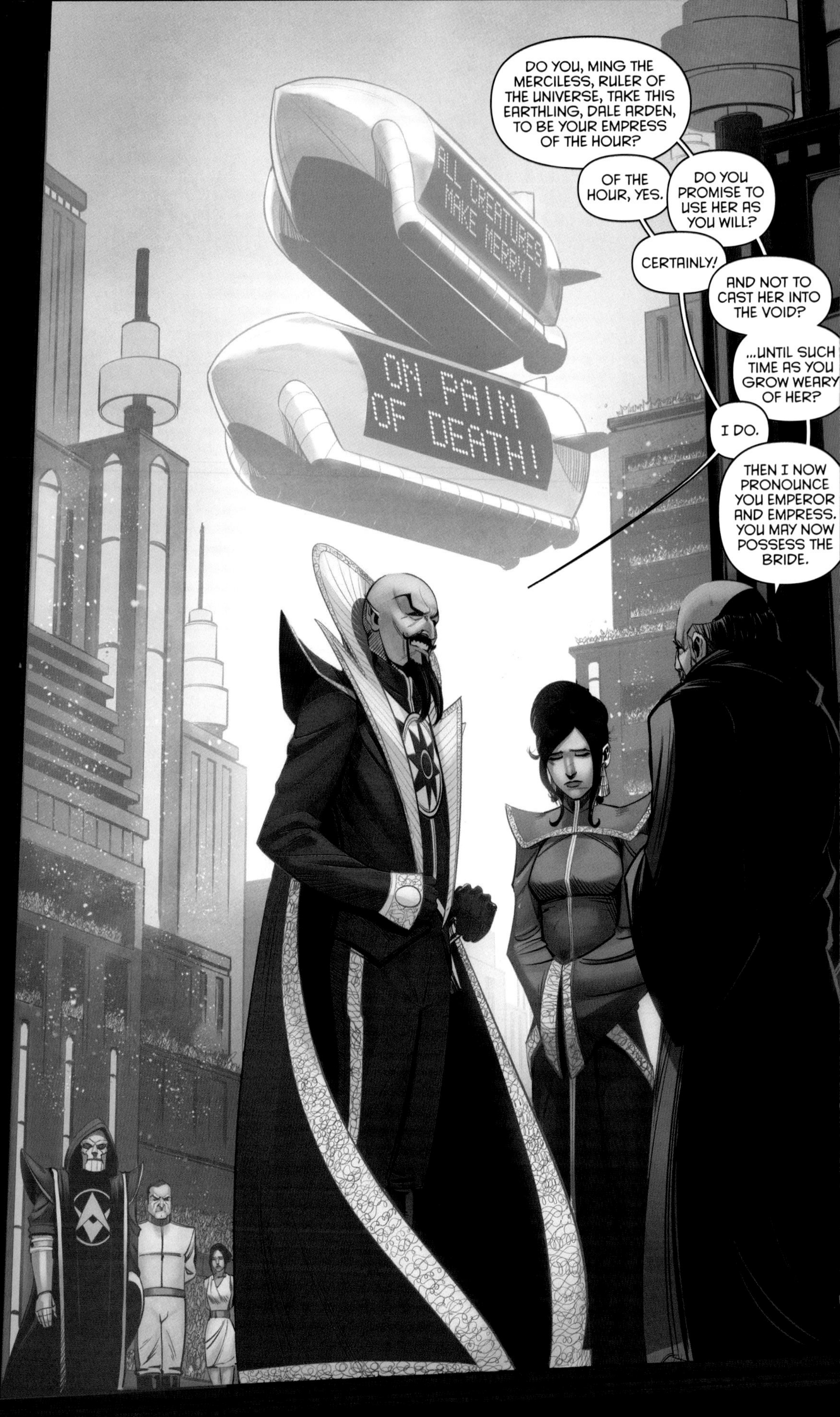
ALL CREATURES MAKE MERRY!
ON PAIN OF DEATH!
DO YOU, MING THE MERCILESS, RULER OF THE UNIVERSE, TAKE THIS EARTHLING, DALE ARDEN, TO BE YOUR EMPRESS OF THE HOUR?
OF THE HOUR, YES.
DO YOU PROMISE TO USE HER AS YOU WILL?
CERTAINLY!
AND NOT TO CAST HER INTO THE VOID?
...UNTIL SUCH TIME AS YOU GROW WEARY OF HER?
I DO.
THEN I NOW PRONOUNCE YOU EMPEROR AND EMPRESS. YOU MAY NOW POSSESS THE BRIDE.

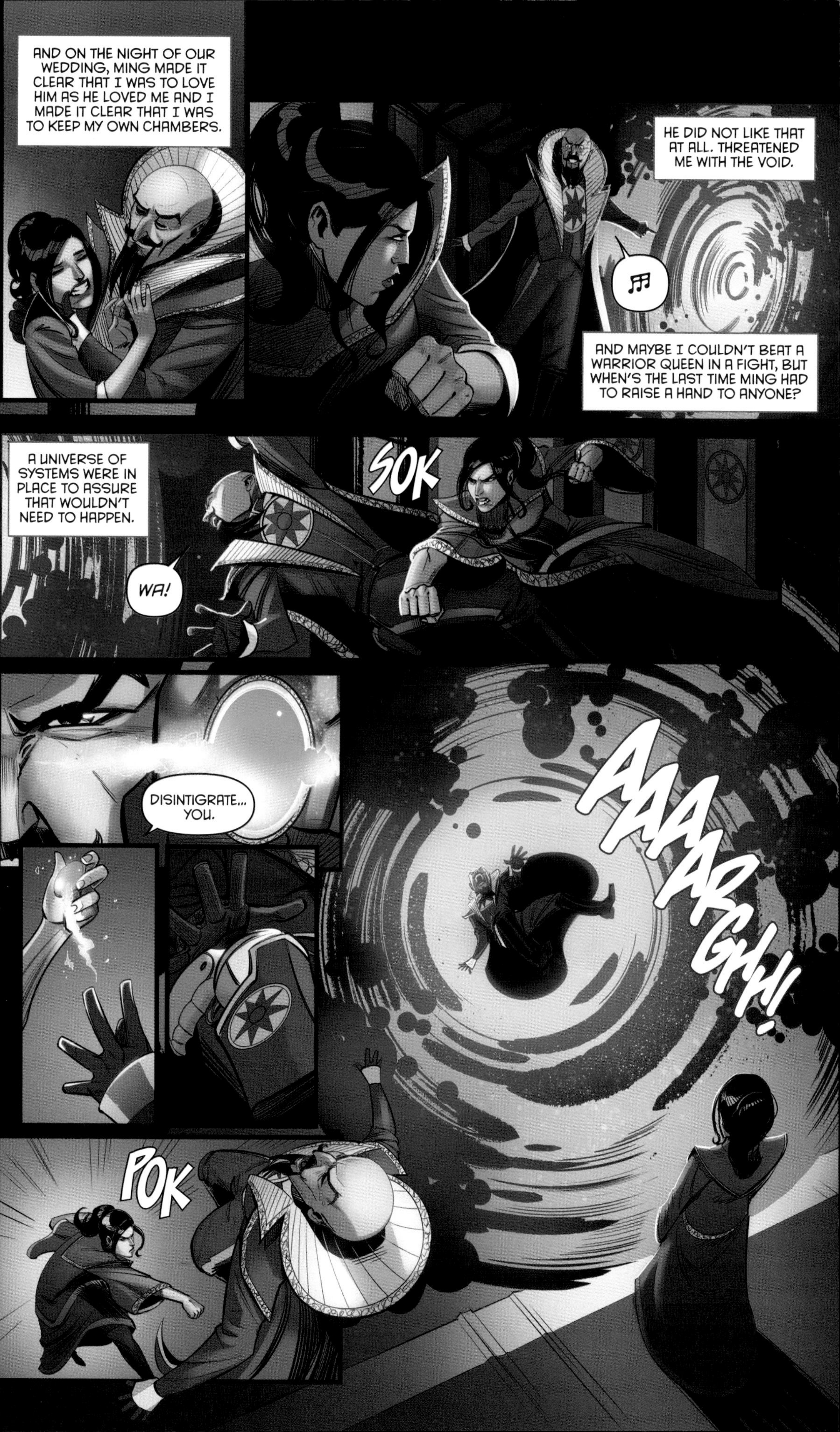
AND ON THE NIGHT OF OUR WEDDING, MING MADE IT CLEAR THAT I WAS TO LOVE HIM AS HE LOVED ME AND I MADE IT CLEAR THAT I WAS TO KEEP MY OWN CHAMBERS.
HE DID NOT LIKE THAT AT ALL. THREATENED ME WITH THE VOID.
♬
AND MAYBE I COULDN'T BEAT A WARRIOR QUEEN IN A FIGHT, BUT WHEN'S THE LAST TIME MING HAD TO RAISE A HAND TO ANYONE?
A UNIVERSE OF SYSTEMS WERE IN PLACE TO ASSURE THAT WOULDN'T NEED TO HAPPEN.
SOK
WA!
DISINTIGRATE... YOU.
AAAARGHH!
POK

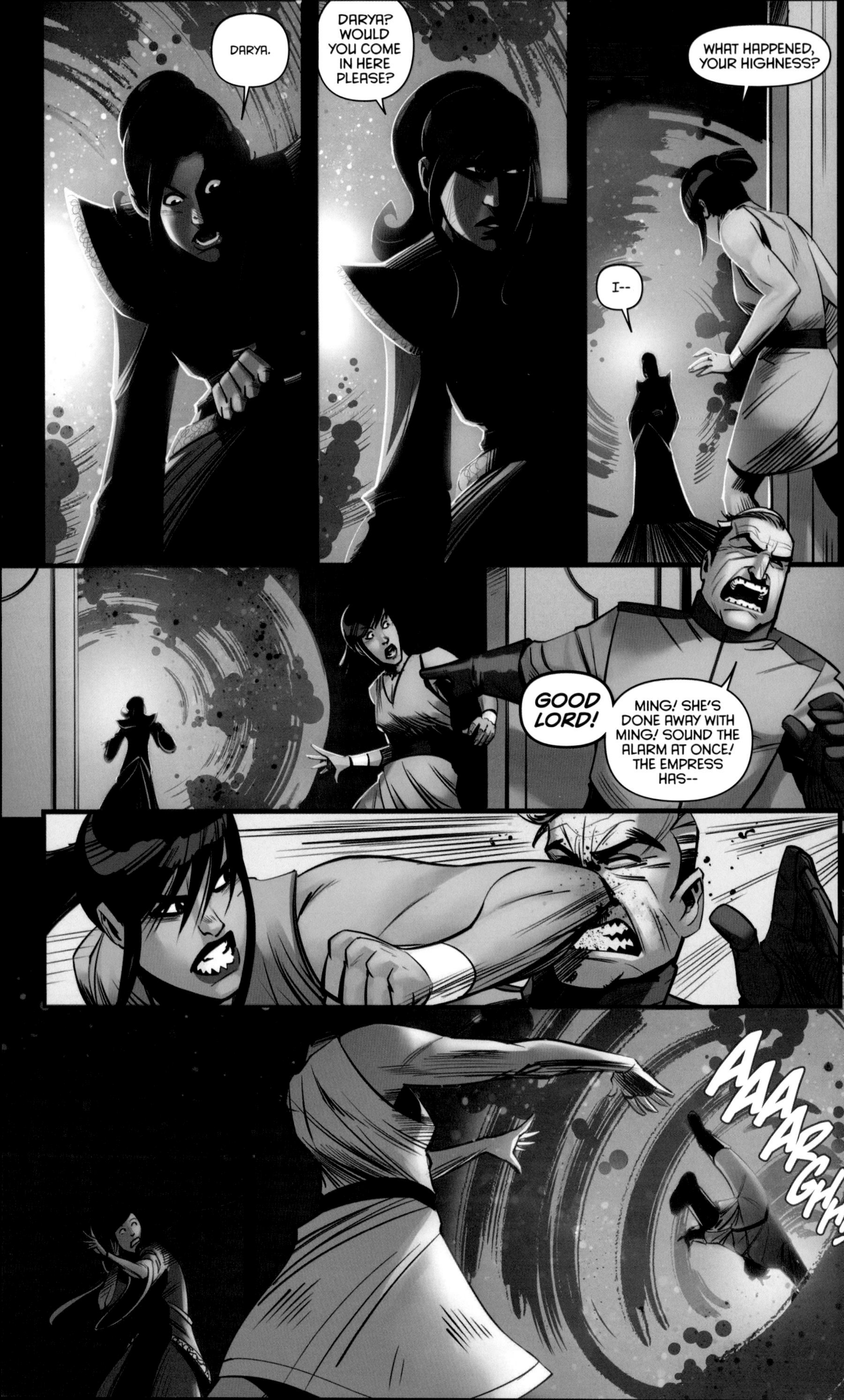
DARYA.
DARYA? WOULD YOU COME IN HERE PLEASE?
WHAT HAPPENED, YOUR HIGHNESS?
I--
GOOD LORD!
MING! SHE'S DONE AWAY WITH MING! SOUND THE ALARM AT ONCE! THE EMPRESS HAS--
AAAARGH!

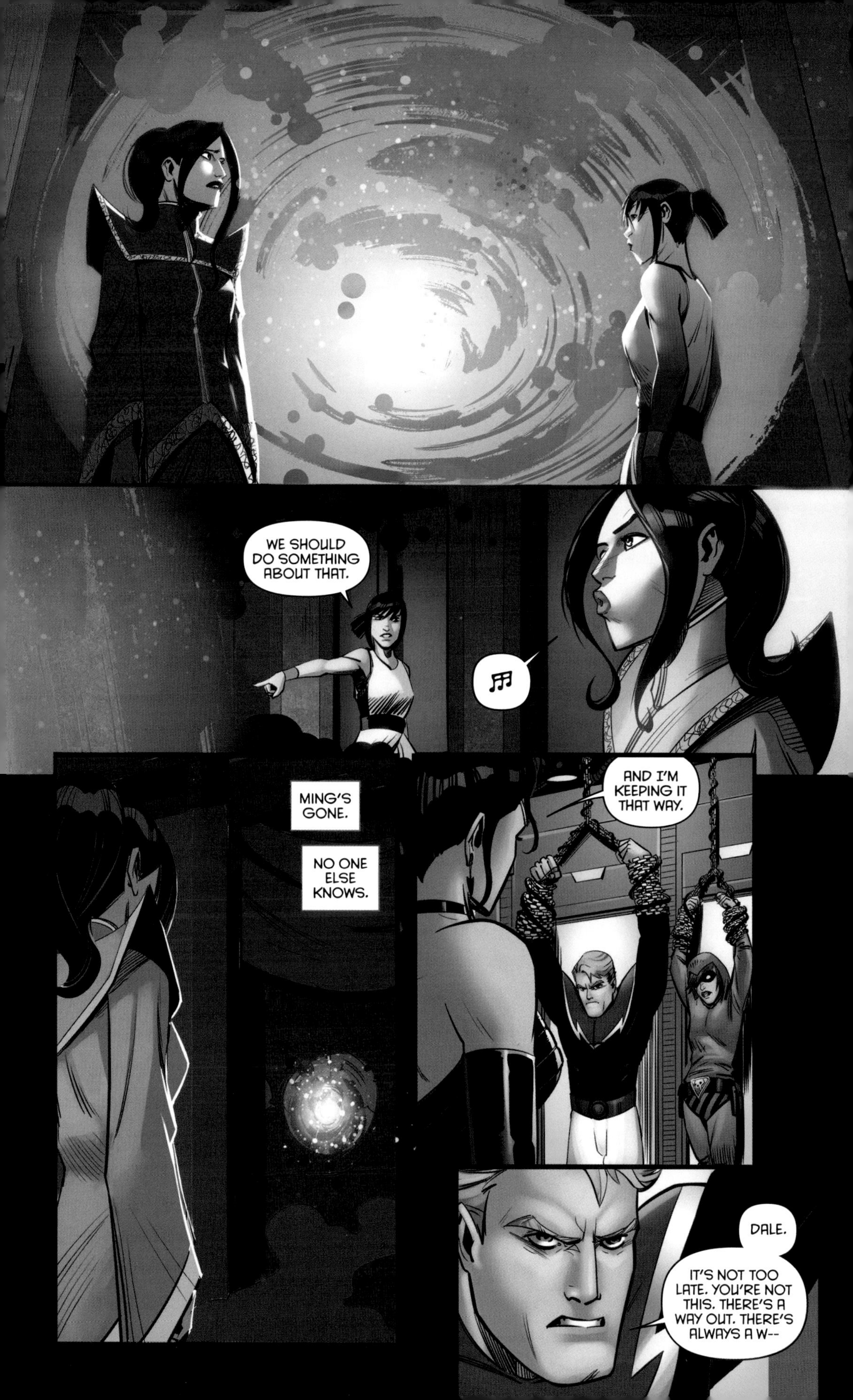

WE SHOULD DO SOMETHING ABOUT THAT.
♬
MING'S GONE.
NO ONE ELSE KNOWS.
AND I'M KEEPING IT THAT WAY.
DALE.
IT'S NOT TOO LATE. YOU'RE NOT THIS. THERE'S A WAY OUT. THERE'S ALWAYS A W--

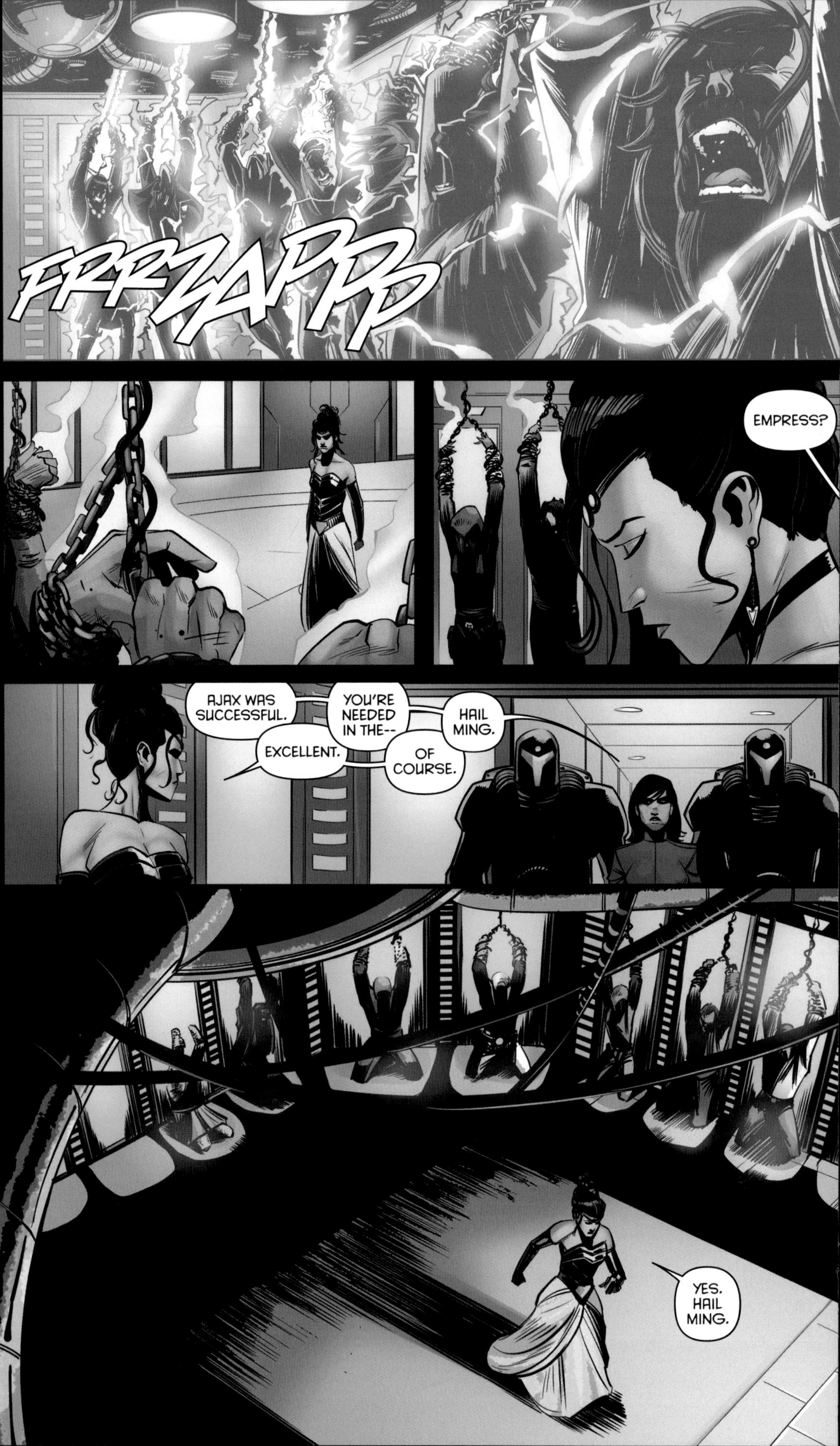
FRRZAPPP
EMPRESS?
AJAX WAS SUCCESSFUL.
EXCELLENT.
YOU'RE NEEDED IN THE--
OF COURSE.
HAIL MING.
YES. HAIL MING.

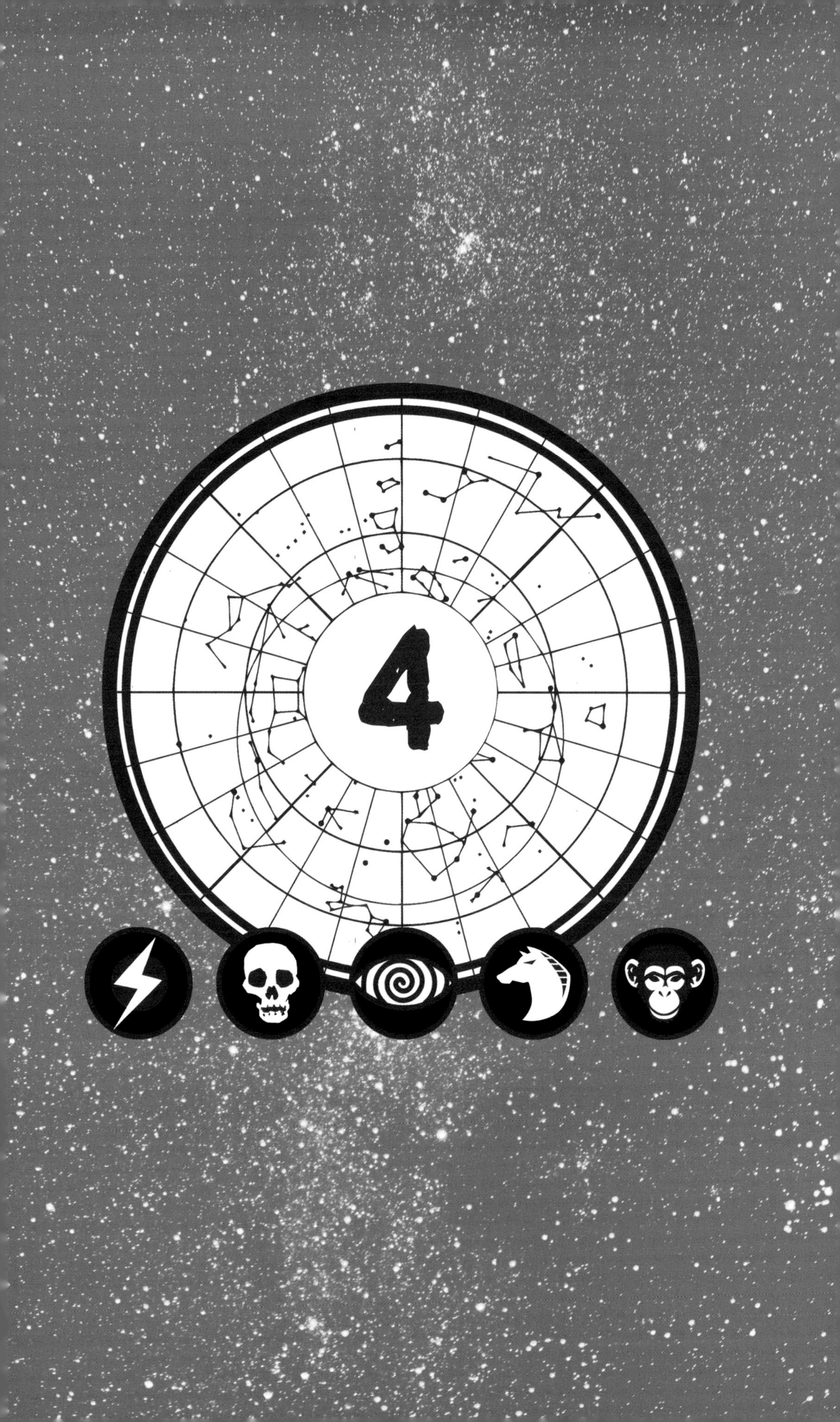
4

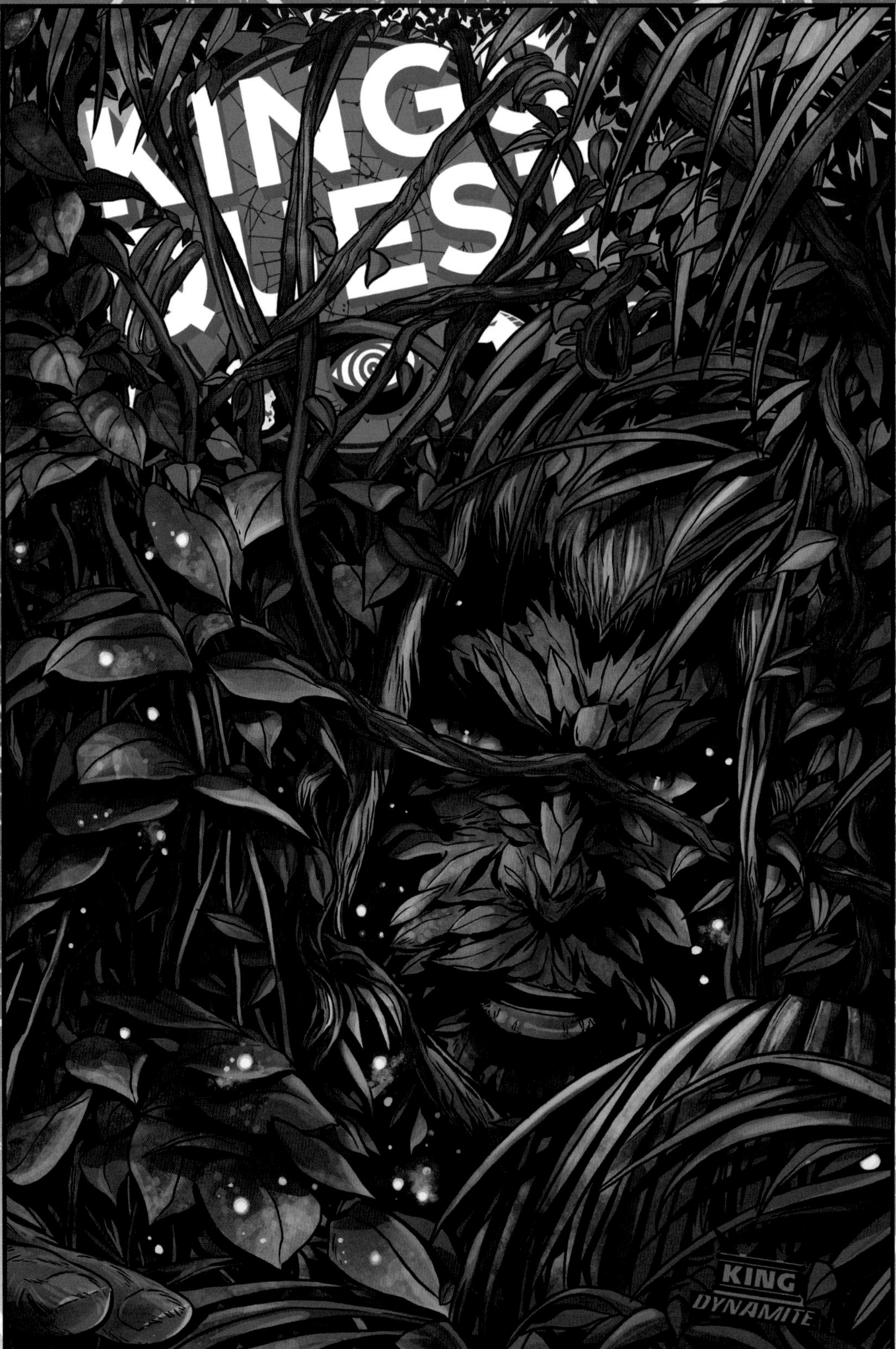
KING
DYNAMITE

Issue #4 cover
Art by **MARC LAMING**

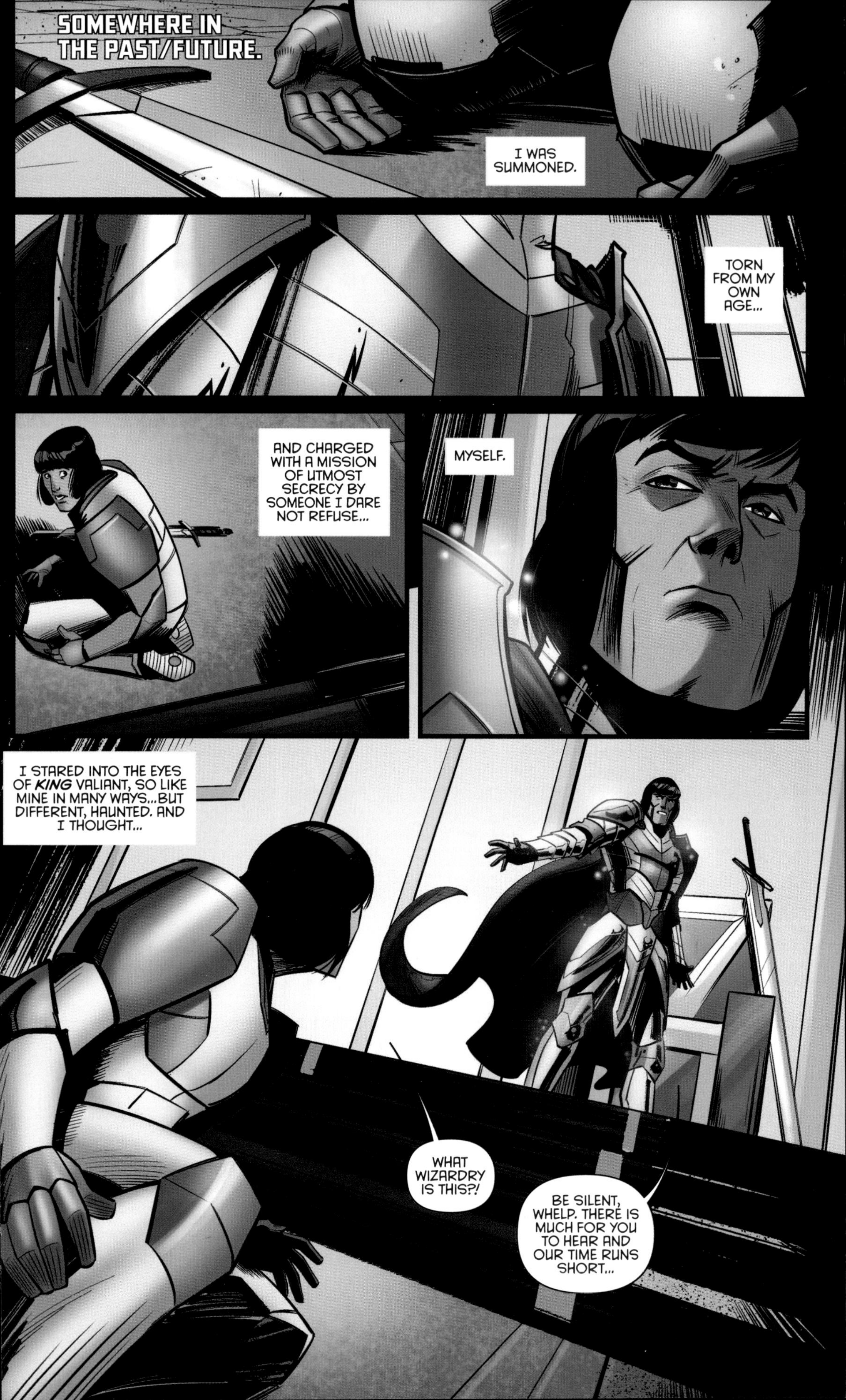
SOMEWHERE IN THE PAST/FUTURE.
I WAS SUMMONED.
TORN FROM MY OWN AGE...
AND CHARGED WITH A MISSION OF UTMOST SECRECY BY SOMEONE I DARE NOT REFUSE...
MYSELF.
I STARED INTO THE EYES OF KING VALIANT, SO LIKE MINE IN MANY WAYS...BUT DIFFERENT, HAUNTED. AND I THOUGHT...
WHAT WIZARDRY IS THIS?!
BE SILENT, WHELP. THERE IS MUCH FOR YOU TO HEAR AND OUR TIME RUNS SHORT...

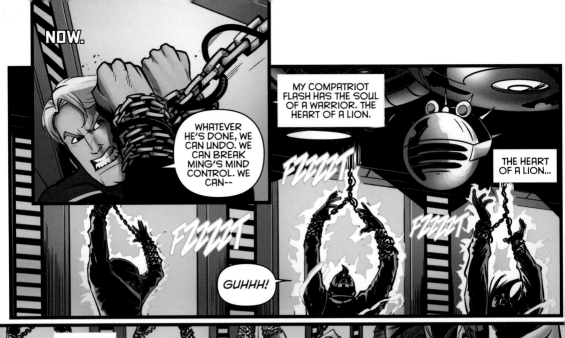

WHATEVER HE'S DONE, WE CAN UNDO. WE CAN BREAK MING'S MIND CONTROL. WE CAN--

MY COMPATRIOT FLASH HAS THE SOUL OF A WARRIOR. THE HEART OF A LION.

THE HEART OF A LION...

FZZZZT

FZZZZT

FZZZZT

GUHHH!

...AND THE BRAINS OF AN OGRE.

UHH... FLASH, STOP... ZARKOV'S INJURIES CAN'T SUSTAIN...

JIM'S WORSE. THIS PLACE IS POISONING HIM.

WHICH PLACE?

THIS PLACE. *THE ENTIRE PLANET!*

PLEASE CONTINUE TO STRUGGLE. I WILL CONTINUE TO INCREASE VOLTAGE. HAIL >CRACKLE< MING.

...NO.

I POSED A QUERY TO YOU, BARBARIAN--

CLOCKWORK MACHINES.

MING RELIES TOO HEAVILY ON THEM.

YOU: SAVAGE. YOU ARE TO BE TORTURED TO DEATH.

WHY DO YOU SMILE?

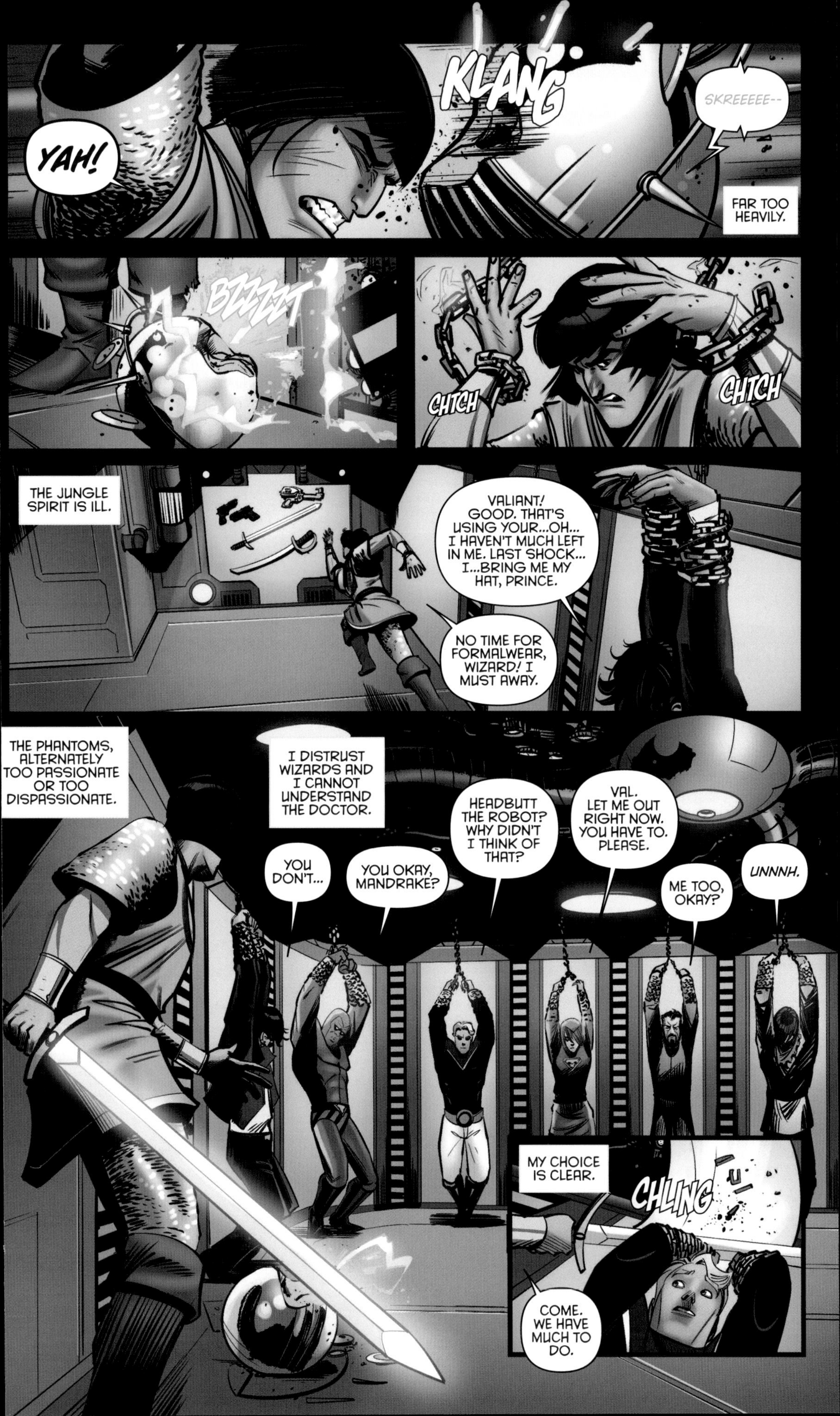
YAH!
KLANG
SKREEEEE--
FAR TOO HEAVILY.
BZZZZT
CHTCH
CHTCH
THE JUNGLE SPIRIT IS ILL.
VALIANT! GOOD. THAT'S USING YOUR...OH... I HAVEN'T MUCH LEFT IN ME. LAST SHOCK... I...BRING ME MY HAT, PRINCE.
NO TIME FOR FORMALWEAR, WIZARD! I MUST AWAY.
THE PHANTOMS, ALTERNATELY TOO PASSIONATE OR TOO DISPASSIONATE.
I DISTRUST WIZARDS AND I CANNOT UNDERSTAND THE DOCTOR.
YOU DON'T...
YOU OKAY, MANDRAKE?
HEADBUTT THE ROBOT? WHY DIDN'T I THINK OF THAT?
VAL. LET ME OUT RIGHT NOW. YOU HAVE TO. PLEASE.
ME TOO, OKAY?
UNNNH.
MY CHOICE IS CLEAR.
CHLING
COME. WE HAVE MUCH TO DO.

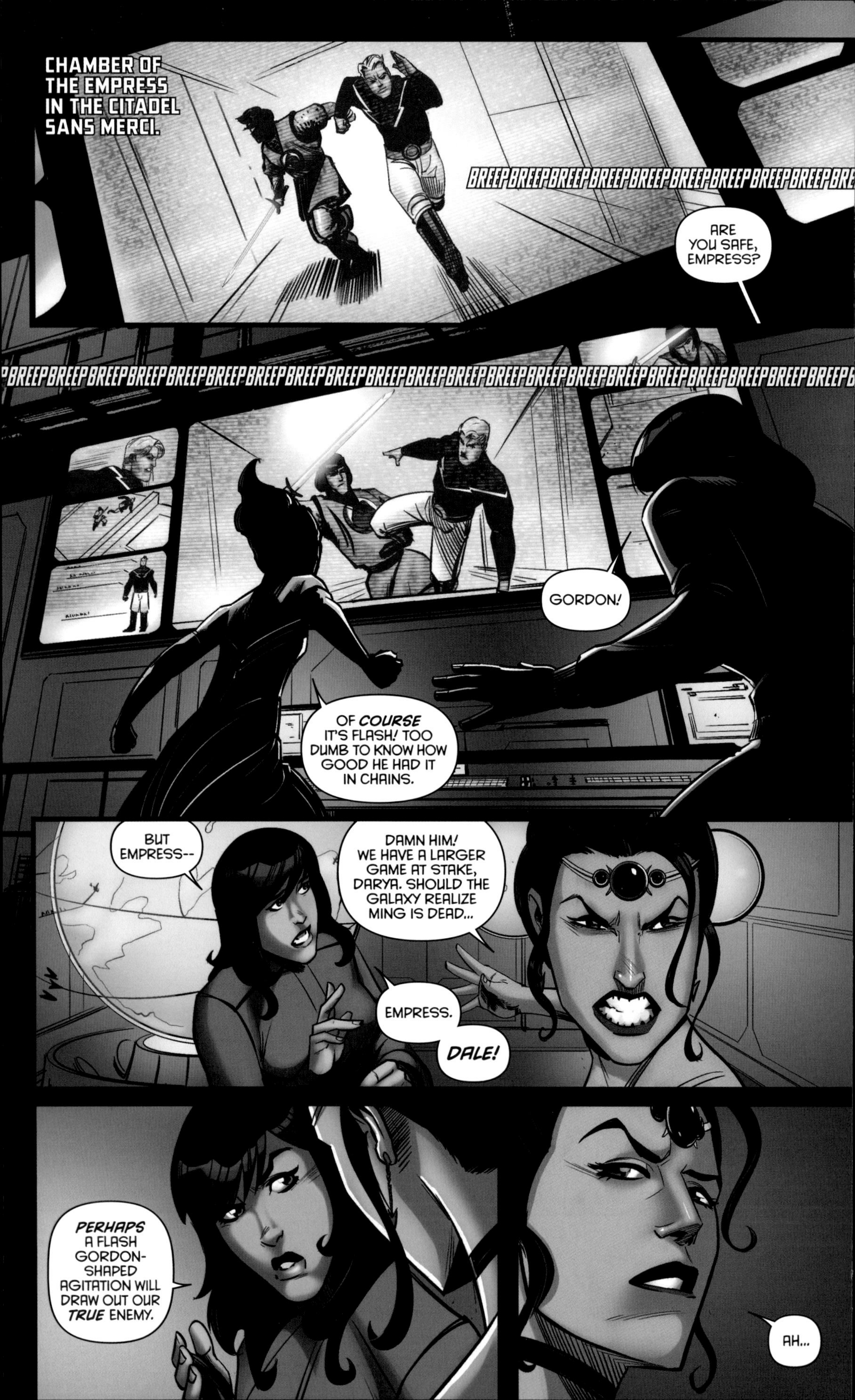
CHAMBER OF THE EMPRESS IN THE CITADEL SANS MERCI.
BREEPBREEPBREEPBREEPBREEPBREEPBREEPBREEPBREEPBRE
ARE YOU SAFE, EMPRESS?
PBREEPBREEPBREEPBREEPBREEPBREEPBREEPBREEPBREEPBREEPBREEPBREEPBREEPBREEPBREEPBREEPBREEPBREEP
GORDON!
OF COURSE IT'S FLASH! TOO DUMB TO KNOW HOW GOOD HE HAD IT IN CHAINS.
BUT EMPRESS--
DAMN HIM! WE HAVE A LARGER GAME AT STAKE, DARYA. SHOULD THE GALAXY REALIZE MING IS DEAD...
EMPRESS.
DALE!
PERHAPS A FLASH GORDON-SHAPED AGITATION WILL DRAW OUT OUR TRUE ENEMY.
AH...

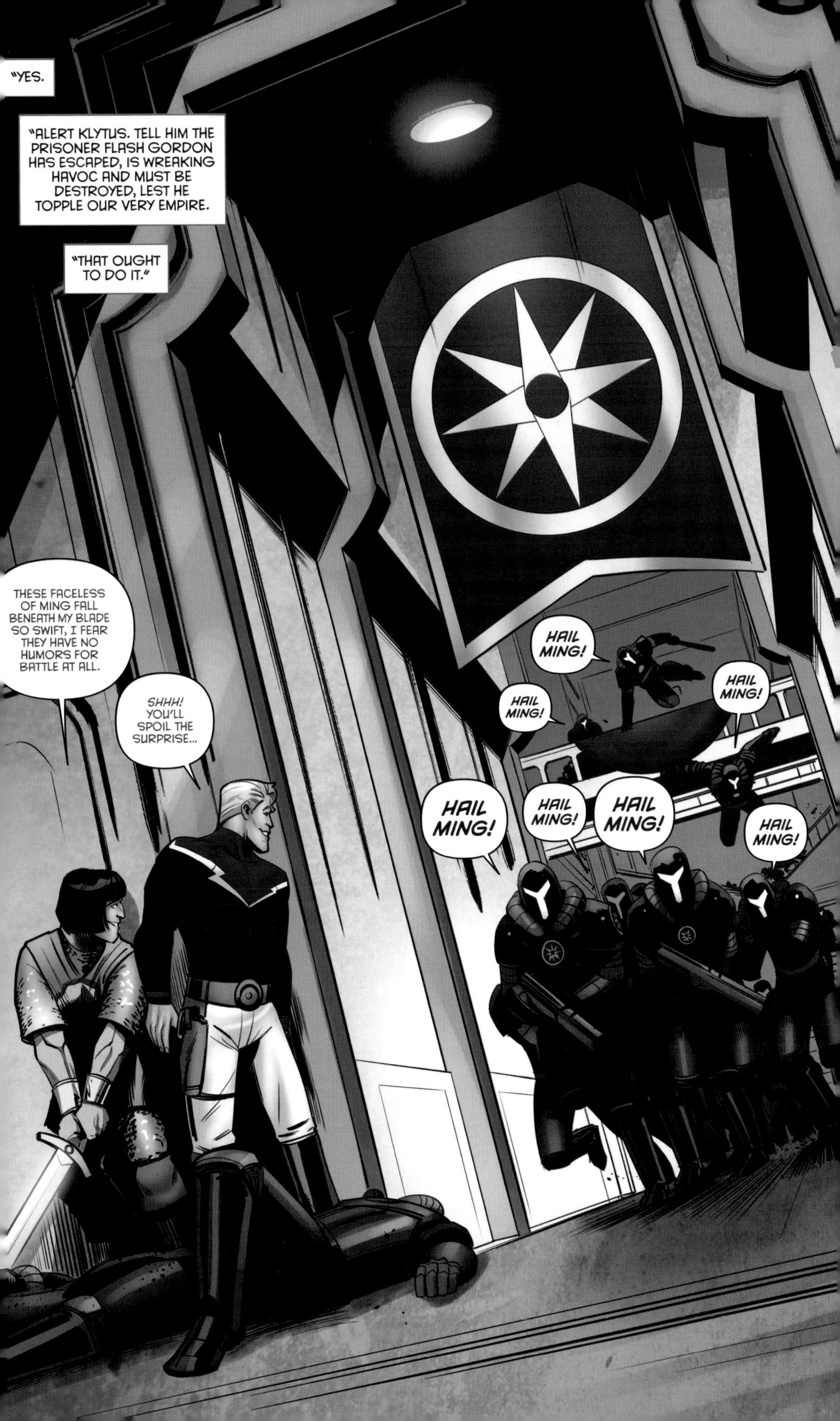
"YES.
"ALERT KLYTUS. TELL HIM THE PRISONER FLASH GORDON HAS ESCAPED, IS WREAKING HAVOC AND MUST BE DESTROYED, LEST HE TOPPLE OUR VERY EMPIRE.
"THAT OUGHT TO DO IT."
THESE FACELESS OF MING FALL BENEATH MY BLADE SO SWIFT, I FEAR THEY HAVE NO HUMORS FOR BATTLE AT ALL.
SHHH! YOU'LL SPOIL THE SURPRISE...
HAIL MING!
HAIL MING!
HAIL MING!
HAIL MING!
HAIL MING!
HAIL MING!
HAIL MING!

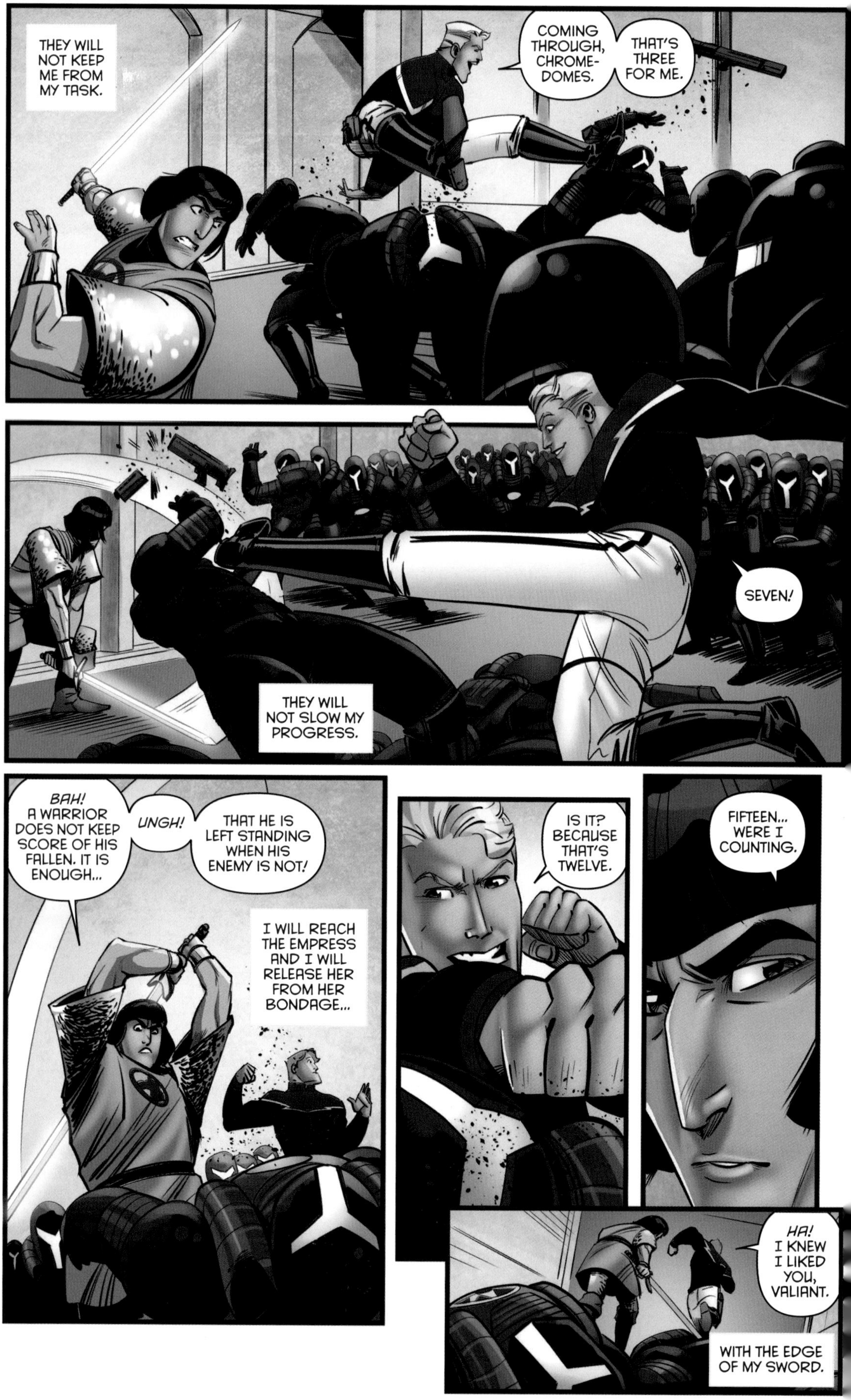
THEY WILL NOT KEEP ME FROM MY TASK.
COMING THROUGH, CHROME-DOMES.
THAT'S THREE FOR ME.
SEVEN!
THEY WILL NOT SLOW MY PROGRESS.
BAH! A WARRIOR DOES NOT KEEP SCORE OF HIS FALLEN. IT IS ENOUGH...
UNGH!
THAT HE IS LEFT STANDING WHEN HIS ENEMY IS NOT!
I WILL REACH THE EMPRESS AND I WILL RELEASE HER FROM HER BONDAGE...
IS IT? BECAUSE THAT'S TWELVE.
FIFTEEN... WERE I COUNTING.
HA! I KNEW I LIKED YOU, VALIANT.
WITH THE EDGE OF MY SWORD.

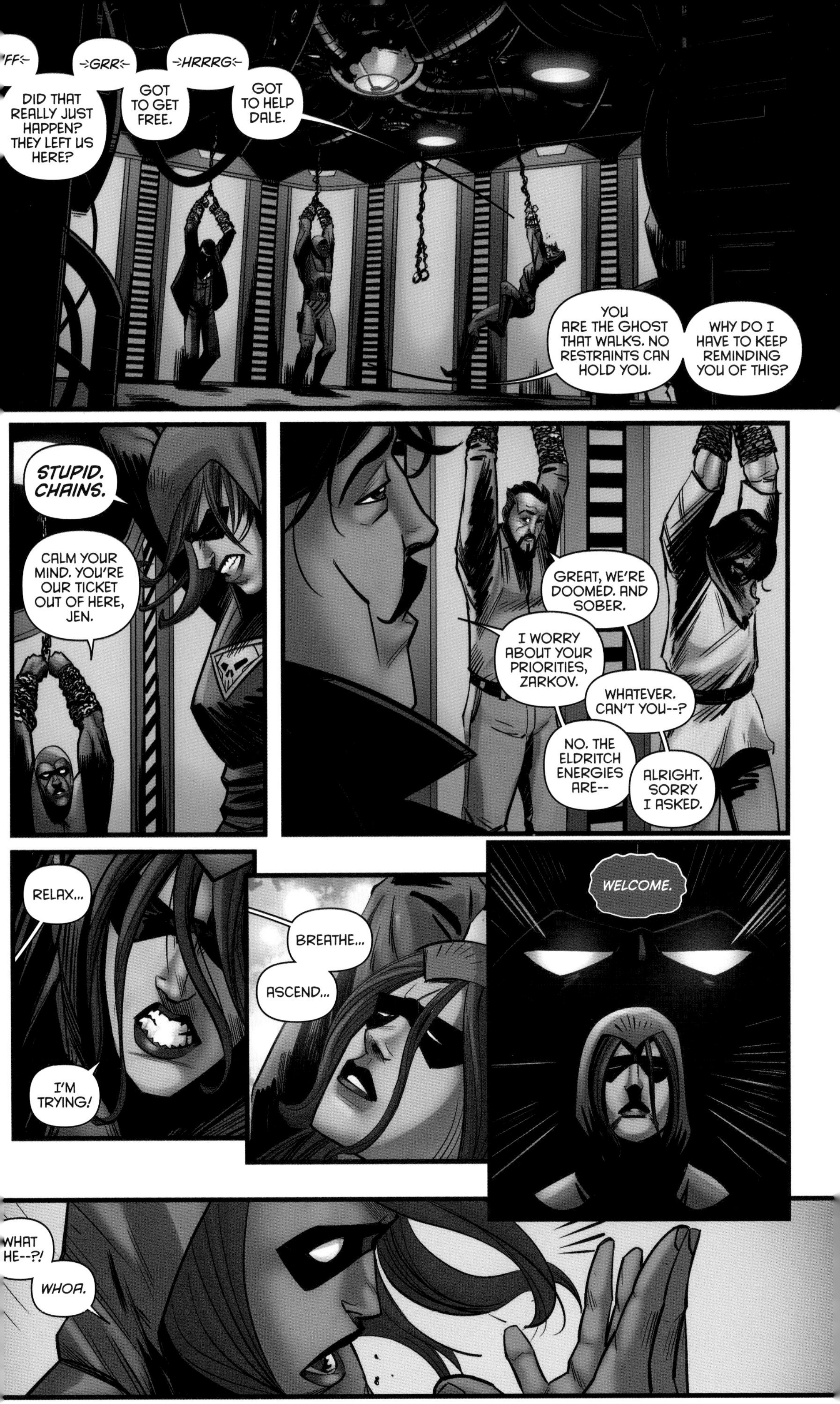

FF
GRR
HRRRG
DID THAT REALLY JUST HAPPEN? THEY LEFT US HERE?
GOT TO GET FREE.
GOT TO HELP DALE.
YOU ARE THE GHOST THAT WALKS. NO RESTRAINTS CAN HOLD YOU.
WHY DO I HAVE TO KEEP REMINDING YOU OF THIS?
STUPID. CHAINS.
CALM YOUR MIND. YOU'RE OUR TICKET OUT OF HERE, JEN.
GREAT, WE'RE DOOMED. AND SOBER.
I WORRY ABOUT YOUR PRIORITIES, ZARKOV.
WHATEVER. CAN'T YOU--?
NO. THE ELDRITCH ENERGIES ARE--
ALRIGHT. SORRY I ASKED.
RELAX...
I'M TRYING!
BREATHE...
ASCEND...
WELCOME.
WHAT HE--?!
WHOA.

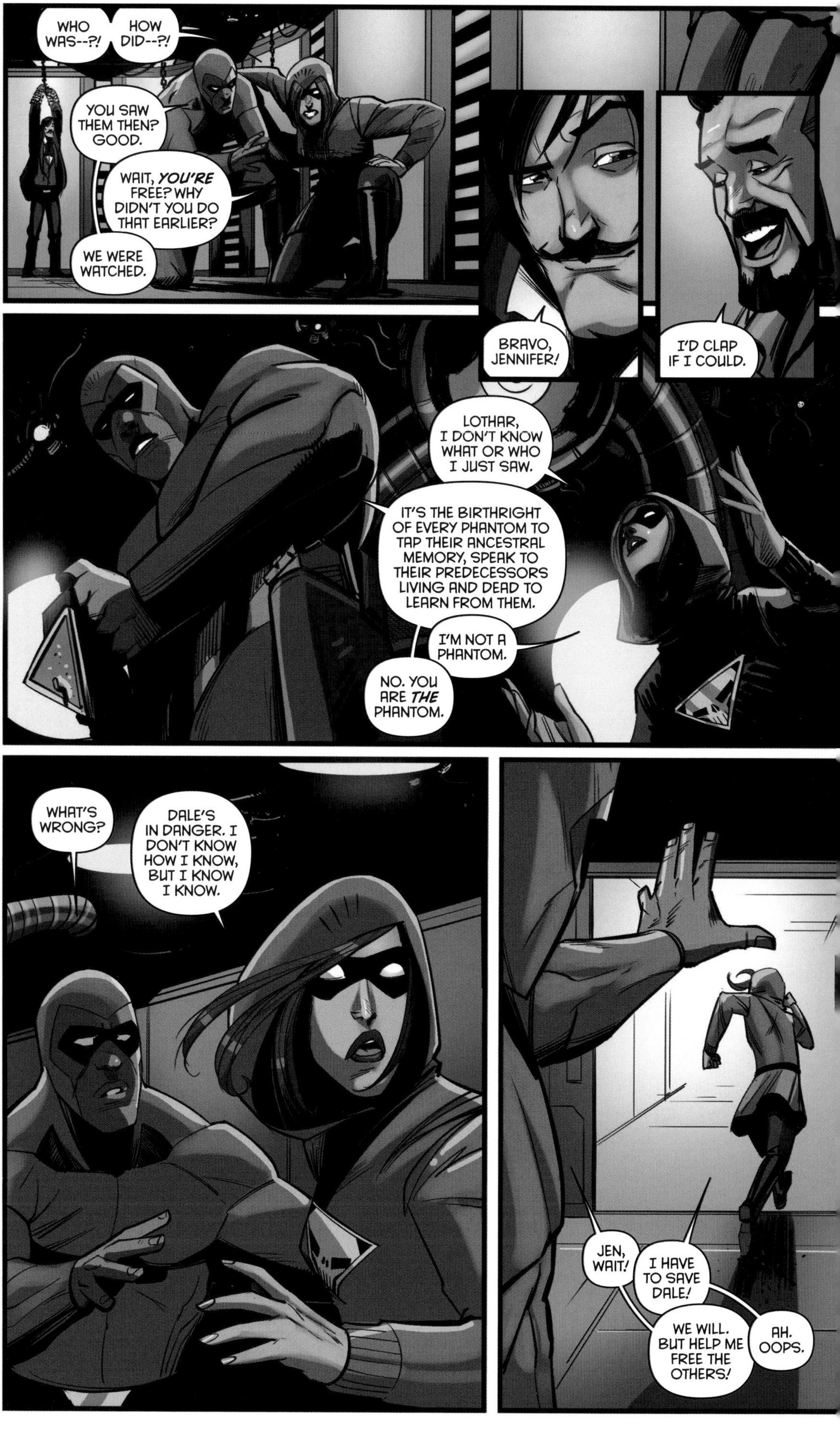
WHO WAS--?!
HOW DID--?!
YOU SAW THEM THEN? GOOD.
WAIT, *YOU'RE* FREE? WHY DIDN'T YOU DO THAT EARLIER?
WE WERE WATCHED.
BRAVO, JENNIFER!
I'D CLAP IF I COULD.
LOTHAR, I DON'T KNOW WHAT OR WHO I JUST SAW.
IT'S THE BIRTHRIGHT OF EVERY PHANTOM TO TAP THEIR ANCESTRAL MEMORY, SPEAK TO THEIR PREDECESSORS LIVING AND DEAD TO LEARN FROM THEM.
I'M NOT A PHANTOM.
NO. YOU ARE *THE* PHANTOM.
WHAT'S WRONG?
DALE'S IN DANGER. I DON'T KNOW HOW I KNOW, BUT I KNOW I KNOW.
JEN, WAIT!
I HAVE TO SAVE DALE!
WE WILL. BUT HELP ME FREE THE OTHERS!
AH. OOPS.

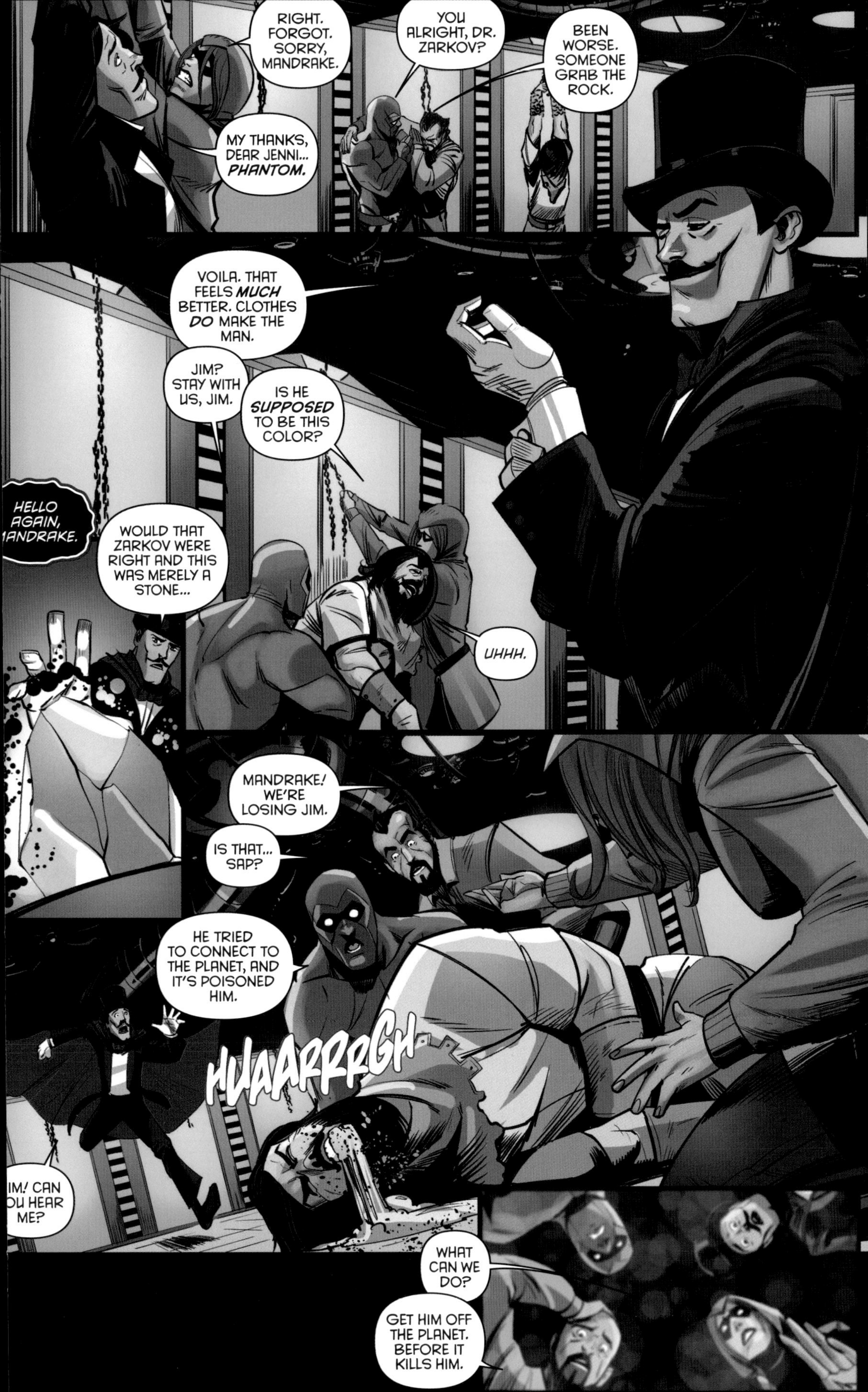
RIGHT. FORGOT. SORRY, MANDRAKE.
MY THANKS, DEAR JENNI... PHANTOM.
YOU ALRIGHT, DR. ZARKOV?
BEEN WORSE. SOMEONE GRAB THE ROCK.
VOILA. THAT FEELS MUCH BETTER. CLOTHES DO MAKE THE MAN.
JIM? STAY WITH US, JIM.
IS HE SUPPOSED TO BE THIS COLOR?
UHHH.
HELLO AGAIN, MANDRAKE.
WOULD THAT ZARKOV WERE RIGHT AND THIS WAS MERELY A STONE...
MANDRAKE! WE'RE LOSING JIM.
IS THAT... SAP?
HE TRIED TO CONNECT TO THE PLANET, AND IT'S POISONED HIM.
HUAARRRGH
WHAT CAN WE DO?
GET HIM OFF THE PLANET. BEFORE IT KILLS HIM.

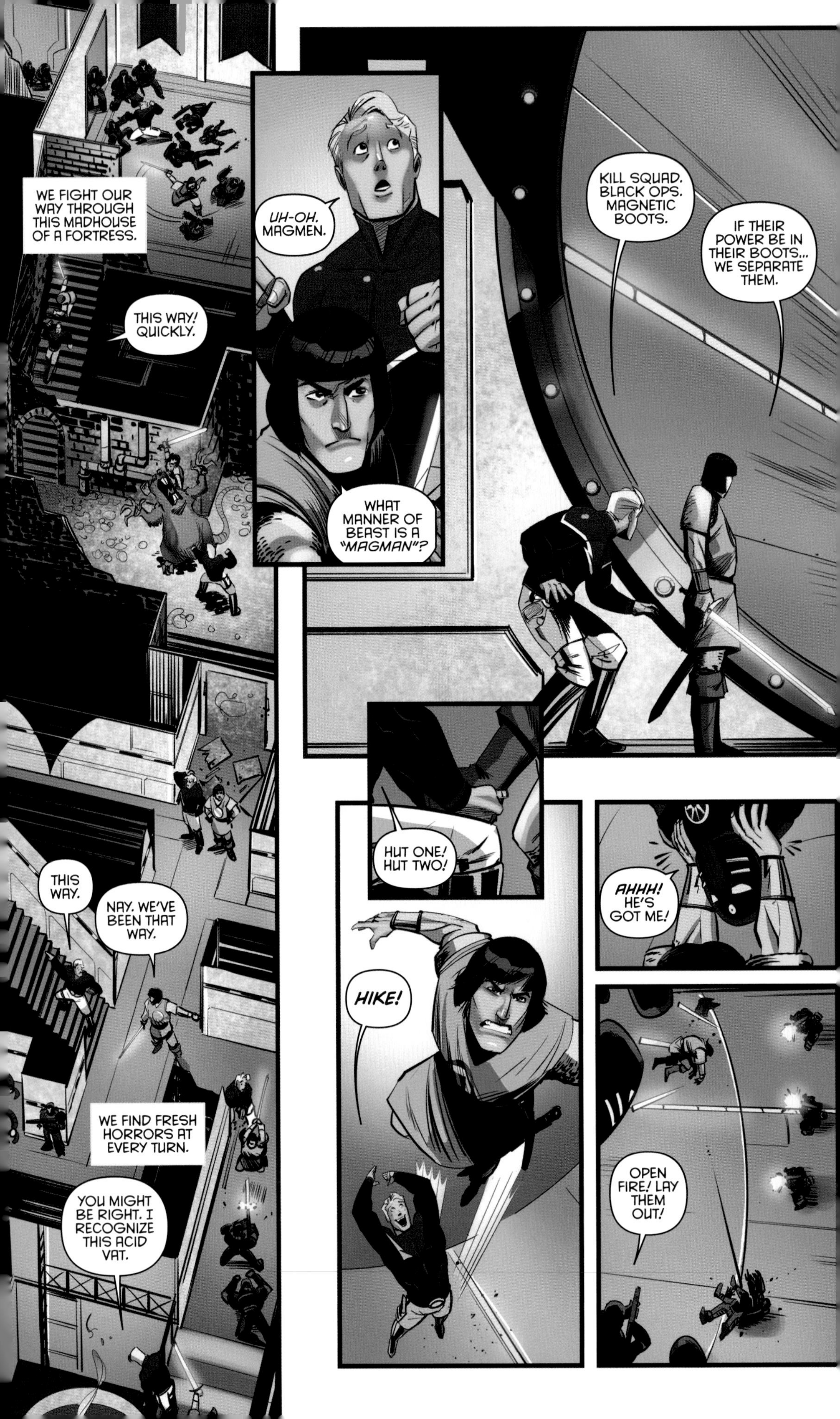
WE FIGHT OUR WAY THROUGH THIS MADHOUSE OF A FORTRESS.
THIS WAY! QUICKLY.
UH-OH. MAGMEN.
WHAT MANNER OF BEAST IS A "MAGMAN"?
KILL SQUAD. BLACK OPS. MAGNETIC BOOTS.
IF THEIR POWER BE IN THEIR BOOTS... WE SEPARATE THEM.
THIS WAY.
NAY. WE'VE BEEN THAT WAY.
WE FIND FRESH HORRORS AT EVERY TURN.
YOU MIGHT BE RIGHT. I RECOGNIZE THIS ACID VAT.
HUT ONE! HUT TWO!
HIKE!
AHHH! HE'S GOT ME!
OPEN FIRE! LAY THEM OUT!

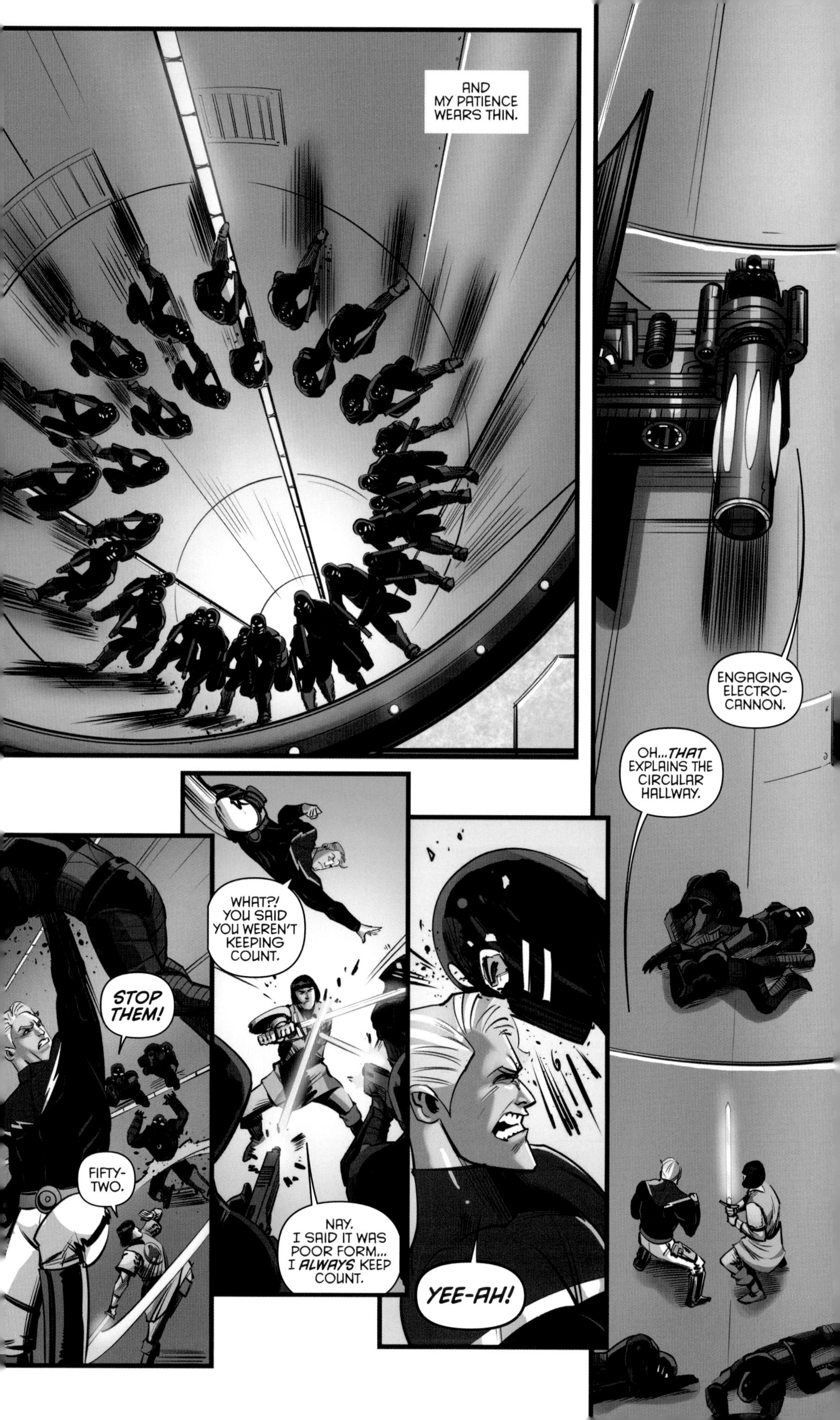
AND MY PATIENCE WEARS THIN.
ENGAGING ELECTRO-CANNON.
OH...THAT EXPLAINS THE CIRCULAR HALLWAY.
STOP THEM!
FIFTY-TWO.
WHAT?! YOU SAID YOU WEREN'T KEEPING COUNT.
NAY. I SAID IT WAS POOR FORM... I ALWAYS KEEP COUNT.
YEE-AH!

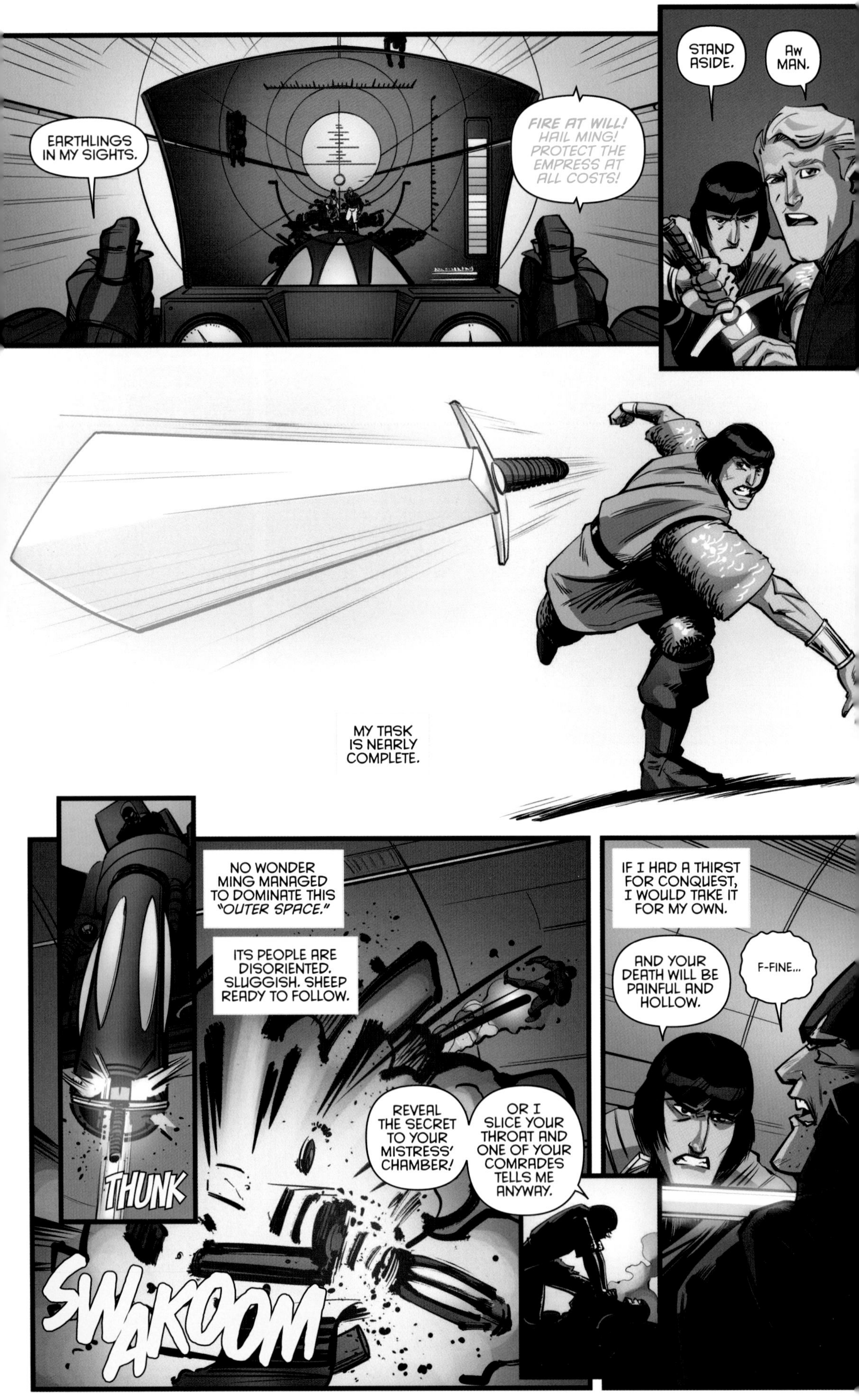
EARTHLINGS IN MY SIGHTS.
FIRE AT WILL! HAIL MING! PROTECT THE EMPRESS AT ALL COSTS!
STAND ASIDE.
AW MAN.
MY TASK IS NEARLY COMPLETE.
THUNK
NO WONDER MING MANAGED TO DOMINATE THIS "OUTER SPACE."
ITS PEOPLE ARE DISORIENTED. SLUGGISH. SHEEP READY TO FOLLOW.
SWAKOOM
REVEAL THE SECRET TO YOUR MISTRESS' CHAMBER!
OR I SLICE YOUR THROAT AND ONE OF YOUR COMRADES TELLS ME ANYWAY.
IF I HAD A THIRST FOR CONQUEST, I WOULD TAKE IT FOR MY OWN.
AND YOUR DEATH WILL BE PAINFUL AND HOLLOW.
F-FINE...

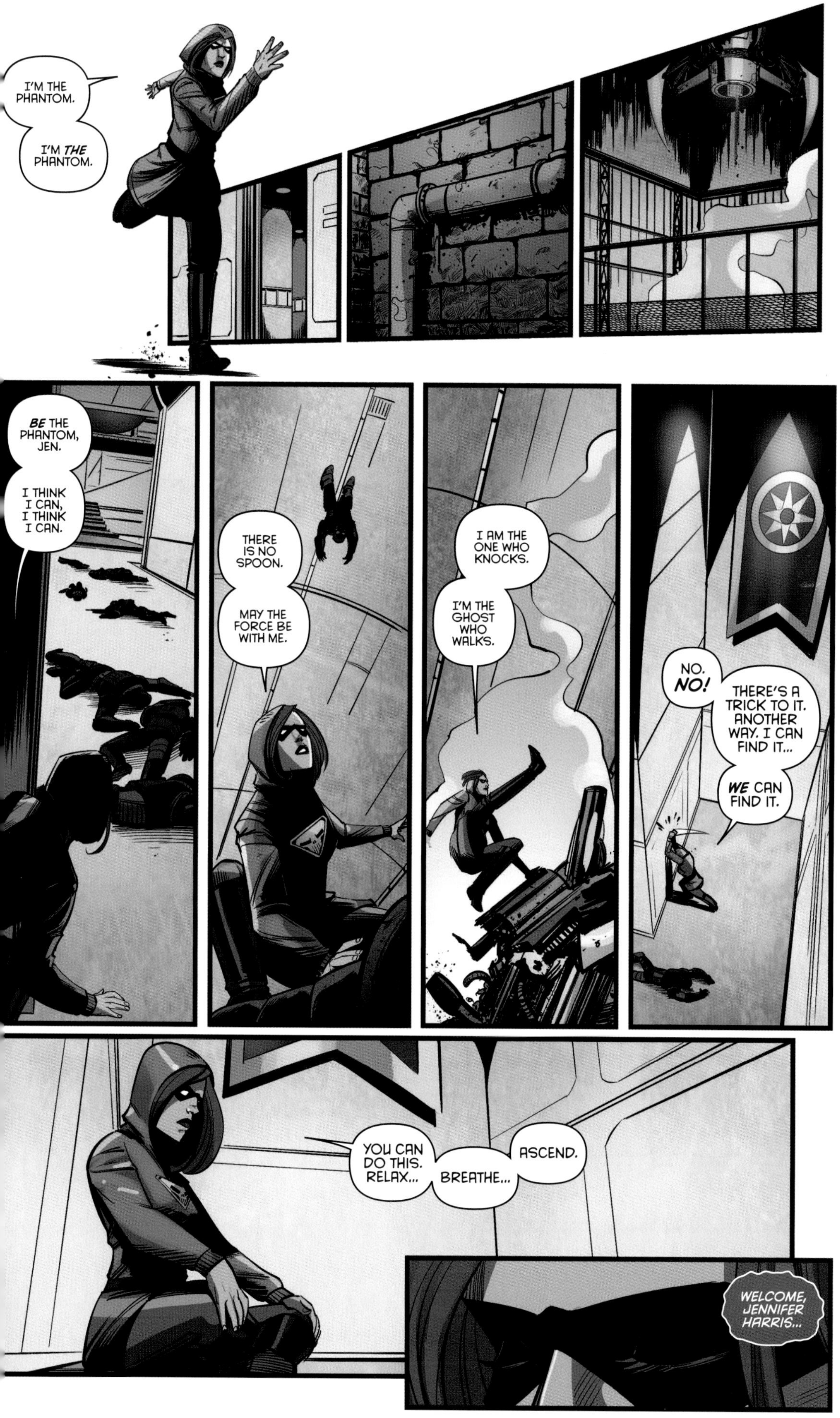
I'M THE PHANTOM.
I'M *THE* PHANTOM.
BE THE PHANTOM, JEN.
I THINK I CAN, I THINK I CAN.
THERE IS NO SPOON.
MAY THE FORCE BE WITH ME.
I AM THE ONE WHO KNOCKS.
I'M THE GHOST WHO WALKS.
NO. ***NO!***
THERE'S A TRICK TO IT. ANOTHER WAY. I CAN FIND IT...
WE CAN FIND IT.
YOU CAN DO THIS. RELAX...
BREATHE...
ASCEND.
WELCOME, JENNIFER HARRIS...

WELCOME, PHANTOM.

WELCOME TO THIS, THE PLACE OF PHANTOMS. I AM SO PLEASED TO MEET YOU.

LET ME LOOK UPON YOU, MY FIERCE AND CLEVER DAUGHTER.

COOL, YEAH MAN, BUT I ALREADY HAVE A FATHER. HE RAISED ME AND WE'VE NEVER MET. SO.

YOUR FATHER IS A GREAT MAN, SURELY.

YEAH. HE REALLY IS, GUY.

OH JENNIFER. YOU ARE AMAZING. I AM SO PROUD OF YOU. EVEN IF YOU WEREN'T A PHANTOM, I WOULD BE.

NOW FIGHT FOR YOUR LOVE, MY LOVE. TAKE TO THE CANOPY AND YOUR PATH WILL BE CLEAR.

THANK YOU... PHANTOM.

CANOPY. AIR DUCT. I'M GONNA SAY SAME THING.

NOW WE'RE-- UGHHH. WHY DID I LOOK DOWN?

PLEASE DON'T PUKE AGAIN.

SLOWLY. DON'T LOOK DOWN.

WHOF WHOF

NG

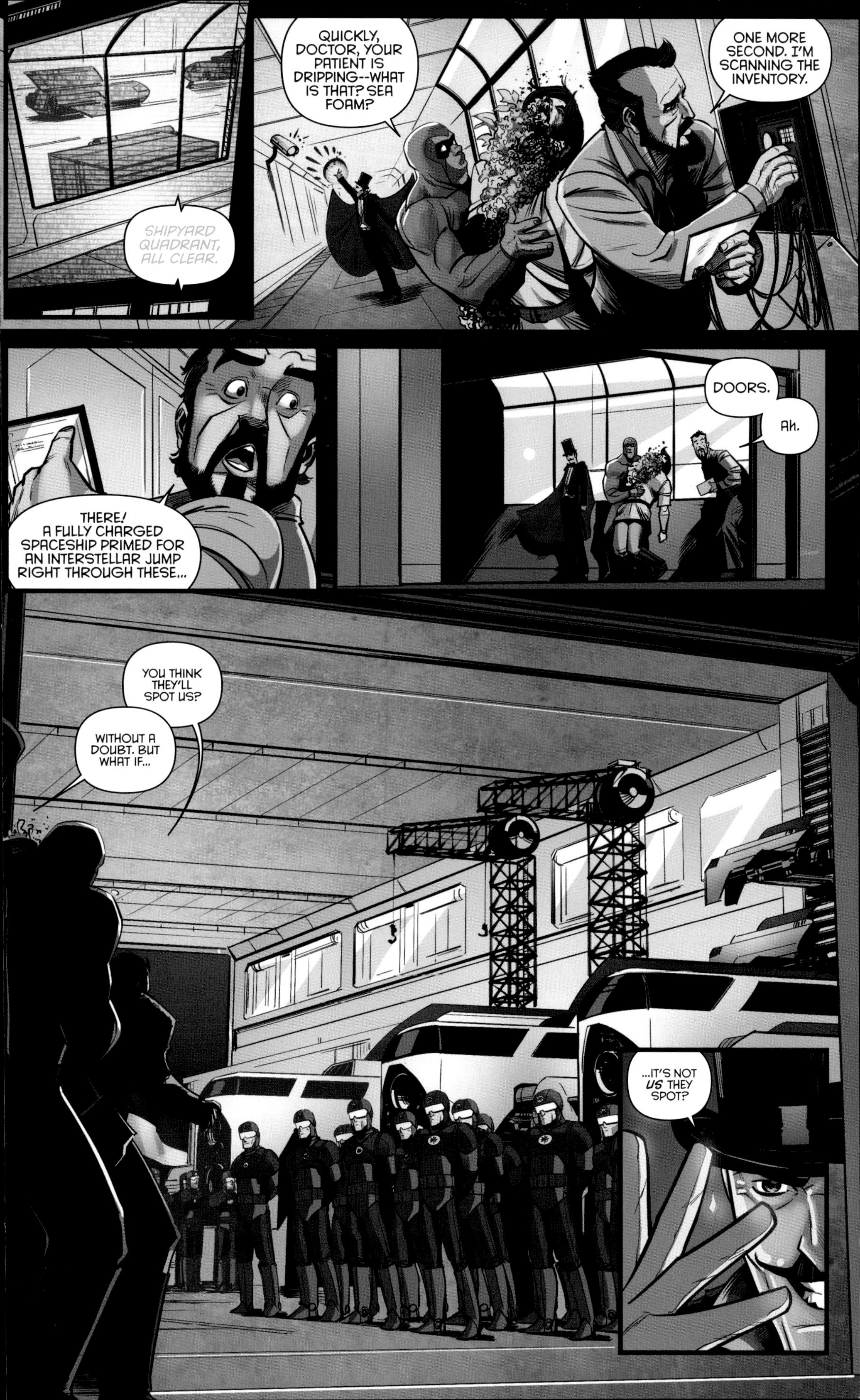
SHIPYARD QUADRANT, ALL CLEAR.
QUICKLY, DOCTOR, YOUR PATIENT IS DRIPPING--WHAT IS THAT? SEA FOAM?
ONE MORE SECOND. I'M SCANNING THE INVENTORY.
THERE! A FULLY CHARGED SPACESHIP PRIMED FOR AN INTERSTELLAR JUMP RIGHT THROUGH THESE...
DOORS.
AH.
YOU THINK THEY'LL SPOT US?
WITHOUT A DOUBT. BUT WHAT IF...
...IT'S NOT US THEY SPOT?

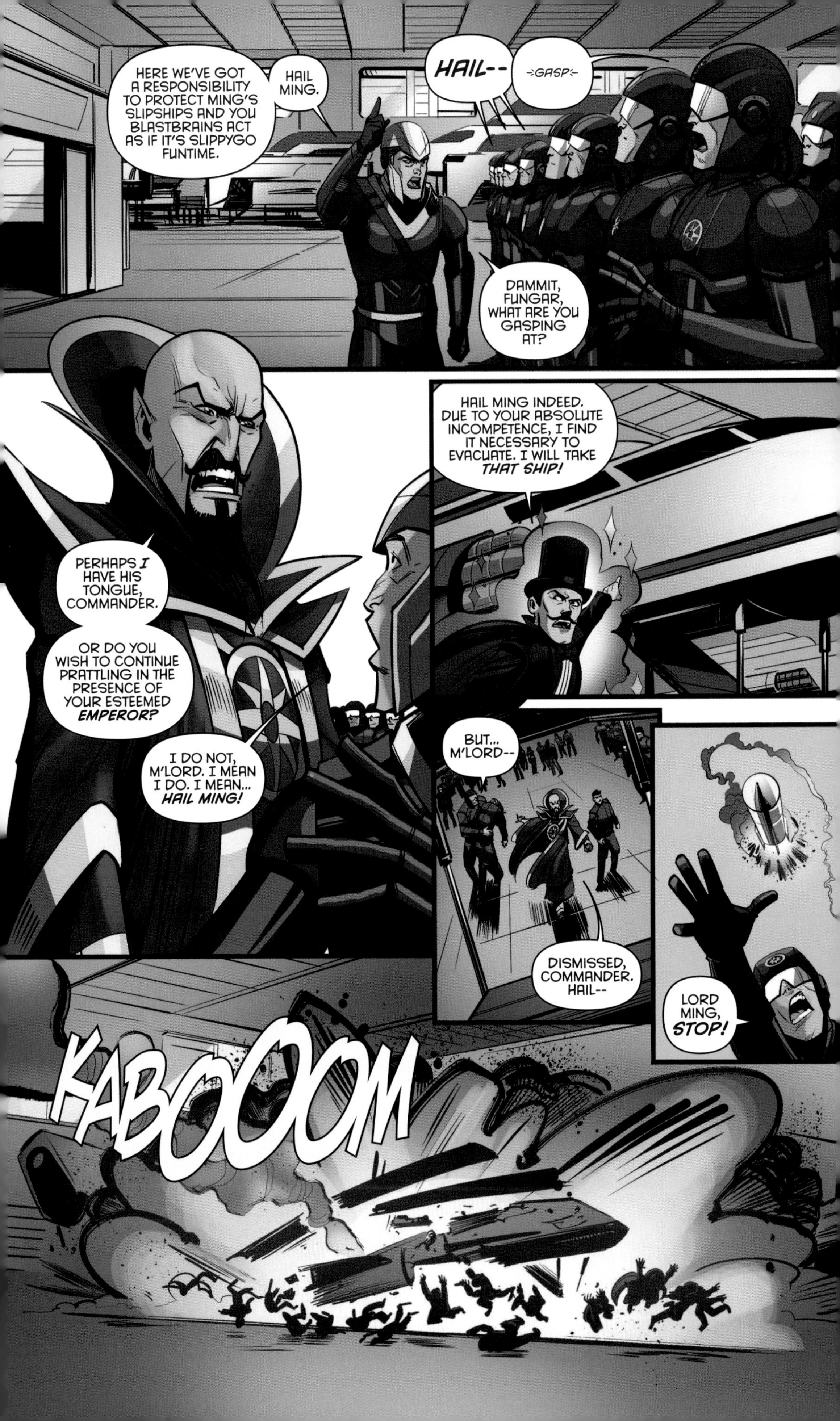
HERE WE'VE GOT A RESPONSIBILITY TO PROTECT MING'S SLIPSHIPS AND YOU BLASTBRAINS ACT AS IF IT'S SLIPPYGO FUNTIME.
HAIL MING.
HAIL--
GASP
DAMMIT, FUNGAR, WHAT ARE YOU GASPING AT?
PERHAPS I HAVE HIS TONGUE, COMMANDER.
OR DO YOU WISH TO CONTINUE PRATTLING IN THE PRESENCE OF YOUR ESTEEMED EMPEROR?
I DO NOT, M'LORD. I MEAN I DO. I MEAN... HAIL MING!
HAIL MING INDEED. DUE TO YOUR ABSOLUTE INCOMPETENCE, I FIND IT NECESSARY TO EVACUATE. I WILL TAKE THAT SHIP!
BUT... M'LORD--
DISMISSED, COMMANDER. HAIL--
LORD MING, STOP!
KABOOOOM

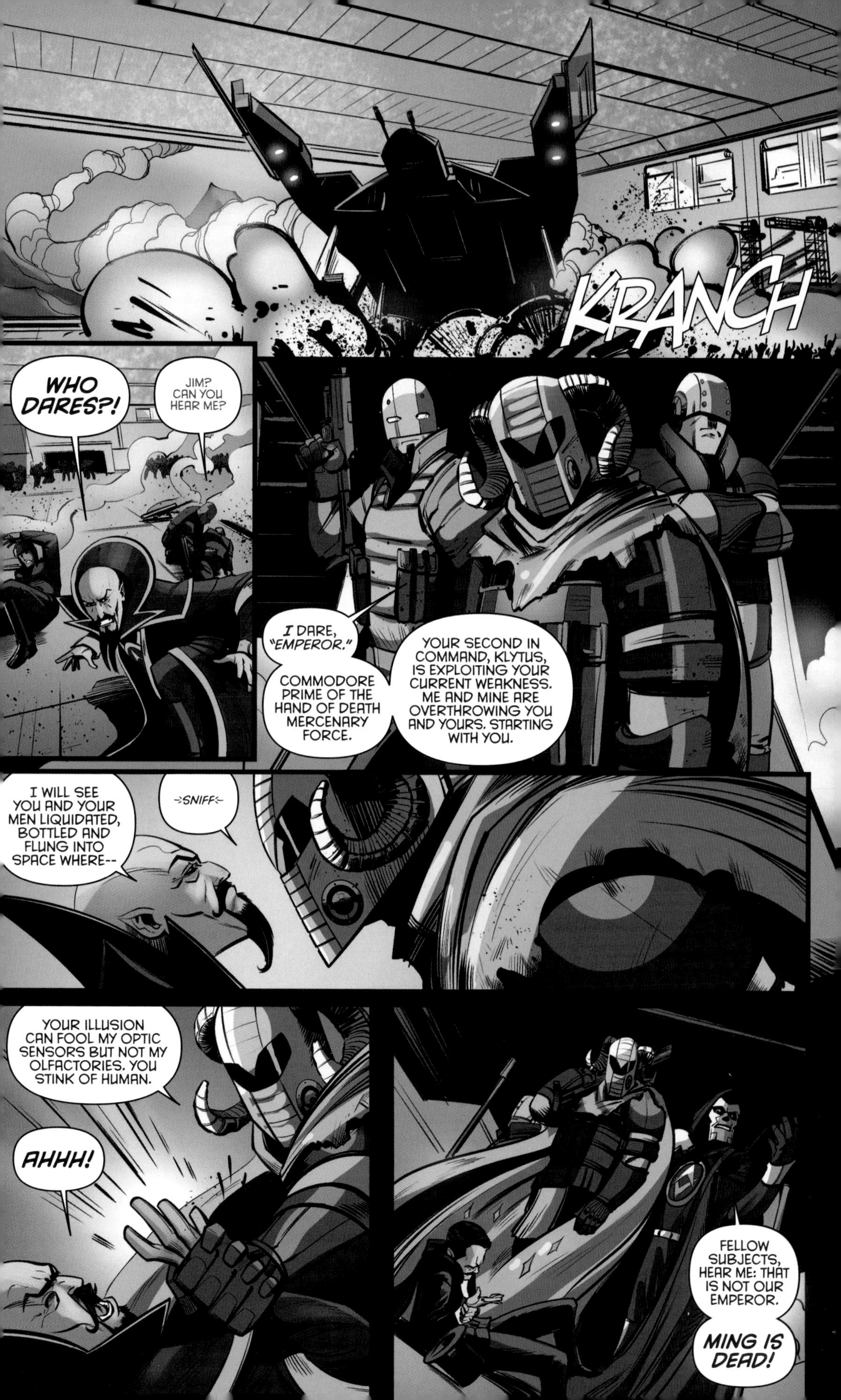
KRANCH
WHO DARES?!
JIM? CAN YOU HEAR ME?
I DARE, "EMPEROR."
COMMODORE PRIME OF THE HAND OF DEATH MERCENARY FORCE.
YOUR SECOND IN COMMAND, KLYTUS, IS EXPLOITING YOUR CURRENT WEAKNESS. ME AND MINE ARE OVERTHROWING YOU AND YOURS. STARTING WITH YOU.
I WILL SEE YOU AND YOUR MEN LIQUIDATED, BOTTLED AND FLUNG INTO SPACE WHERE--
SNIFF
YOUR ILLUSION CAN FOOL MY OPTIC SENSORS BUT NOT MY OLFACTORIES. YOU STINK OF HUMAN.
AHHH!
FELLOW SUBJECTS, HEAR ME: THAT IS NOT OUR EMPEROR.
MING IS DEAD!

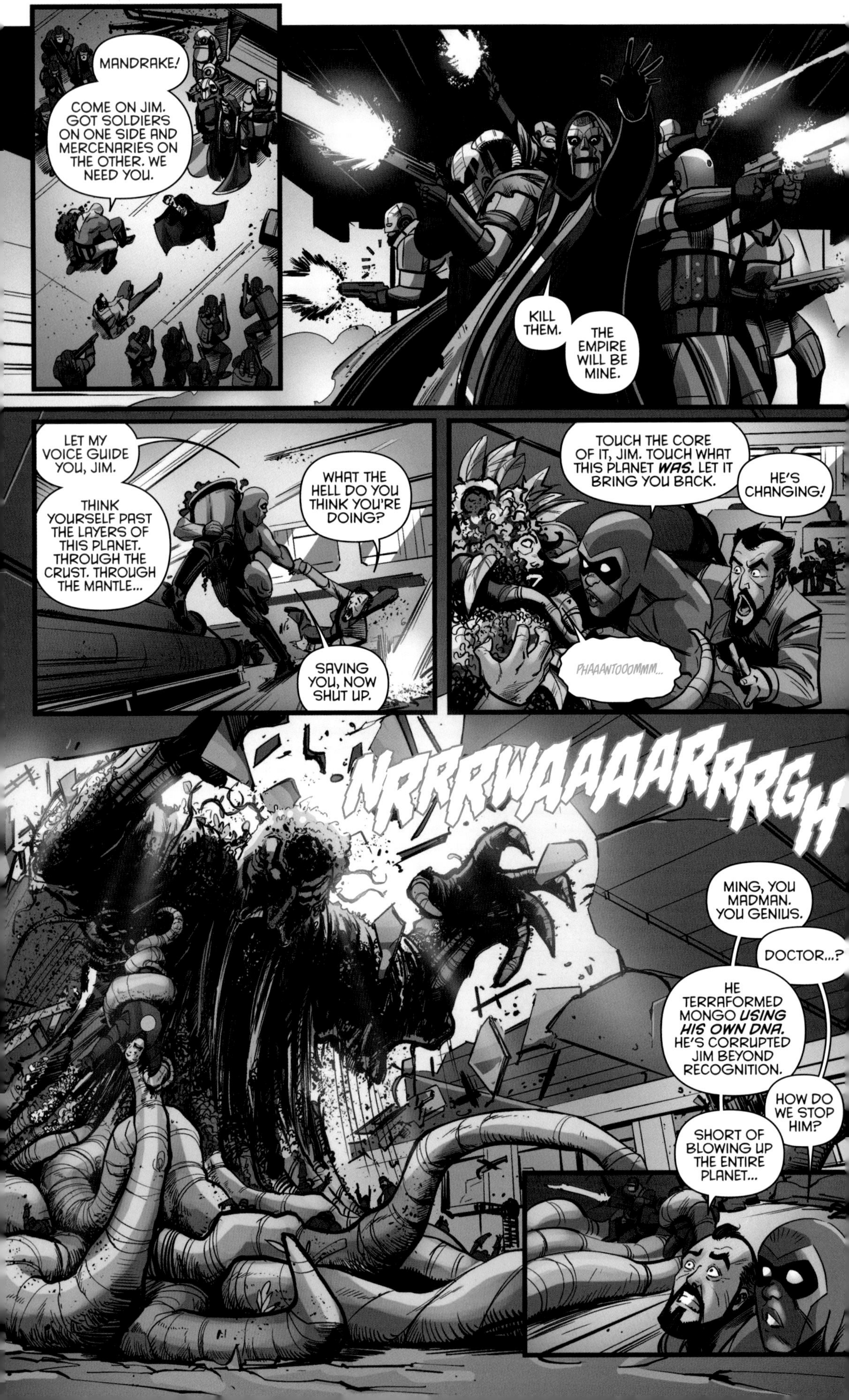
MANDRAKE!
COME ON JIM. GOT SOLDIERS ON ONE SIDE AND MERCENARIES ON THE OTHER. WE NEED YOU.
KILL THEM.
THE EMPIRE WILL BE MINE.
LET MY VOICE GUIDE YOU, JIM.
THINK YOURSELF PAST THE LAYERS OF THIS PLANET. THROUGH THE CRUST. THROUGH THE MANTLE...
WHAT THE HELL DO YOU THINK YOU'RE DOING?
SAVING YOU, NOW SHUT UP.
TOUCH THE CORE OF IT, JIM. TOUCH WHAT THIS PLANET ***WAS.*** LET IT BRING YOU BACK.
HE'S CHANGING!
PHAAANTOOOMMM...
NRRRWAAAAARRRGH
MING, YOU MADMAN. YOU GENIUS.
DOCTOR...?
HE TERRAFORMED MONGO ***USING HIS OWN DNA.*** HE'S CORRUPTED JIM BEYOND RECOGNITION.
HOW DO WE STOP HIM?
SHORT OF BLOWING UP THE ENTIRE PLANET...

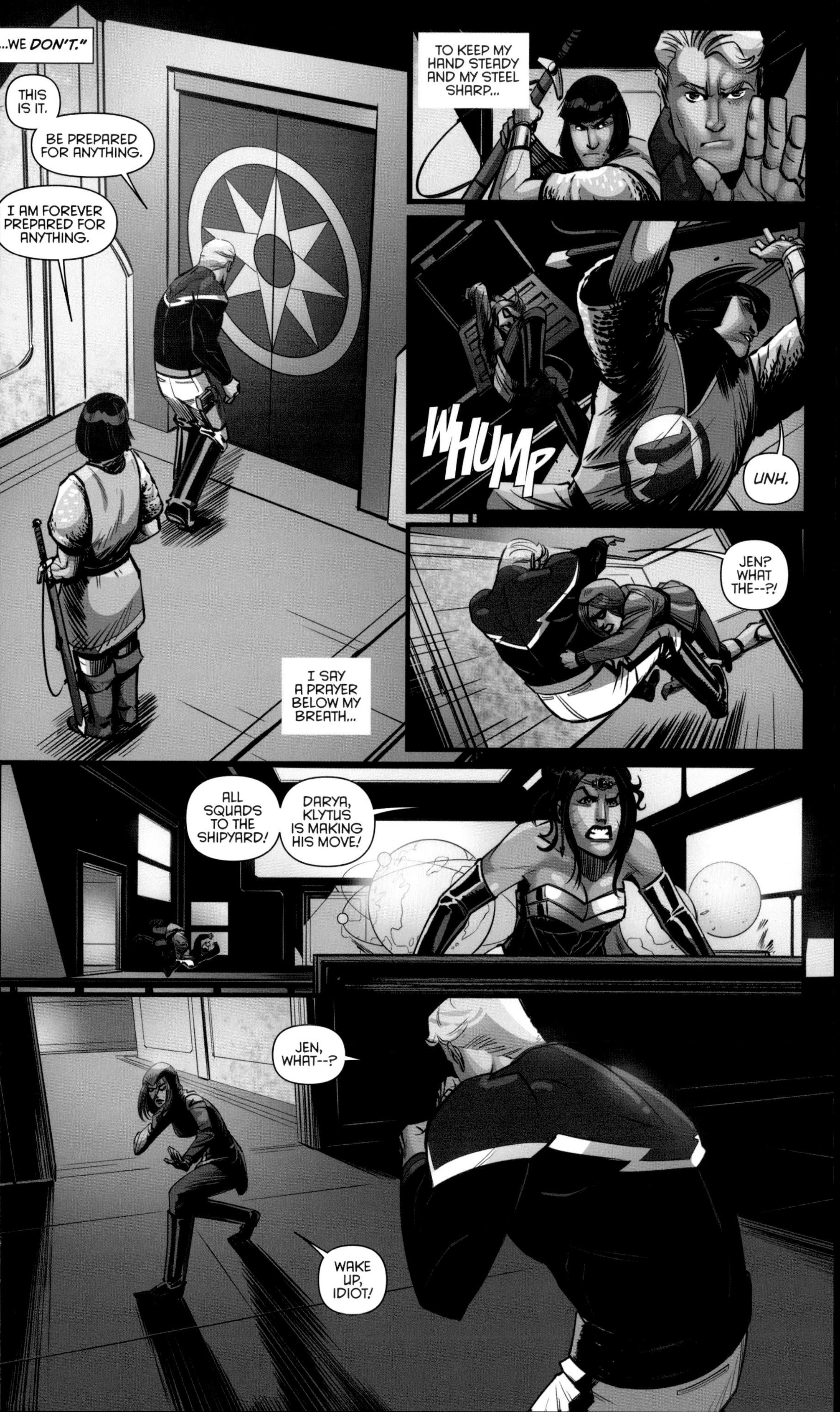
...WE DON'T."
THIS IS IT.
BE PREPARED FOR ANYTHING.
I AM FOREVER PREPARED FOR ANYTHING.
TO KEEP MY HAND STEADY AND MY STEEL SHARP...
WHUMP
UNH.
I SAY A PRAYER BELOW MY BREATH...
JEN? WHAT THE--?!
ALL SQUADS TO THE SHIPYARD!
DARYA, KLYTUS IS MAKING HIS MOVE!
JEN, WHAT--?
WAKE UP, IDIOT!

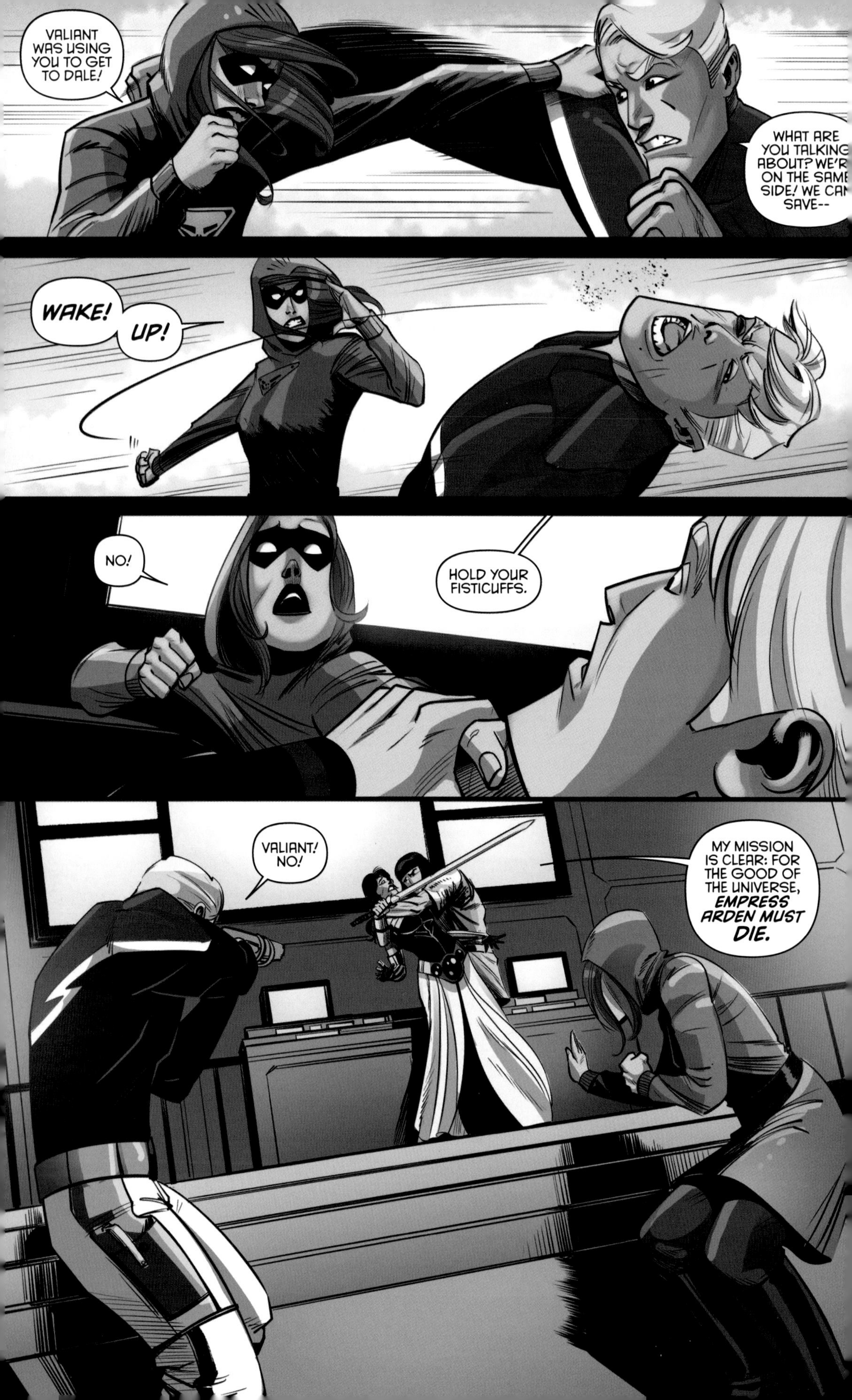
VALIANT WAS USING YOU TO GET TO DALE!
WHAT ARE YOU TALKING ABOUT? WE'RE ON THE SAME SIDE! WE CAN SAVE--
WAKE!
UP!
NO!
HOLD YOUR FISTICUFFS.
VALIANT! NO!
MY MISSION IS CLEAR: FOR THE GOOD OF THE UNIVERSE, EMPRESS ARDEN MUST DIE.

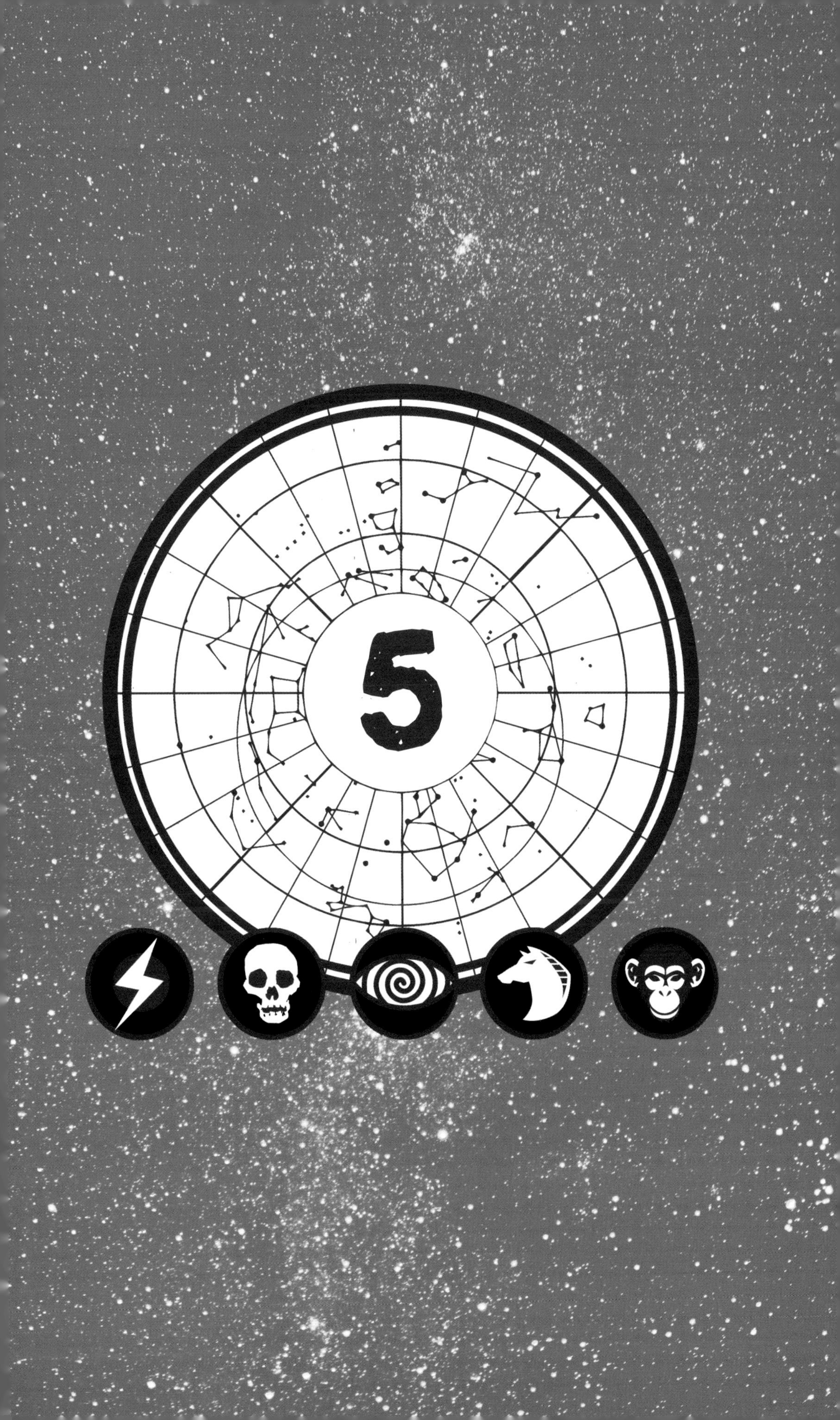
5

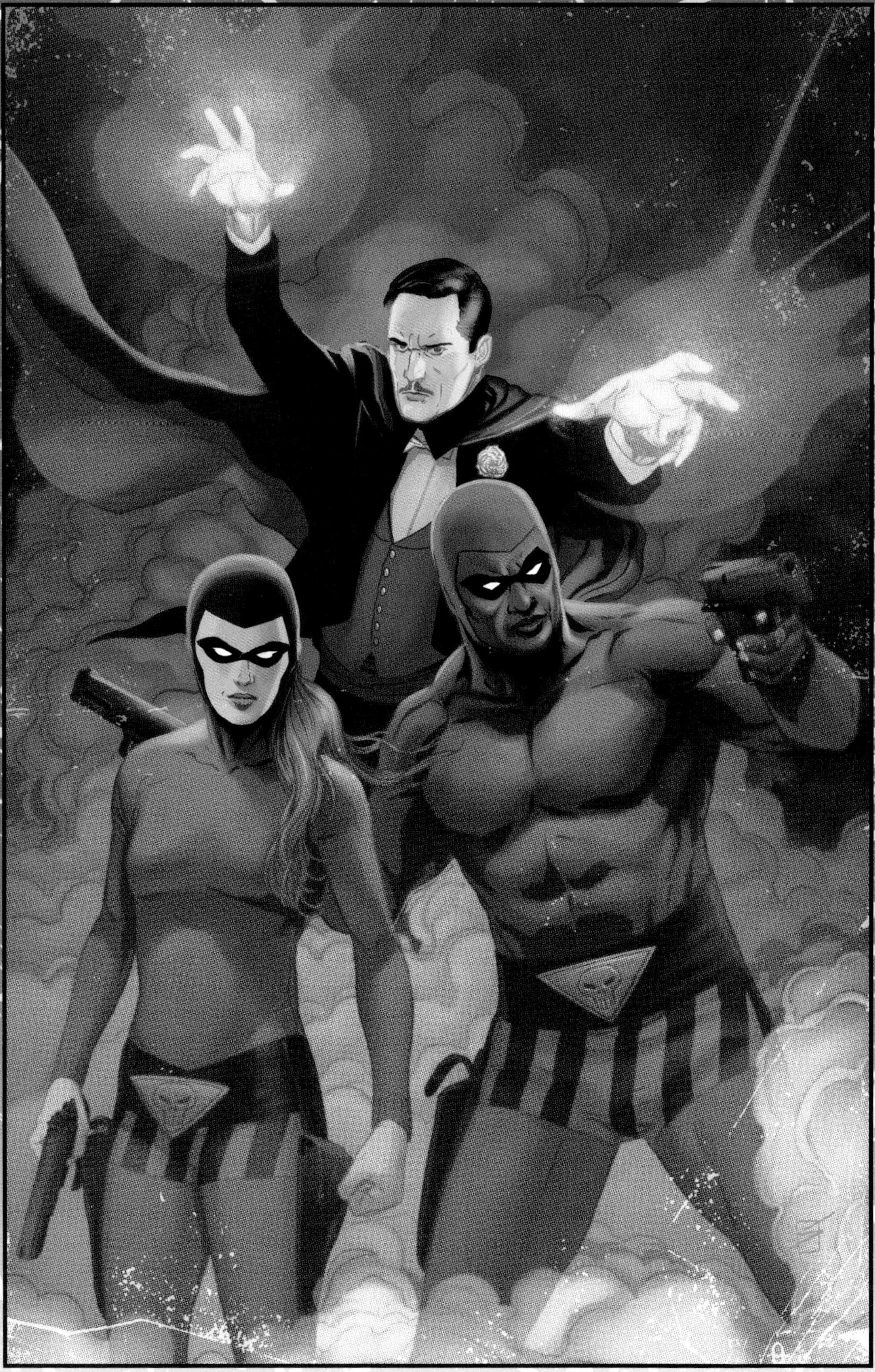

Issue #5 cover
Art by **MARC LAMING**

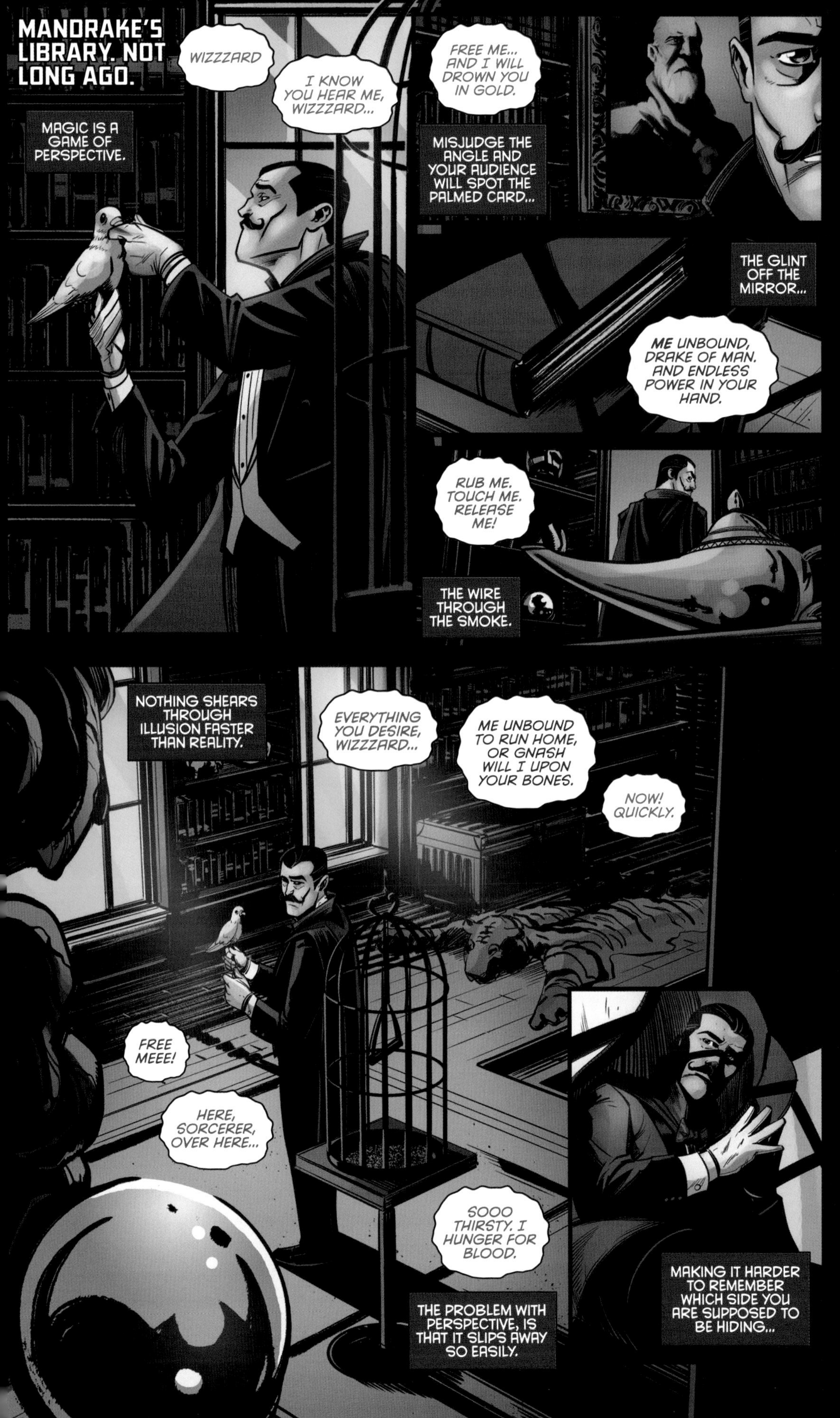
MANDRAKE'S LIBRARY. NOT LONG AGO.
MAGIC IS A GAME OF PERSPECTIVE.
WIZZZARD
I KNOW YOU HEAR ME, WIZZZARD...
FREE ME... AND I WILL DROWN YOU IN GOLD.
MISJUDGE THE ANGLE AND YOUR AUDIENCE WILL SPOT THE PALMED CARD...
THE GLINT OFF THE MIRROR...
ME UNBOUND, DRAKE OF MAN. AND ENDLESS POWER IN YOUR HAND.
RUB ME. TOUCH ME. RELEASE ME!
THE WIRE THROUGH THE SMOKE.
NOTHING SHEARS THROUGH ILLUSION FASTER THAN REALITY.
EVERYTHING YOU DESIRE, WIZZZARD...
ME UNBOUND TO RUN HOME, OR GNASH WILL I UPON YOUR BONES.
NOW! QUICKLY.
FREE MEEE!
HERE, SORCERER, OVER HERE...
SOOO THIRSTY. I HUNGER FOR BLOOD.
THE PROBLEM WITH PERSPECTIVE, IS THAT IT SLIPS AWAY SO EASILY.
MAKING IT HARDER TO REMEMBER WHICH SIDE YOU ARE SUPPOSED TO BE HIDING...

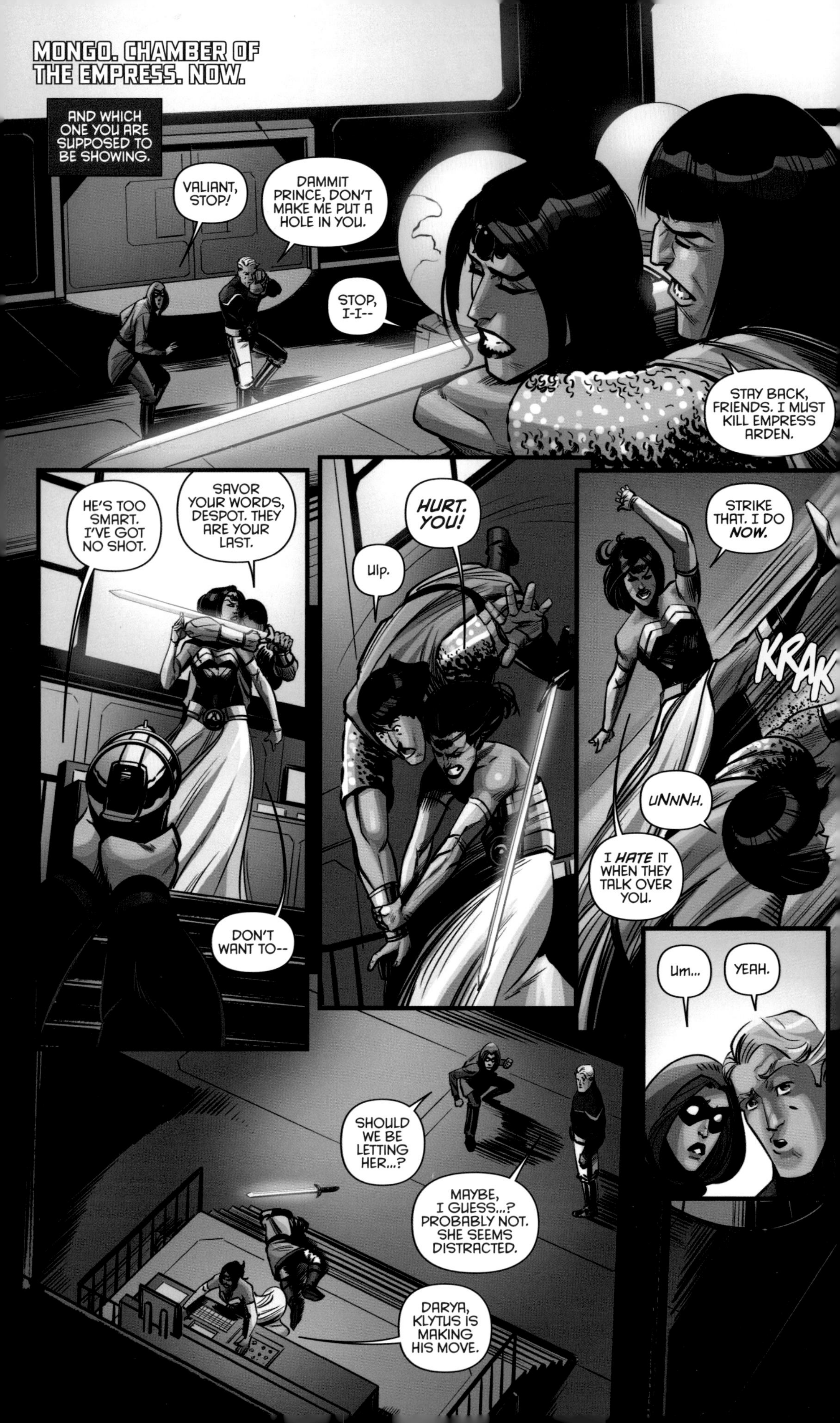
MONGO. CHAMBER OF THE EMPRESS. NOW.
AND WHICH ONE YOU ARE SUPPOSED TO BE SHOWING.
VALIANT, STOP!
DAMMIT PRINCE, DON'T MAKE ME PUT A HOLE IN YOU.
STOP, I-I--
STAY BACK, FRIENDS. I MUST KILL EMPRESS ARDEN.
HE'S TOO SMART. I'VE GOT NO SHOT.
SAVOR YOUR WORDS, DESPOT. THEY ARE YOUR LAST.
DON'T WANT TO--
HURT. YOU!
Ulp.
STRIKE THAT. I DO NOW.
KRAK
UNNNH.
I HATE IT WHEN THEY TALK OVER YOU.
Um...
YEAH.
SHOULD WE BE LETTING HER...?
MAYBE, I GUESS...? PROBABLY NOT. SHE SEEMS DISTRACTED.
DARYA, KLYTUS IS MAKING HIS MOVE.

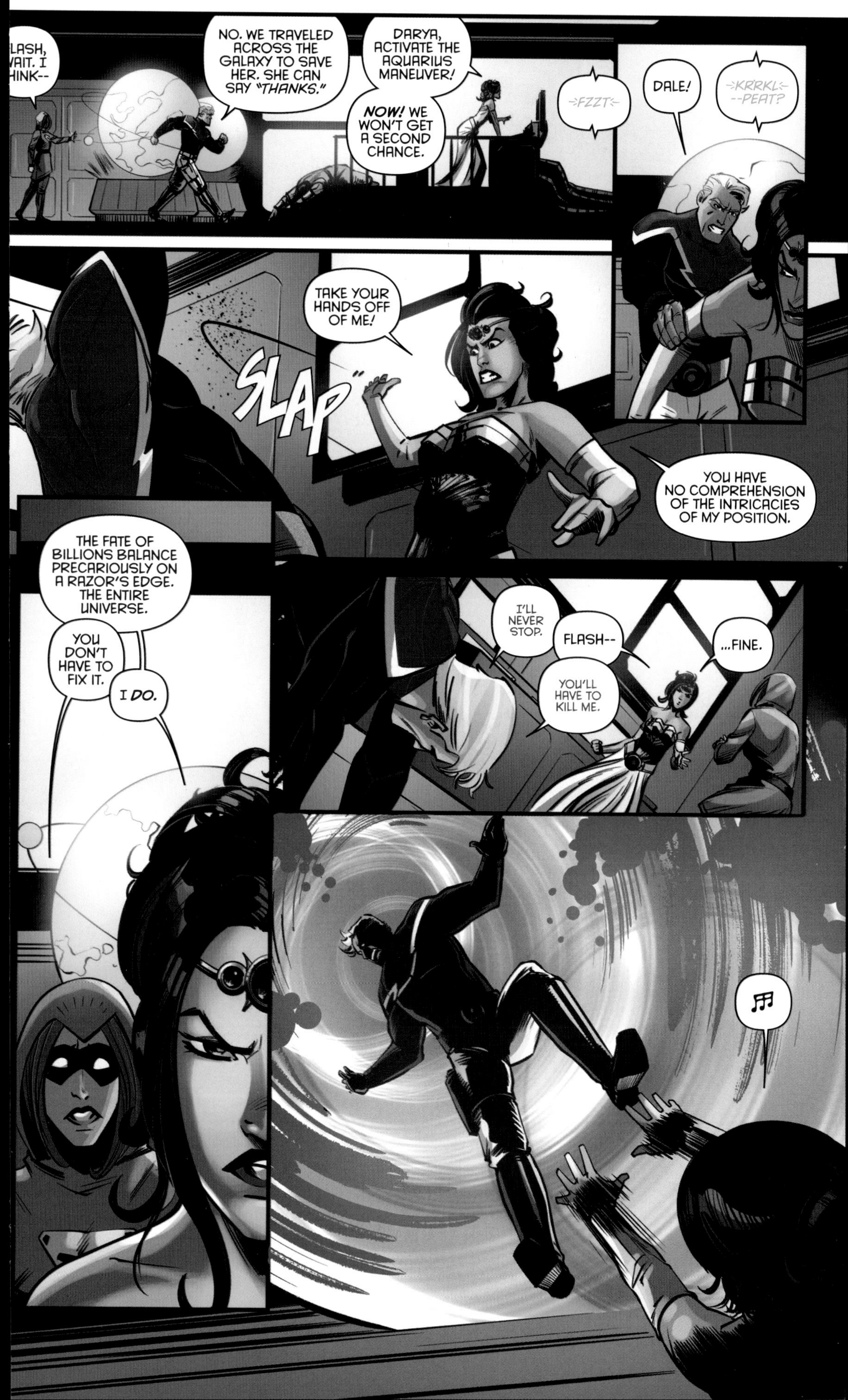

LASH, WAIT. I HINK--
NO. WE TRAVELED ACROSS THE GALAXY TO SAVE HER. SHE CAN SAY "THANKS."
DARYA, ACTIVATE THE AQUARIUS MANEUVER!
NOW! WE WON'T GET A SECOND CHANCE.
FZZT
DALE!
KRRKL --PEAT?
TAKE YOUR HANDS OFF OF ME!
SLAP
YOU HAVE NO COMPREHENSION OF THE INTRICACIES OF MY POSITION.
THE FATE OF BILLIONS BALANCE PRECARIOUSLY ON A RAZOR'S EDGE. THE ENTIRE UNIVERSE.
YOU DON'T HAVE TO FIX IT.
I DO.
I'LL NEVER STOP.
FLASH--
YOU'LL HAVE TO KILL ME.
...FINE.

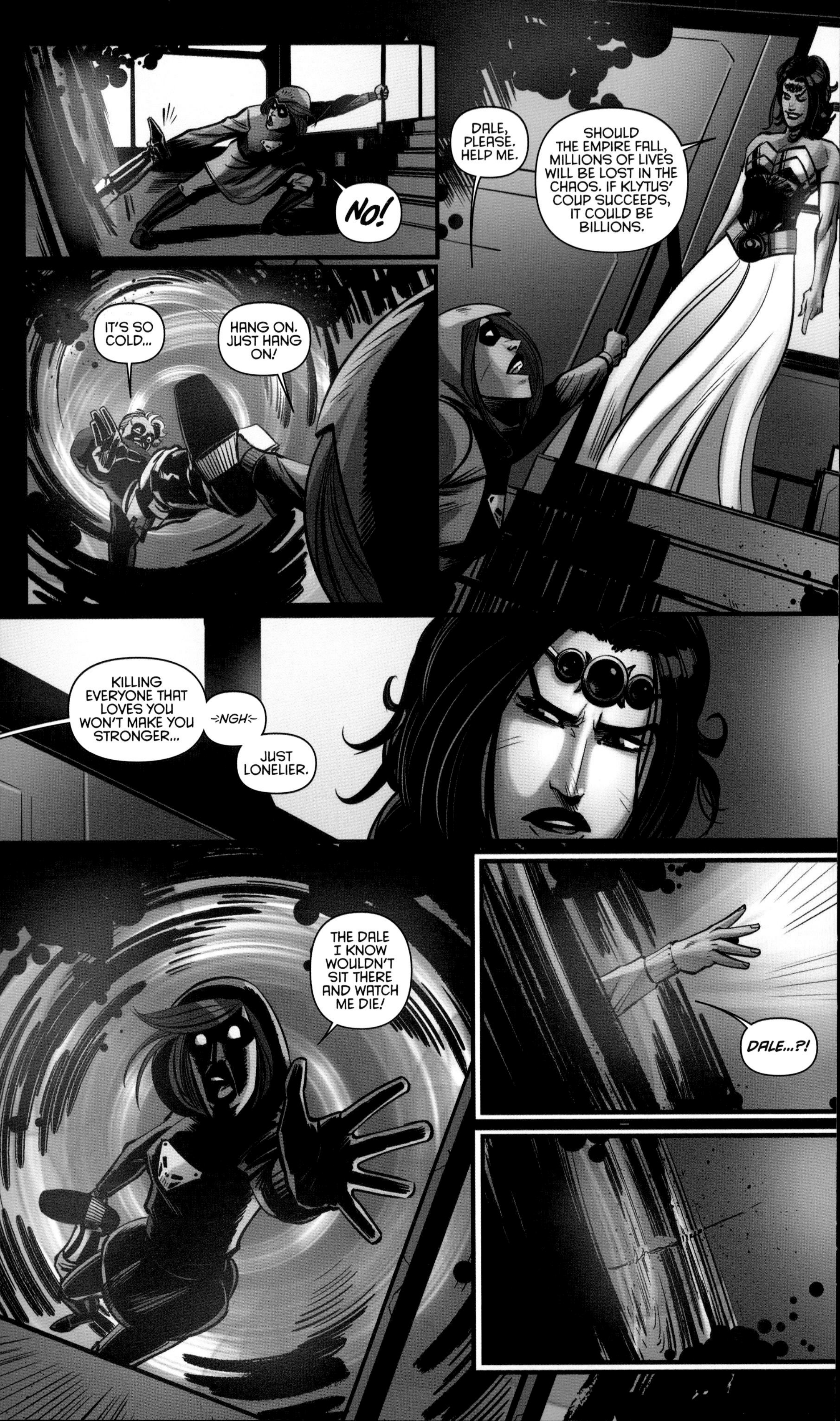
NO!
DALE, PLEASE. HELP ME.
SHOULD THE EMPIRE FALL, MILLIONS OF LIVES WILL BE LOST IN THE CHAOS. IF KLYTUS' COUP SUCCEEDS, IT COULD BE BILLIONS.
IT'S SO COLD...
HANG ON. JUST HANG ON!
KILLING EVERYONE THAT LOVES YOU WON'T MAKE YOU STRONGER...
NGH
JUST LONELIER.
THE DALE I KNOW WOULDN'T SIT THERE AND WATCH ME DIE!
DALE...?!

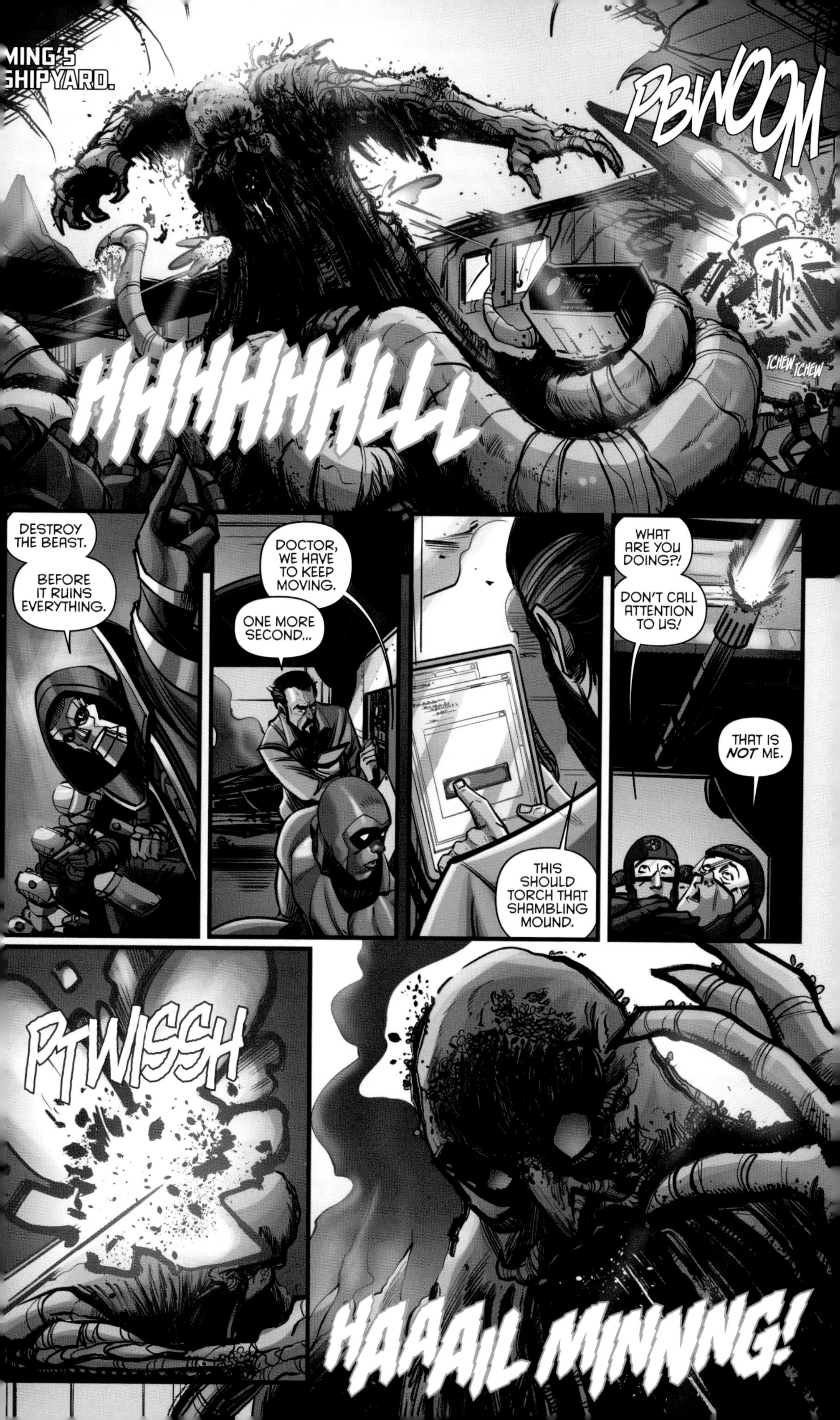
MING'S SHIPYARD.
PBWOOM
HHHHHHLLL
TCHEW TCHEW
DESTROY THE BEAST.
BEFORE IT RUINS EVERYTHING.
DOCTOR, WE HAVE TO KEEP MOVING.
ONE MORE SECOND...
THIS SHOULD TORCH THAT SHAMBLING MOUND.
WHAT ARE YOU DOING?!
DON'T CALL ATTENTION TO US!
THAT IS *NOT* ME.
PTWISSH!
HAAAIL MINNNG!

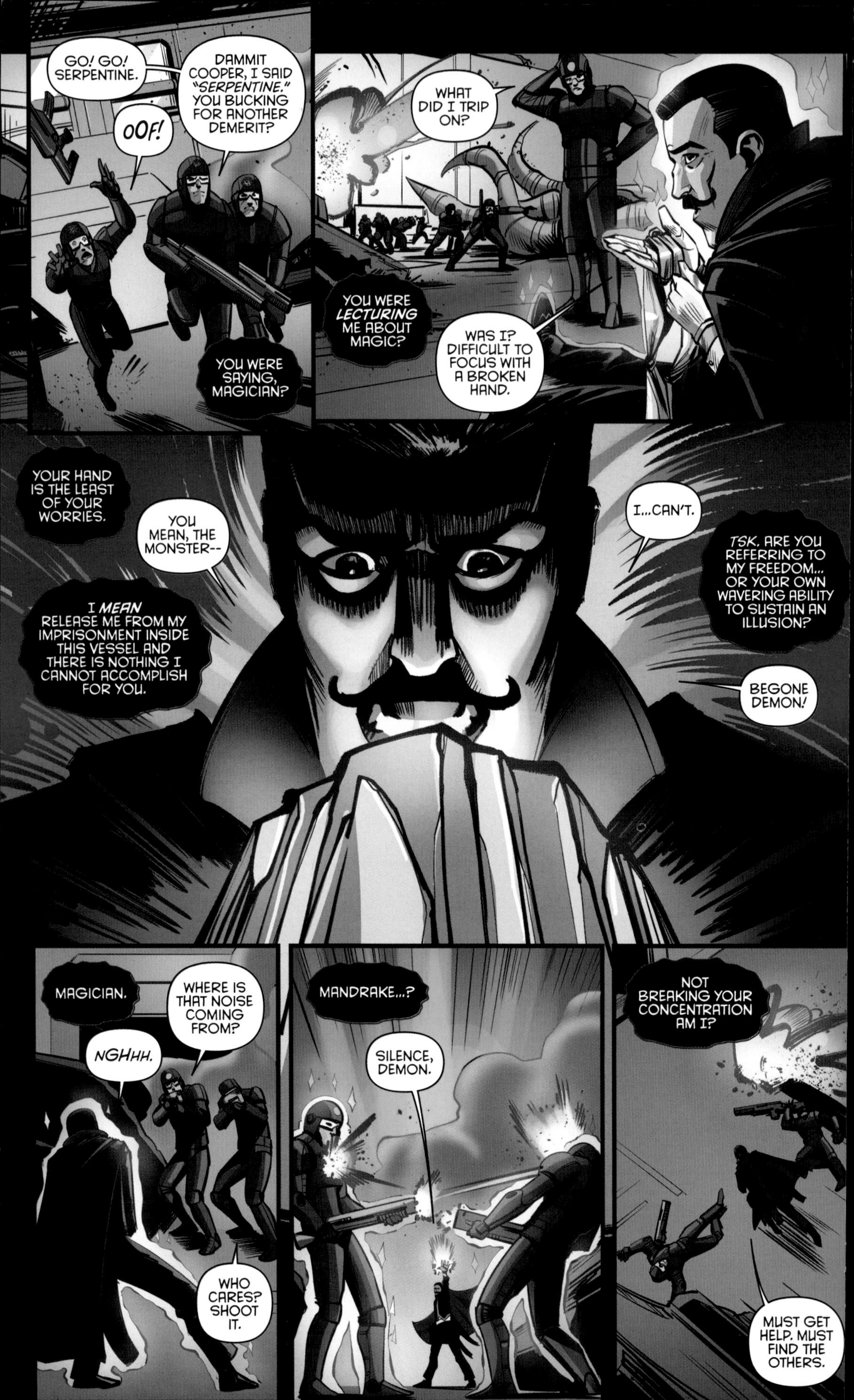
GO! GO! SERPENTINE.
DAMMIT COOPER, I SAID "SERPENTINE." YOU BUCKING FOR ANOTHER DEMERIT?
OOF!
YOU WERE SAYING, MAGICIAN?
WHAT DID I TRIP ON?
YOU WERE LECTURING ME ABOUT MAGIC?
WAS I? DIFFICULT TO FOCUS WITH A BROKEN HAND.
YOUR HAND IS THE LEAST OF YOUR WORRIES.
YOU MEAN, THE MONSTER--
I MEAN RELEASE ME FROM MY IMPRISONMENT INSIDE THIS VESSEL AND THERE IS NOTHING I CANNOT ACCOMPLISH FOR YOU.
I...CAN'T.
TSK. ARE YOU REFERRING TO MY FREEDOM... OR YOUR OWN WAVERING ABILITY TO SUSTAIN AN ILLUSION?
BEGONE DEMON!
MAGICIAN.
WHERE IS THAT NOISE COMING FROM?
NGHHH.
WHO CARES? SHOOT IT.
MANDRAKE...?
SILENCE, DEMON.
NOT BREAKING YOUR CONCENTRATION AM I?
MUST GET HELP. MUST FIND THE OTHERS.

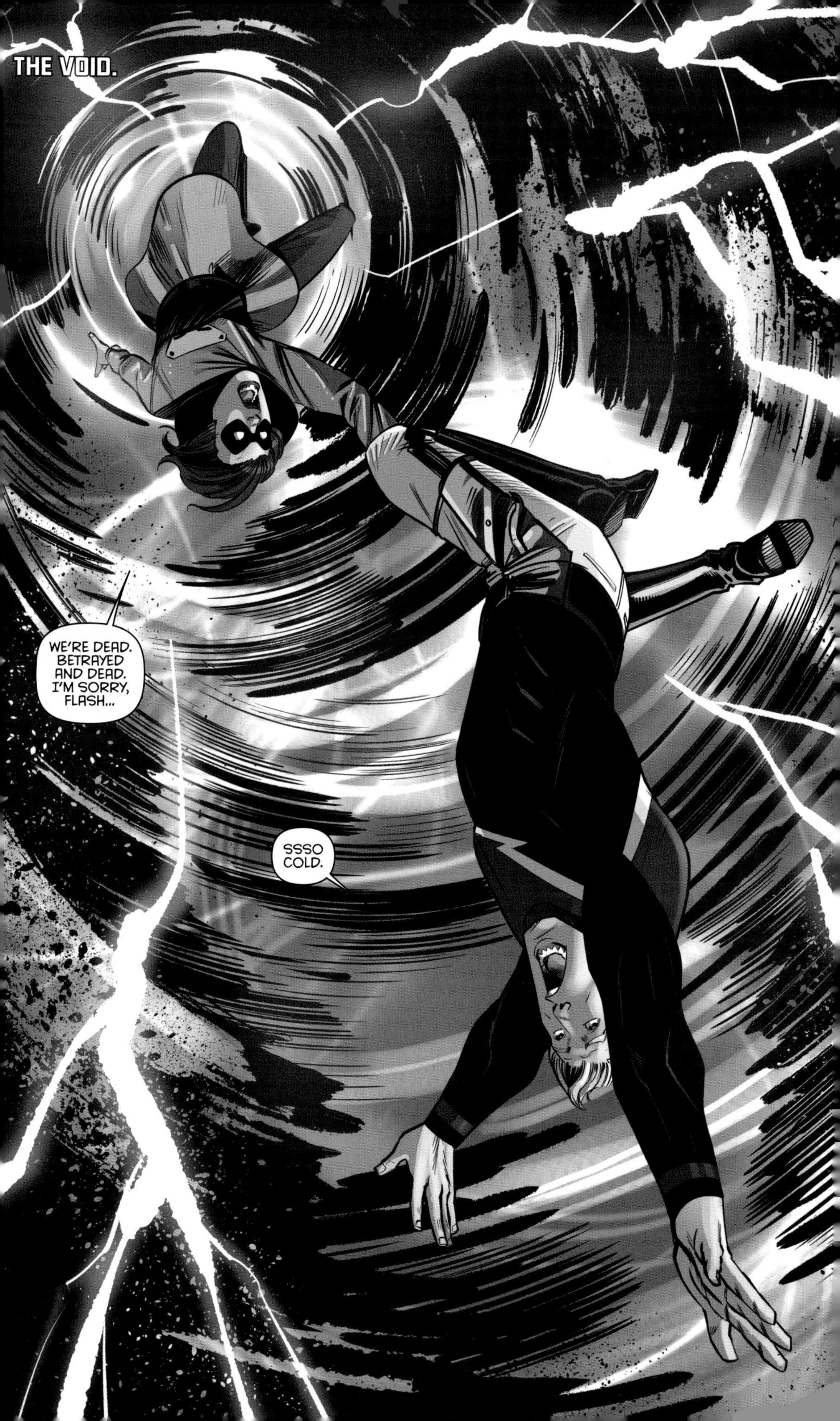
THE VOID.
WE'RE DEAD. BETRAYED AND DEAD. I'M SORRY, FLASH...
SSSO COLD.

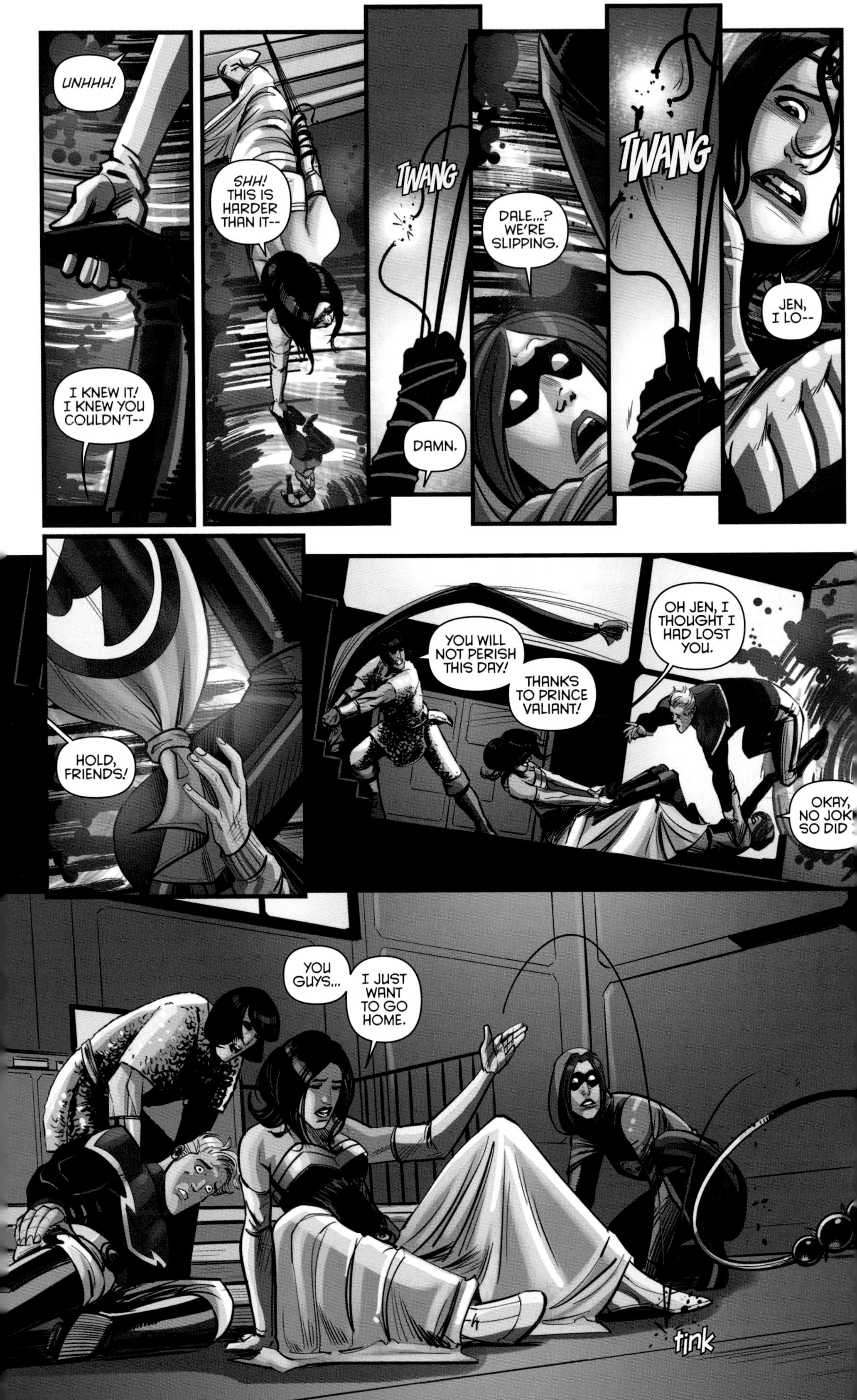
UNHHH!
I KNEW IT! I KNEW YOU COULDN'T--
SHH! THIS IS HARDER THAN IT--
TWANG
DAMN.
DALE...? WE'RE SLIPPING.
TWANG
JEN, I LO--
HOLD, FRIENDS!
YOU WILL NOT PERISH THIS DAY!
THANKS TO PRINCE VALIANT!
OH JEN, I THOUGHT I HAD LOST YOU.
OKAY, NO JOK SO DID
YOU GUYS...
I JUST WANT TO GO HOME.
tink

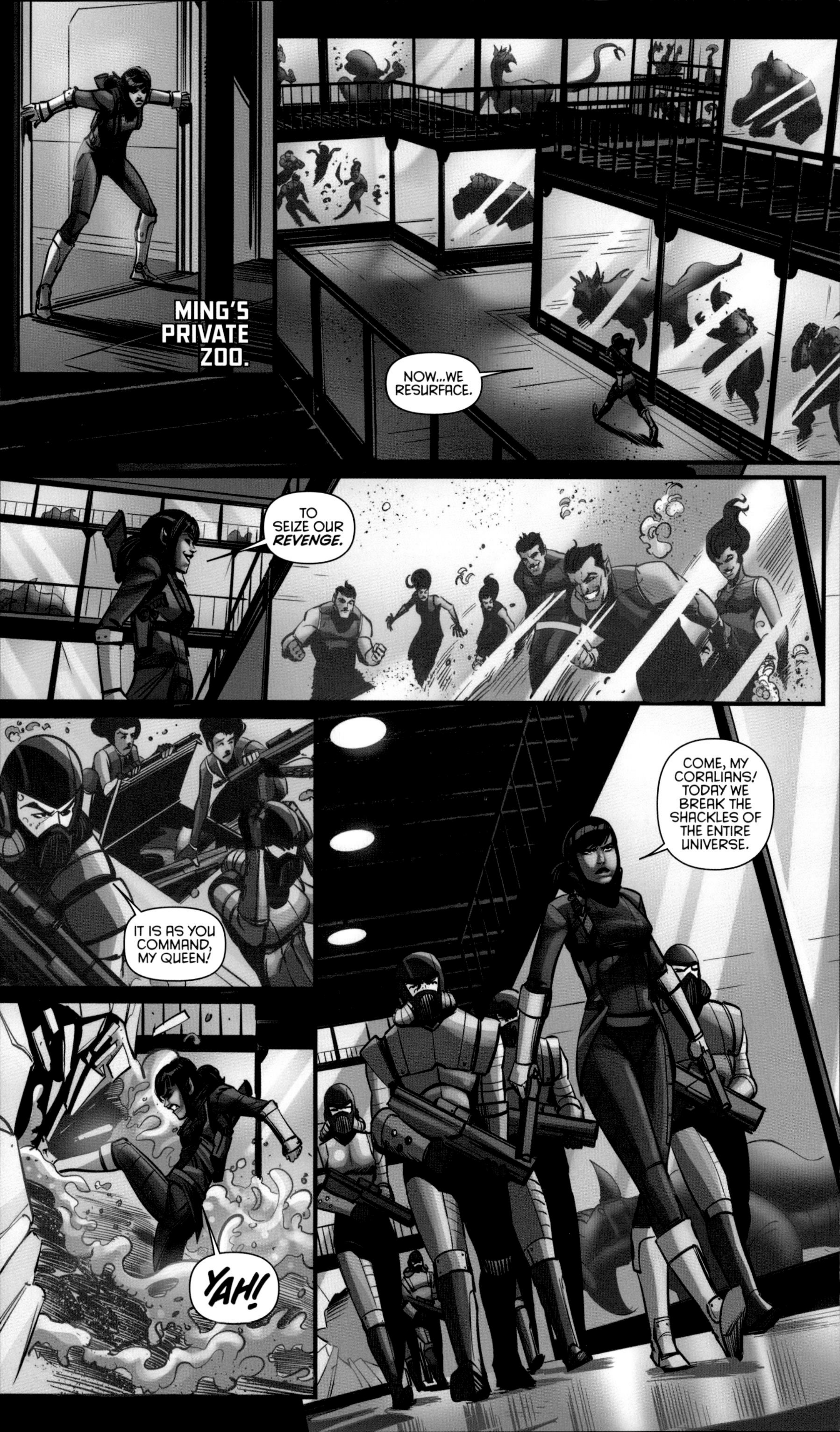
MING'S PRIVATE ZOO.
NOW...WE RESURFACE.
TO SEIZE OUR *REVENGE.*
IT IS AS YOU COMMAND, MY QUEEN!
COME, MY CORALIANS! TODAY WE BREAK THE SHACKLES OF THE ENTIRE UNIVERSE.
YAH!

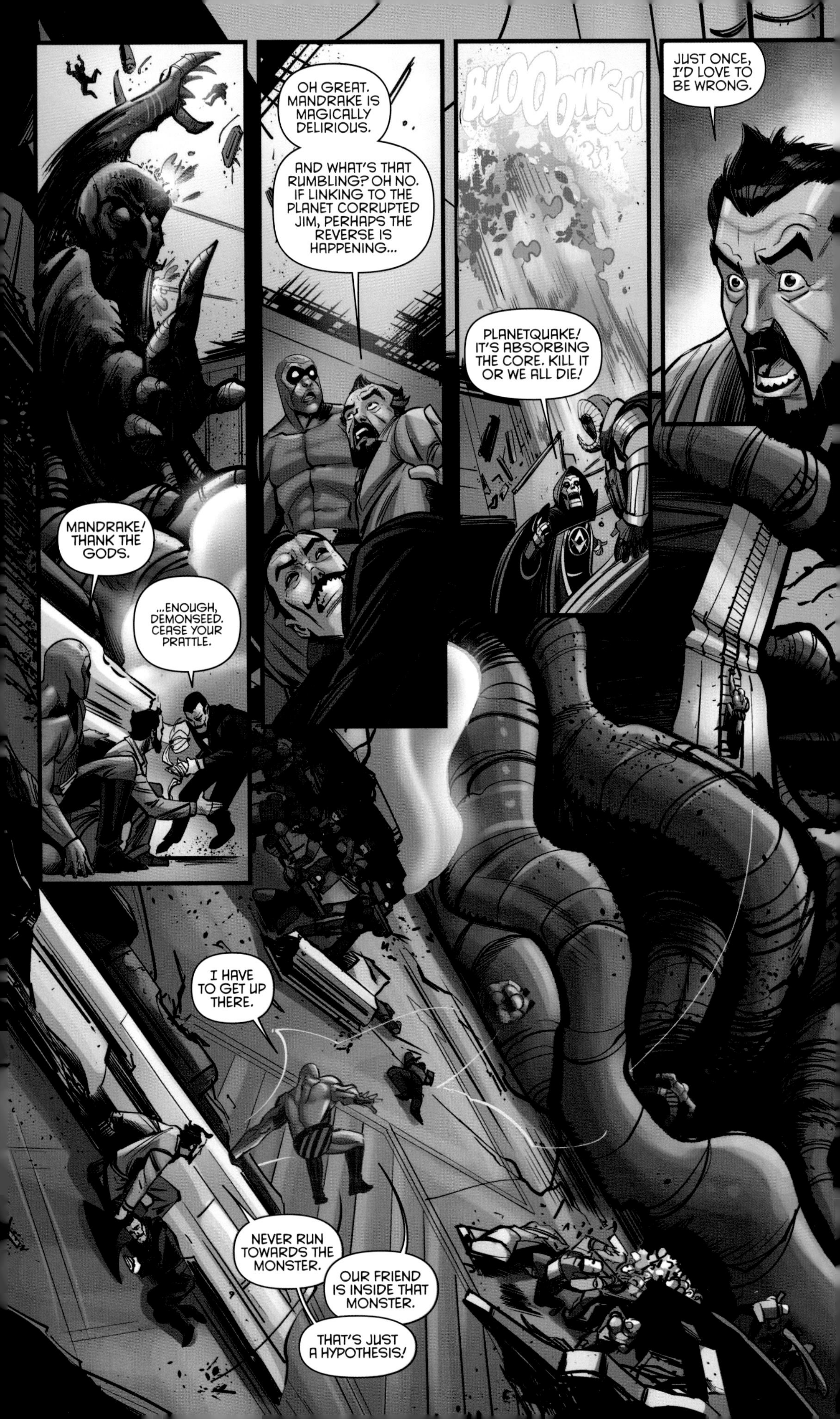
MANDRAKE! THANK THE GODS.
...ENOUGH, DEMONSEED. CEASE YOUR PRATTLE.
OH GREAT. MANDRAKE IS MAGICALLY DELIRIOUS.
AND WHAT'S THAT RUMBLING? OH NO. IF LINKING TO THE PLANET CORRUPTED JIM, PERHAPS THE REVERSE IS HAPPENING...
BLOOOWSH
PLANETQUAKE! IT'S ABSORBING THE CORE. KILL IT OR WE ALL DIE!
JUST ONCE, I'D LOVE TO BE WRONG.
I HAVE TO GET UP THERE.
NEVER RUN TOWARDS THE MONSTER.
OUR FRIEND IS INSIDE THAT MONSTER.
THAT'S JUST A HYPOTHESIS!

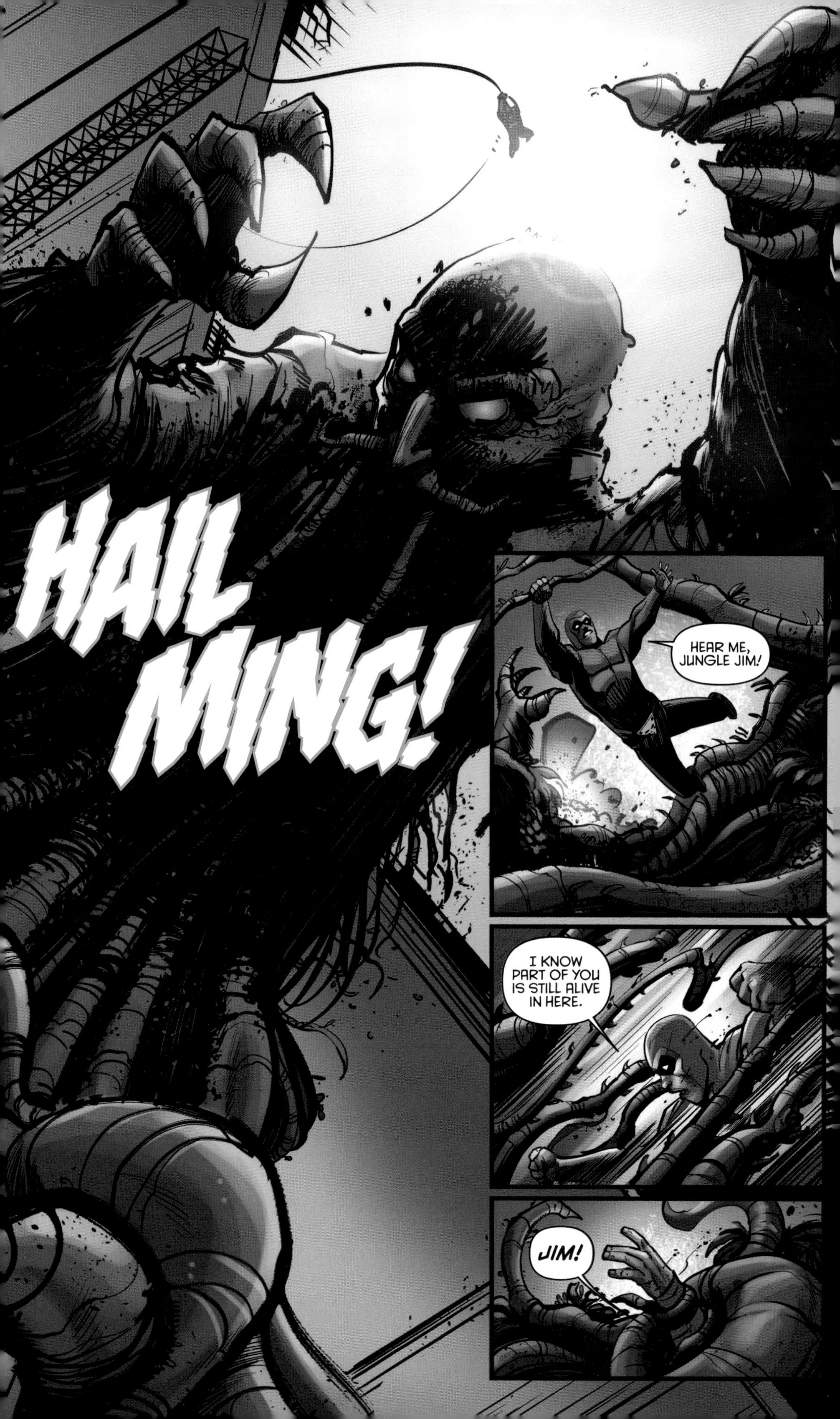
HAIL MING!
HEAR ME, JUNGLE JIM!
I KNOW PART OF YOU IS STILL ALIVE IN HERE.
JIM!

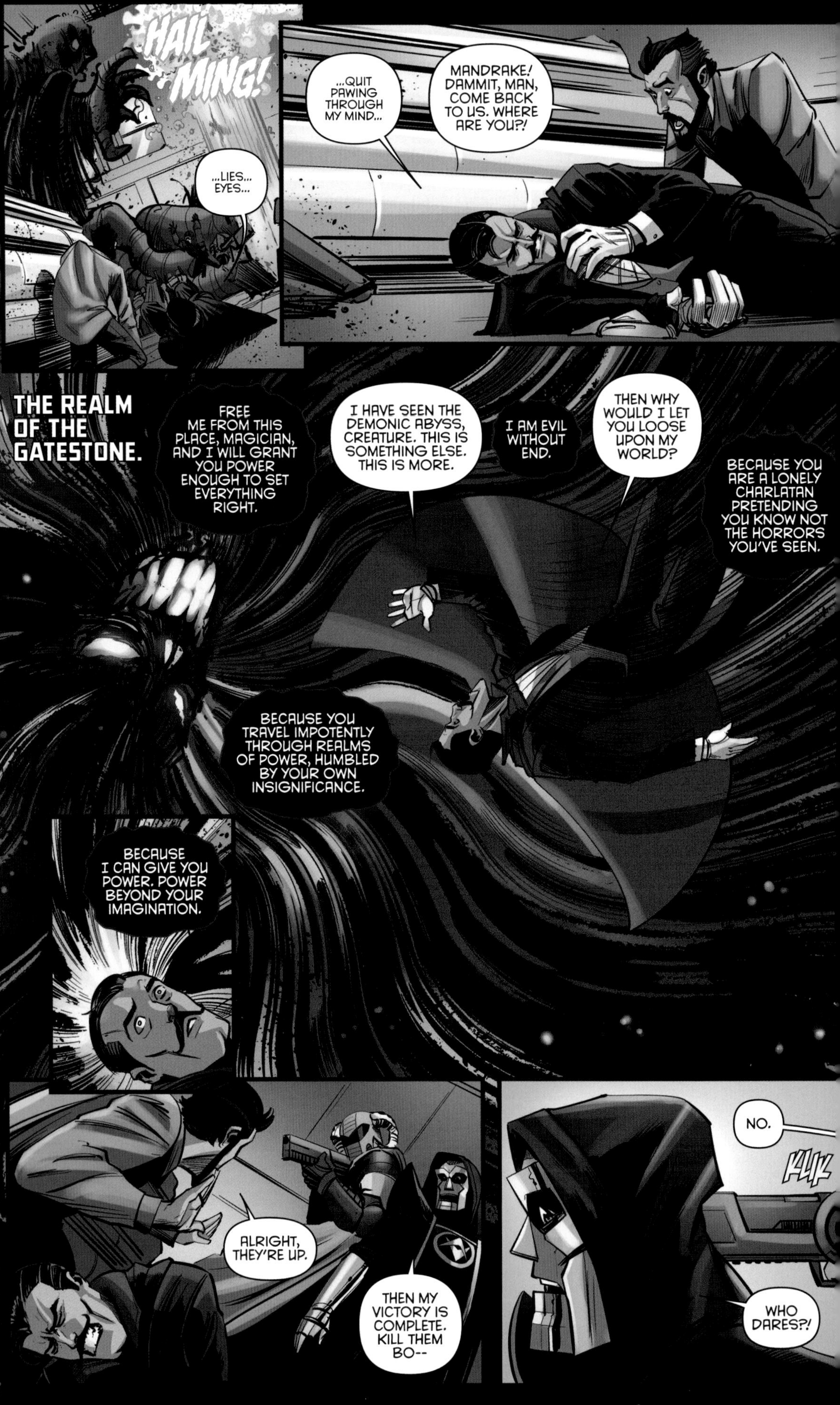
HAIL MING!
...LIES... EYES...
...QUIT PAWING THROUGH MY MIND...
MANDRAKE! DAMMIT, MAN, COME BACK TO US. WHERE ARE YOU?!
THE REALM OF THE GATESTONE.
FREE ME FROM THIS PLACE, MAGICIAN, AND I WILL GRANT YOU POWER ENOUGH TO SET EVERYTHING RIGHT.
I HAVE SEEN THE DEMONIC ABYSS, CREATURE. THIS IS SOMETHING ELSE. THIS IS MORE.
I AM EVIL WITHOUT END.
THEN WHY WOULD I LET YOU LOOSE UPON MY WORLD?
BECAUSE YOU ARE A LONELY CHARLATAN PRETENDING YOU KNOW NOT THE HORRORS YOU'VE SEEN.
BECAUSE YOU TRAVEL IMPOTENTLY THROUGH REALMS OF POWER, HUMBLED BY YOUR OWN INSIGNIFICANCE.
BECAUSE I CAN GIVE YOU POWER. POWER BEYOND YOUR IMAGINATION.
ALRIGHT, THEY'RE UP.
THEN MY VICTORY IS COMPLETE. KILL THEM BO--
NO.
KLIK
WHO DARES?!

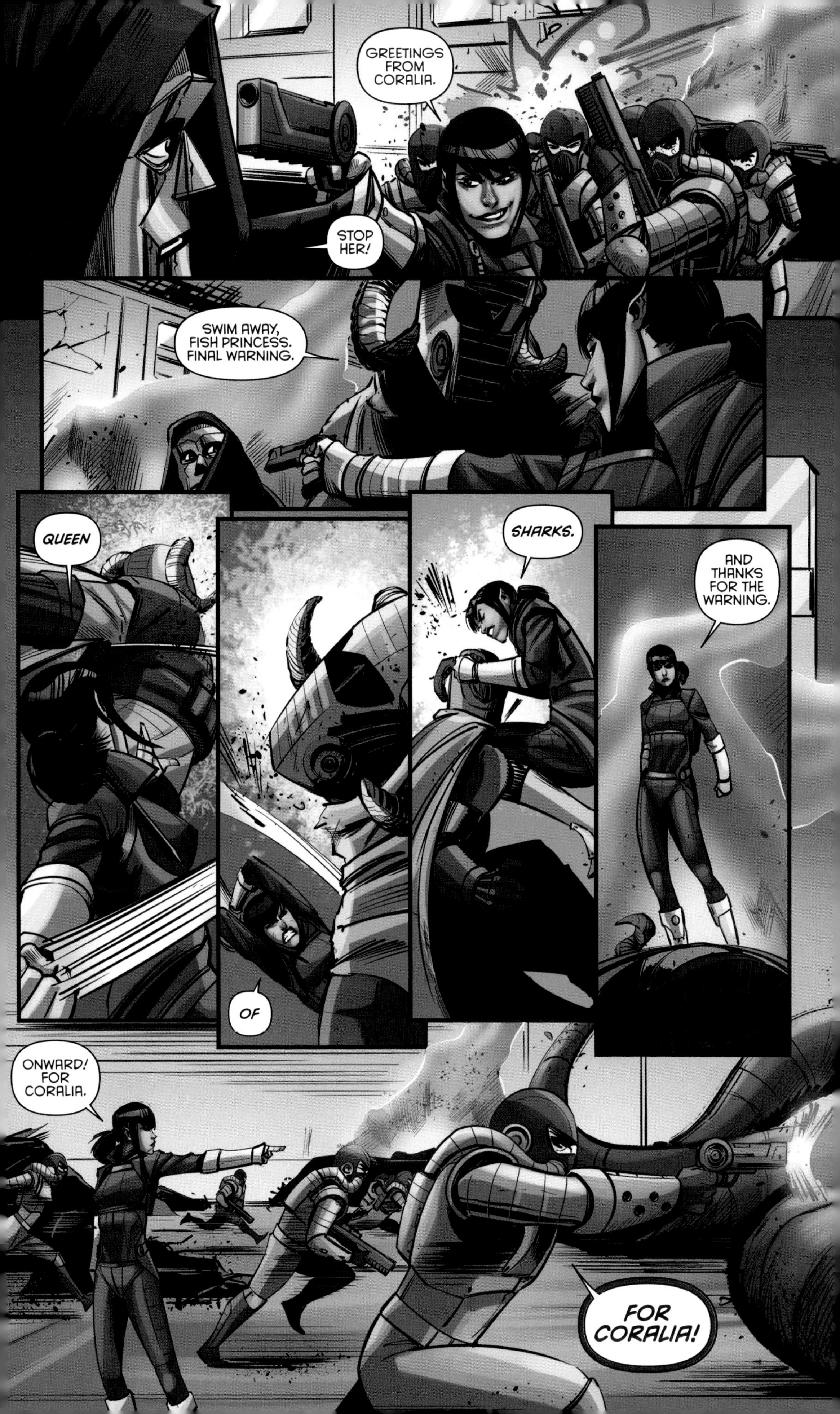
GREETINGS FROM CORALIA.
STOP HER!
SWIM AWAY, FISH PRINCESS. FINAL WARNING.
QUEEN
OF
SHARKS.
AND THANKS FOR THE WARNING.
ONWARD! FOR CORALIA.
FOR CORALIA!

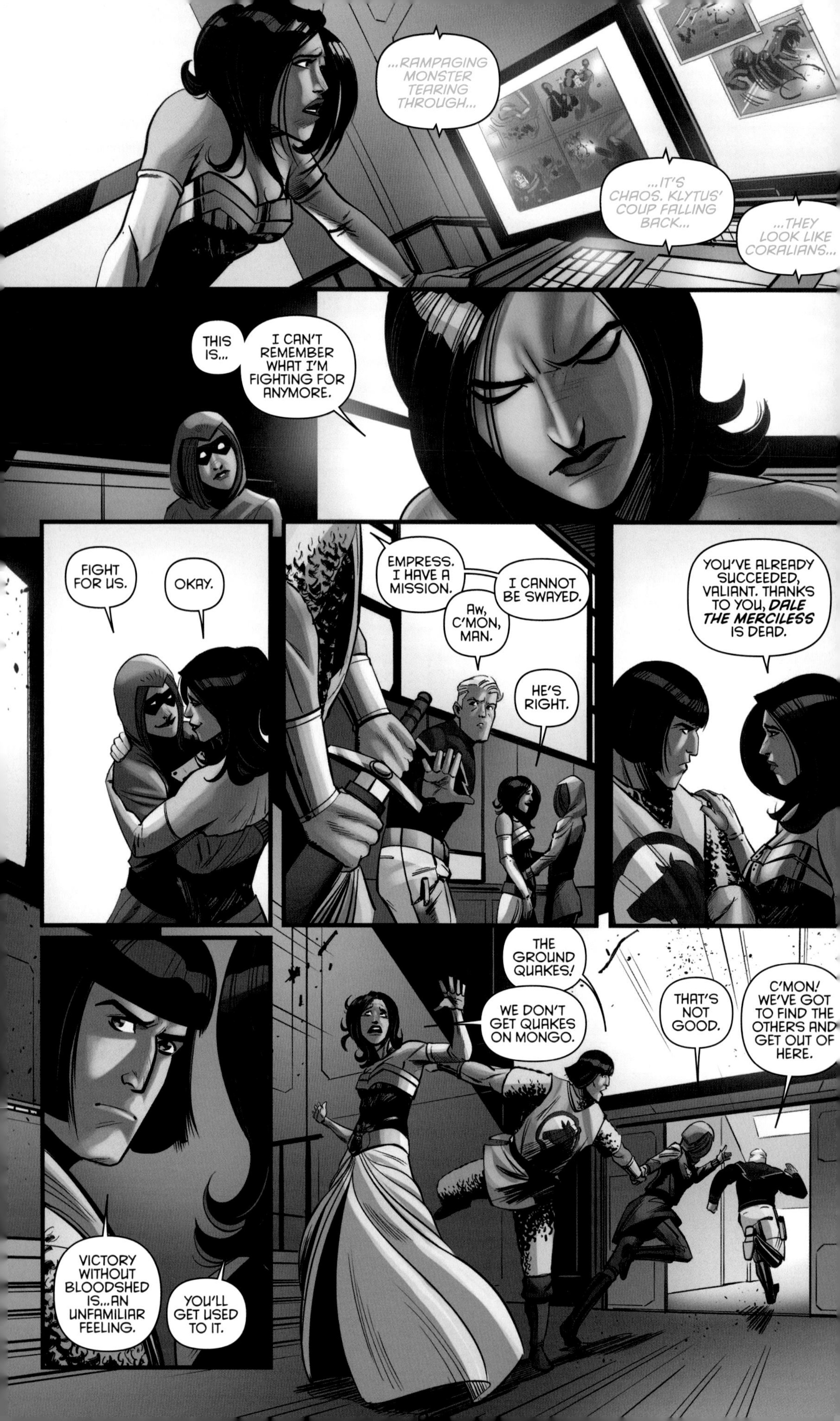
...RAMPAGING MONSTER TEARING THROUGH...
...IT'S CHAOS. KLYTUS' COUP FALLING BACK...
...THEY LOOK LIKE CORALIANS...
THIS IS...
I CAN'T REMEMBER WHAT I'M FIGHTING FOR ANYMORE.
FIGHT FOR US.
OKAY.
EMPRESS. I HAVE A MISSION.
I CANNOT BE SWAYED.
AW, C'MON, MAN.
HE'S RIGHT.
YOU'VE ALREADY SUCCEEDED, VALIANT. THANKS TO YOU, DALE THE MERCILESS IS DEAD.
VICTORY WITHOUT BLOODSHED IS...AN UNFAMILIAR FEELING.
YOU'LL GET USED TO IT.
THE GROUND QUAKES!
WE DON'T GET QUAKES ON MONGO.
THAT'S NOT GOOD.
C'MON! WE'VE GOT TO FIND THE OTHERS AND GET OUT OF HERE.

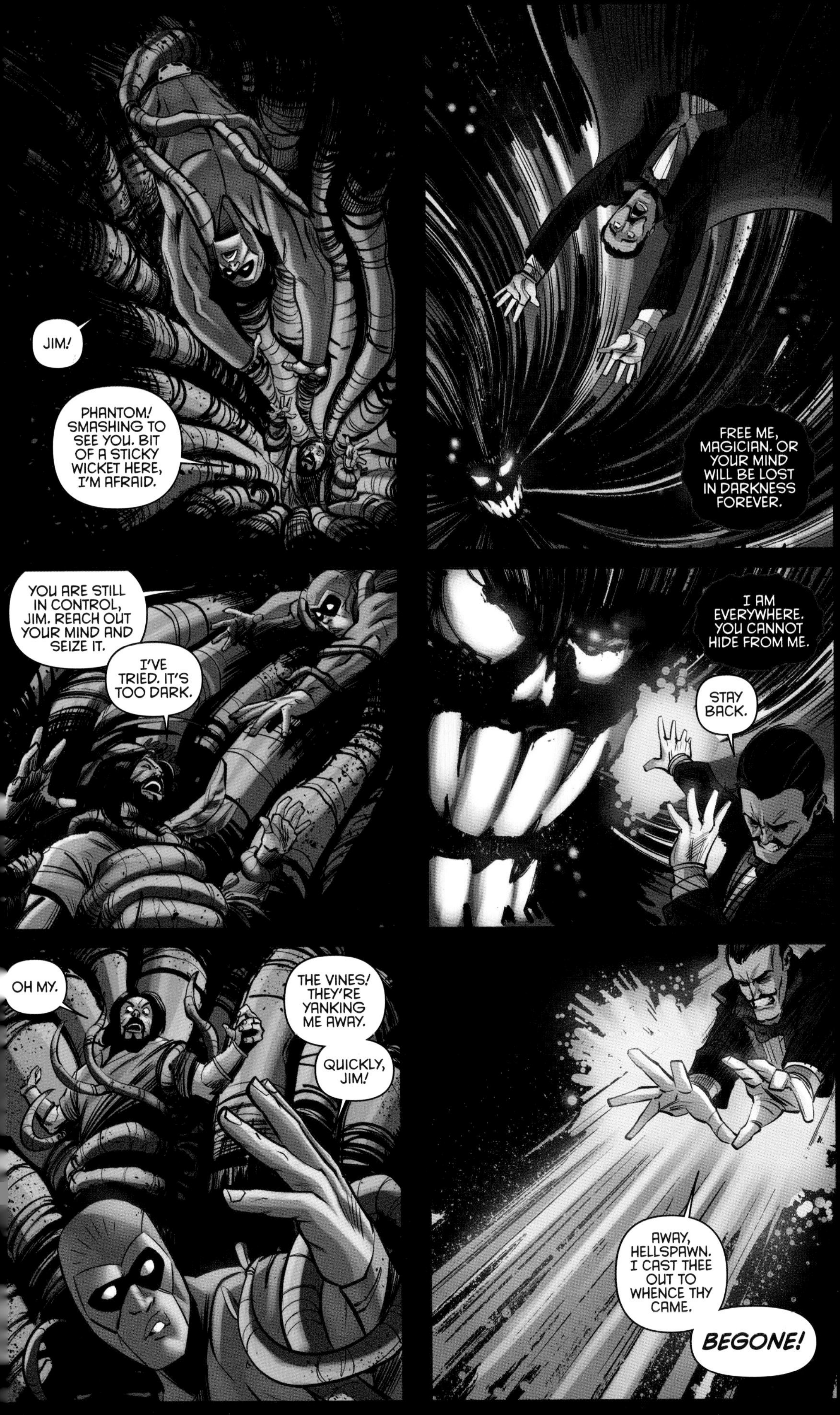
JIM!
PHANTOM! SMASHING TO SEE YOU. BIT OF A STICKY WICKET HERE, I'M AFRAID.
FREE ME, MAGICIAN. OR YOUR MIND WILL BE LOST IN DARKNESS FOREVER.
YOU ARE STILL IN CONTROL, JIM. REACH OUT YOUR MIND AND SEIZE IT.
I'VE TRIED. IT'S TOO DARK.
I AM EVERYWHERE. YOU CANNOT HIDE FROM ME.
STAY BACK.
OH MY.
THE VINES! THEY'RE YANKING ME AWAY.
QUICKLY, JIM!
AWAY, HELLSPAWN. I CAST THEE OUT TO WHENCE THY CAME.
BEGONE!

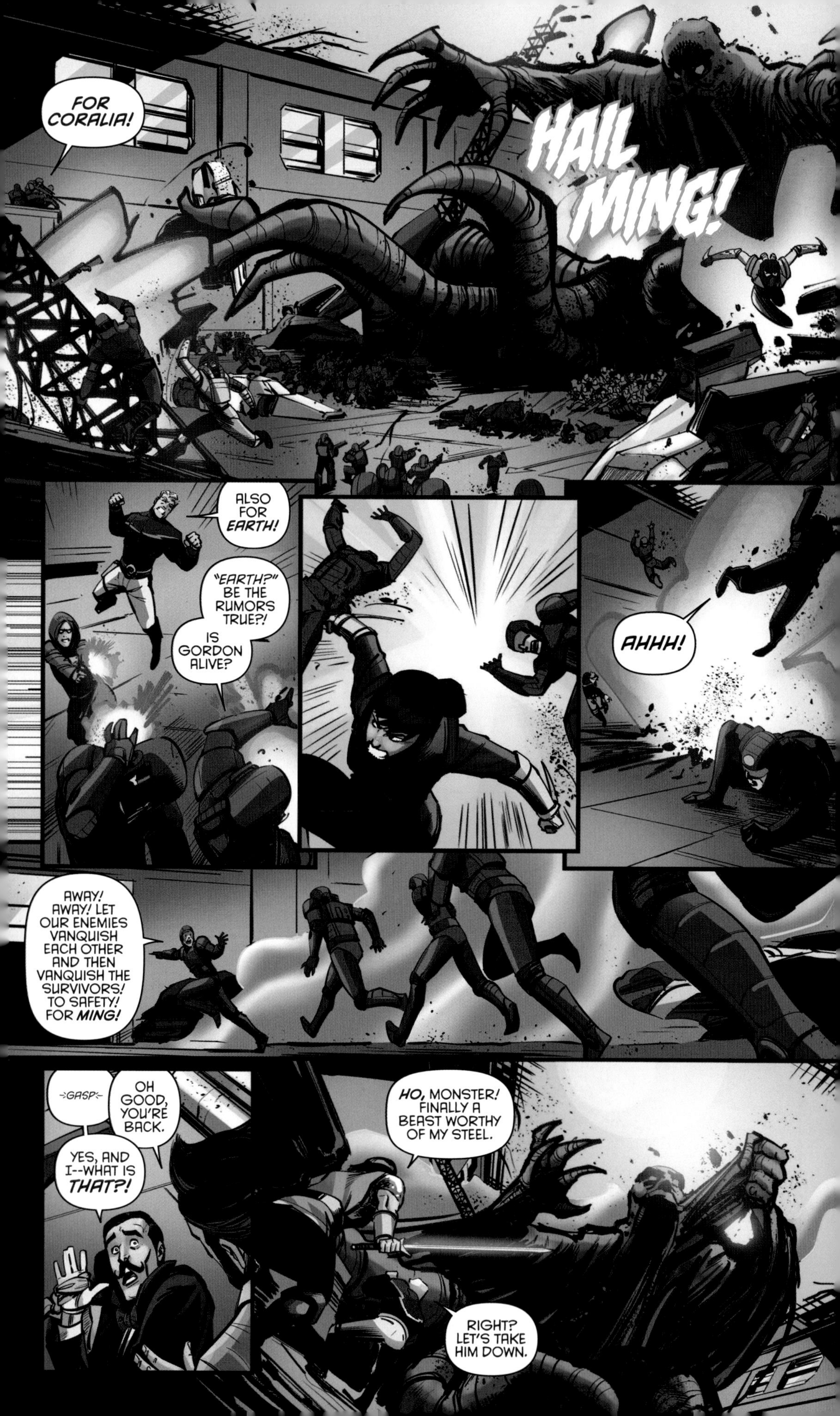
FOR CORALIA!
HAIL MING!
ALSO FOR EARTH!
"EARTH?" BE THE RUMORS TRUE?!
IS GORDON ALIVE?
AHHH!
AWAY! AWAY! LET OUR ENEMIES VANQUISH EACH OTHER AND THEN VANQUISH THE SURVIVORS! TO SAFETY! FOR MING!
GASP
OH GOOD, YOU'RE BACK.
YES, AND I--WHAT IS THAT?!
HO, MONSTER! FINALLY A BEAST WORTHY OF MY STEEL.
RIGHT? LET'S TAKE HIM DOWN.

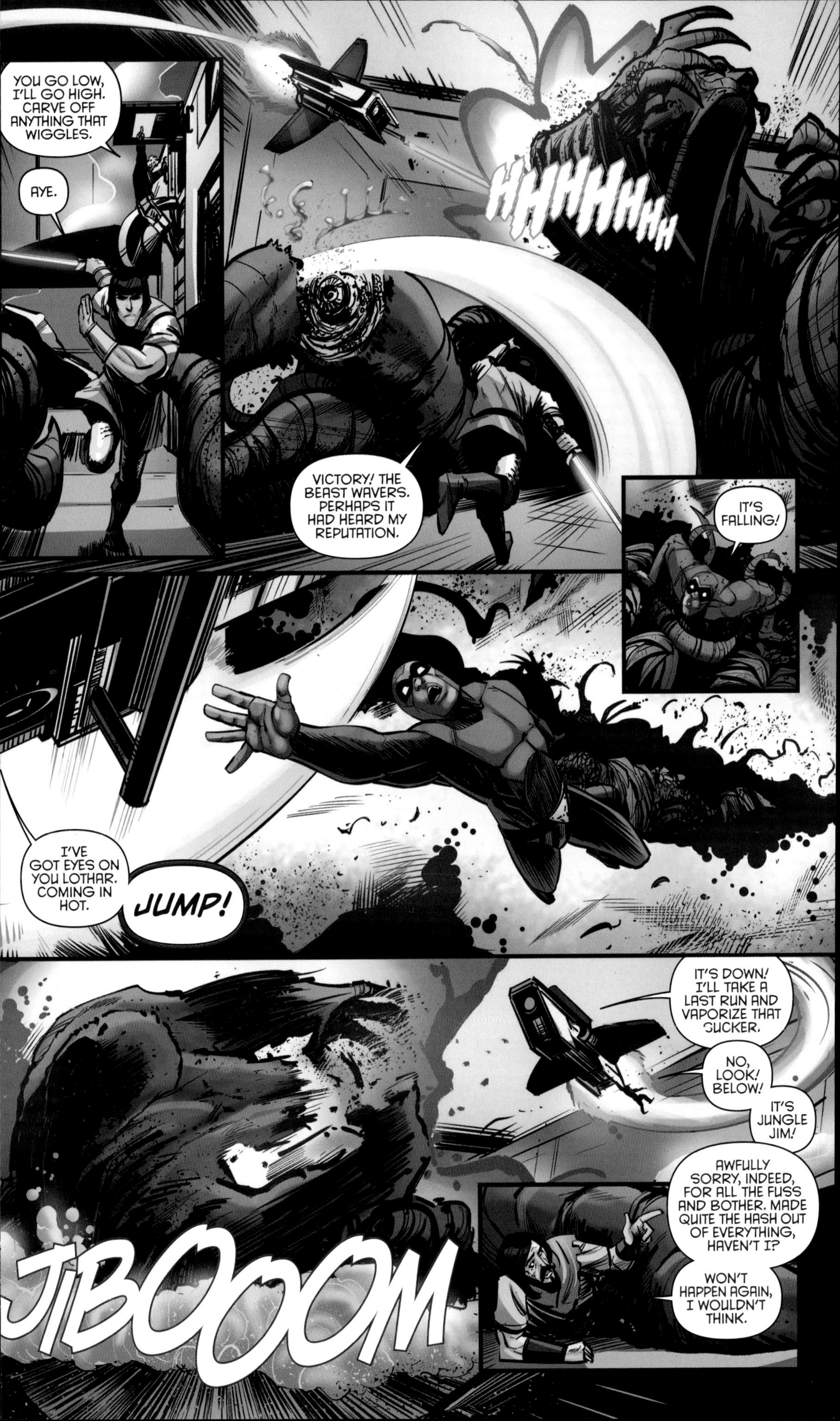
YOU GO LOW, I'LL GO HIGH. CARVE OFF ANYTHING THAT WIGGLES.
AYE.
HHHHHHHHH
VICTORY! THE BEAST WAVERS. PERHAPS IT HAD HEARD MY REPUTATION.
IT'S FALLING!
I'VE GOT EYES ON YOU LOTHAR. COMING IN HOT.
JUMP!
IT'S DOWN! I'LL TAKE A LAST RUN AND VAPORIZE THAT SUCKER.
NO, LOOK! BELOW!
IT'S JUNGLE JIM!
JIBOOOOM
AWFULLY SORRY, INDEED, FOR ALL THE FUSS AND BOTHER. MADE QUITE THE HASH OUT OF EVERYTHING, HAVEN'T I?
WON'T HAPPEN AGAIN, I WOULDN'T THINK.

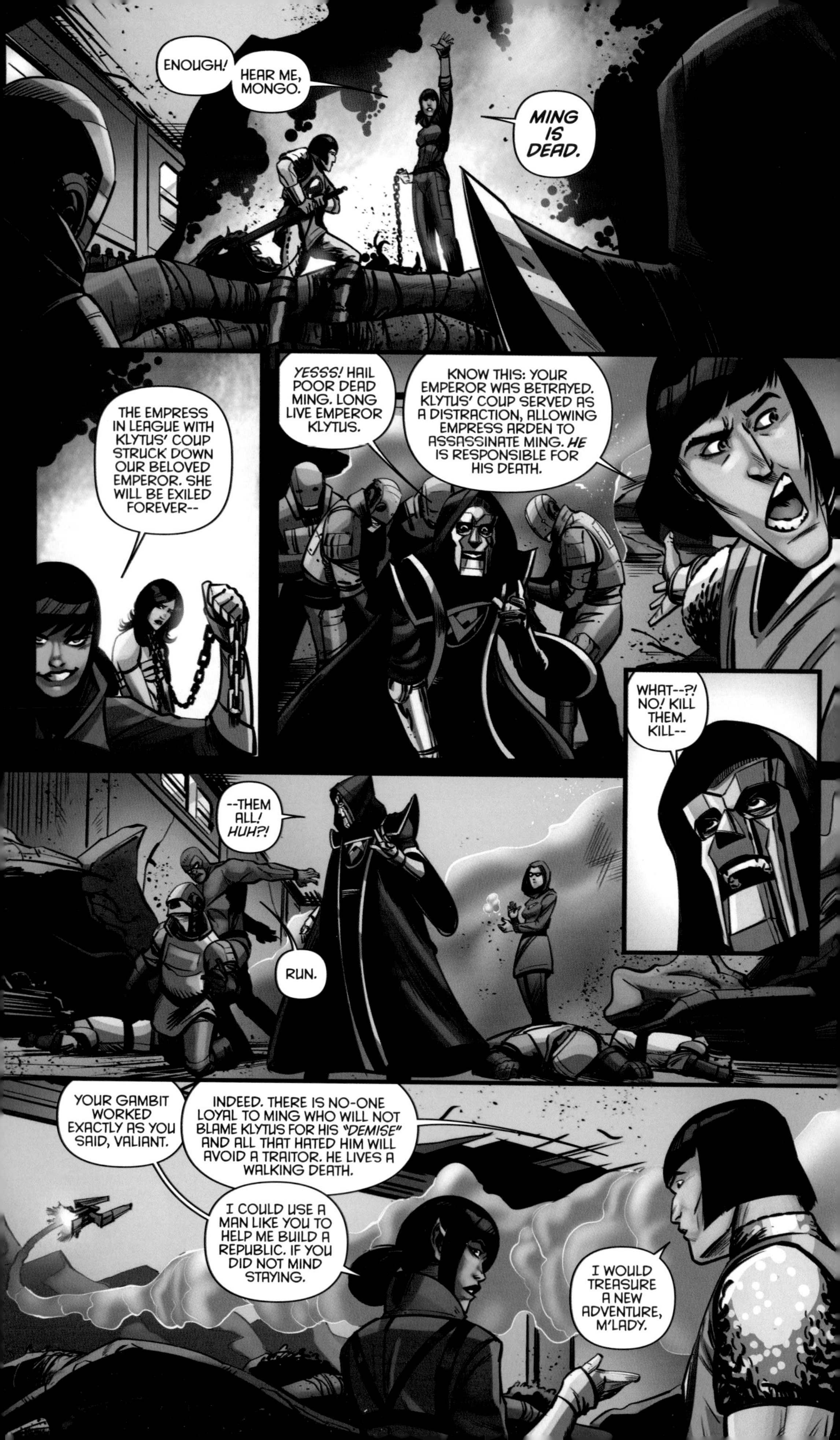
ENOUGH!
HEAR ME, MONGO.
MING IS DEAD.
THE EMPRESS IN LEAGUE WITH KLYTUS' COUP STRUCK DOWN OUR BELOVED EMPEROR. SHE WILL BE EXILED FOREVER--
YESSS! HAIL POOR DEAD MING. LONG LIVE EMPEROR KLYTUS.
KNOW THIS: YOUR EMPEROR WAS BETRAYED. KLYTUS' COUP SERVED AS A DISTRACTION, ALLOWING EMPRESS ARDEN TO ASSASSINATE MING. HE IS RESPONSIBLE FOR HIS DEATH.
WHAT--?! NO! KILL THEM. KILL--
--THEM ALL! HUH?!
RUN.
YOUR GAMBIT WORKED EXACTLY AS YOU SAID, VALIANT.
INDEED. THERE IS NO-ONE LOYAL TO MING WHO WILL NOT BLAME KLYTUS FOR HIS "DEMISE" AND ALL THAT HATED HIM WILL AVOID A TRAITOR. HE LIVES A WALKING DEATH.
I COULD USE A MAN LIKE YOU TO HELP ME BUILD A REPUBLIC. IF YOU DID NOT MIND STAYING.
I WOULD TREASURE A NEW ADVENTURE, M'LADY.

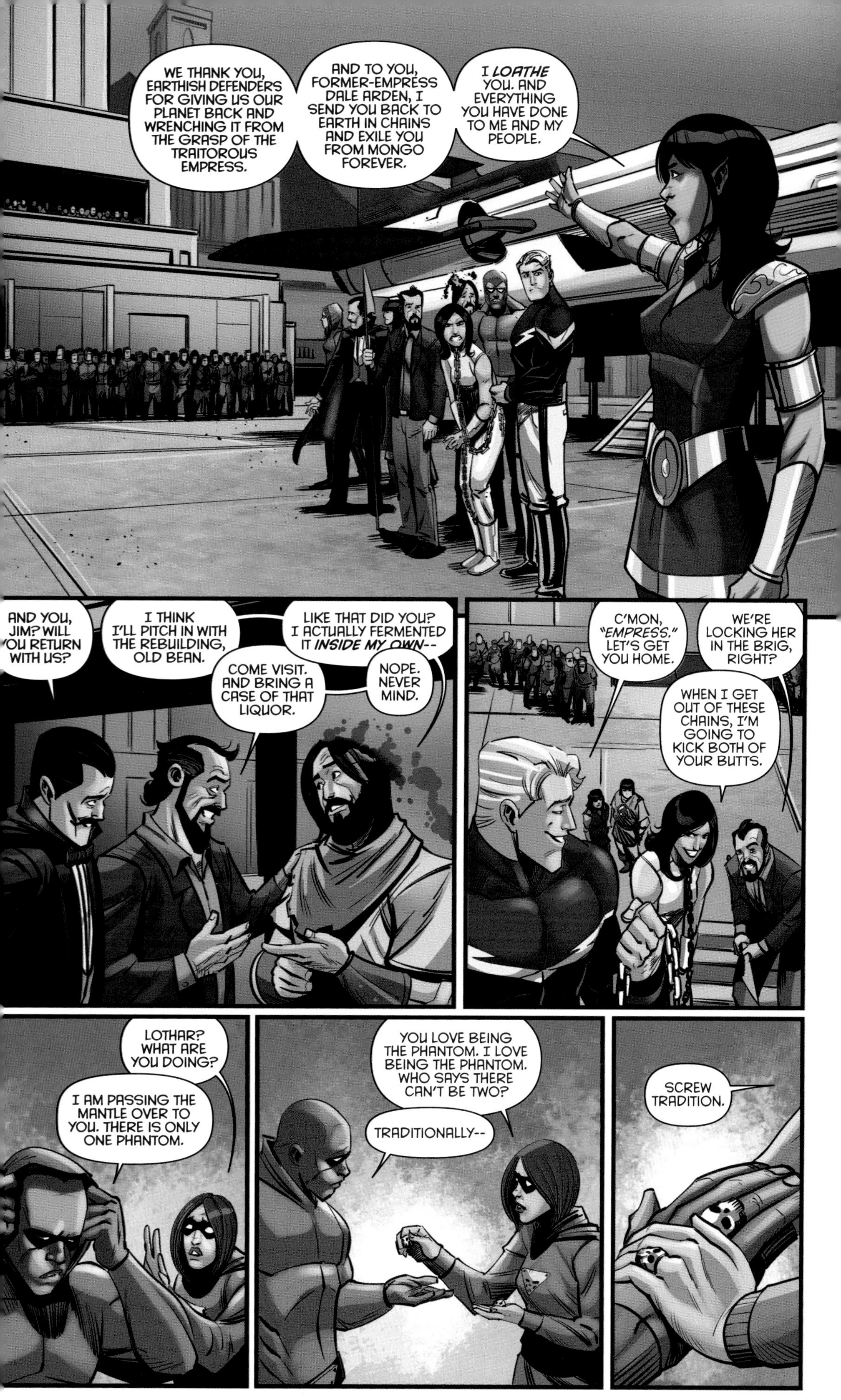
WE THANK YOU, EARTHISH DEFENDERS FOR GIVING US OUR PLANET BACK AND WRENCHING IT FROM THE GRASP OF THE TRAITOROUS EMPRESS.
AND TO YOU, FORMER-EMPRESS DALE ARDEN, I SEND YOU BACK TO EARTH IN CHAINS AND EXILE YOU FROM MONGO FOREVER.
I *LOATHE* YOU. AND EVERYTHING YOU HAVE DONE TO ME AND MY PEOPLE.
AND YOU, JIM? WILL YOU RETURN WITH US?
I THINK I'LL PITCH IN WITH THE REBUILDING, OLD BEAN.
COME VISIT. AND BRING A CASE OF THAT LIQUOR.
LIKE THAT DID YOU? I ACTUALLY FERMENTED IT *INSIDE MY OWN*--
NOPE. NEVER MIND.
C'MON, "*EMPRESS.*" LET'S GET YOU HOME.
WE'RE LOCKING HER IN THE BRIG, RIGHT?
WHEN I GET OUT OF THESE CHAINS, I'M GOING TO KICK BOTH OF YOUR BUTTS.
LOTHAR? WHAT ARE YOU DOING?
I AM PASSING THE MANTLE OVER TO YOU. THERE IS ONLY ONE PHANTOM.
YOU LOVE BEING THE PHANTOM. I LOVE BEING THE PHANTOM. WHO SAYS THERE CAN'T BE TWO?
TRADITIONALLY--
SCREW TRADITION.

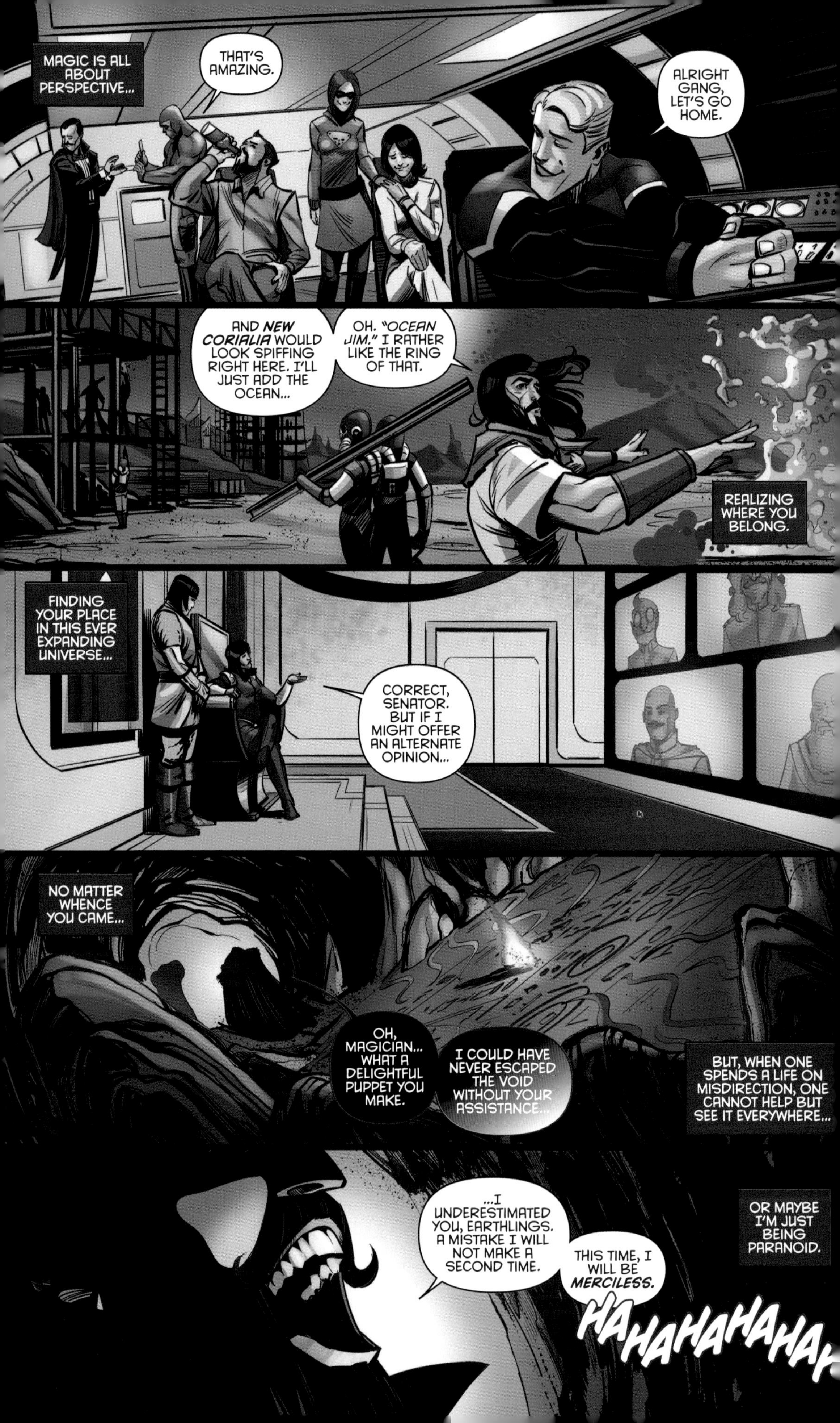
MAGIC IS ALL ABOUT PERSPECTIVE...
THAT'S AMAZING.
ALRIGHT GANG, LET'S GO HOME.
AND NEW CORIALIA WOULD LOOK SPIFFING RIGHT HERE. I'LL JUST ADD THE OCEAN...
OH. "OCEAN JIM." I RATHER LIKE THE RING OF THAT.
REALIZING WHERE YOU BELONG.
FINDING YOUR PLACE IN THIS EVER EXPANDING UNIVERSE...
CORRECT, SENATOR. BUT IF I MIGHT OFFER AN ALTERNATE OPINION...
NO MATTER WHENCE YOU CAME...
OH, MAGICIAN... WHAT A DELIGHTFUL PUPPET YOU MAKE.
I COULD HAVE NEVER ESCAPED THE VOID WITHOUT YOUR ASSISTANCE...
BUT, WHEN ONE SPENDS A LIFE ON MISDIRECTION, ONE CANNOT HELP BUT SEE IT EVERYWHERE...
...I UNDERESTIMATED YOU, EARTHLINGS. A MISTAKE I WILL NOT MAKE A SECOND TIME.
THIS TIME, I WILL BE MERCILESS.
OR MAYBE I'M JUST BEING PARANOID.
HAHAHAHAHAHA

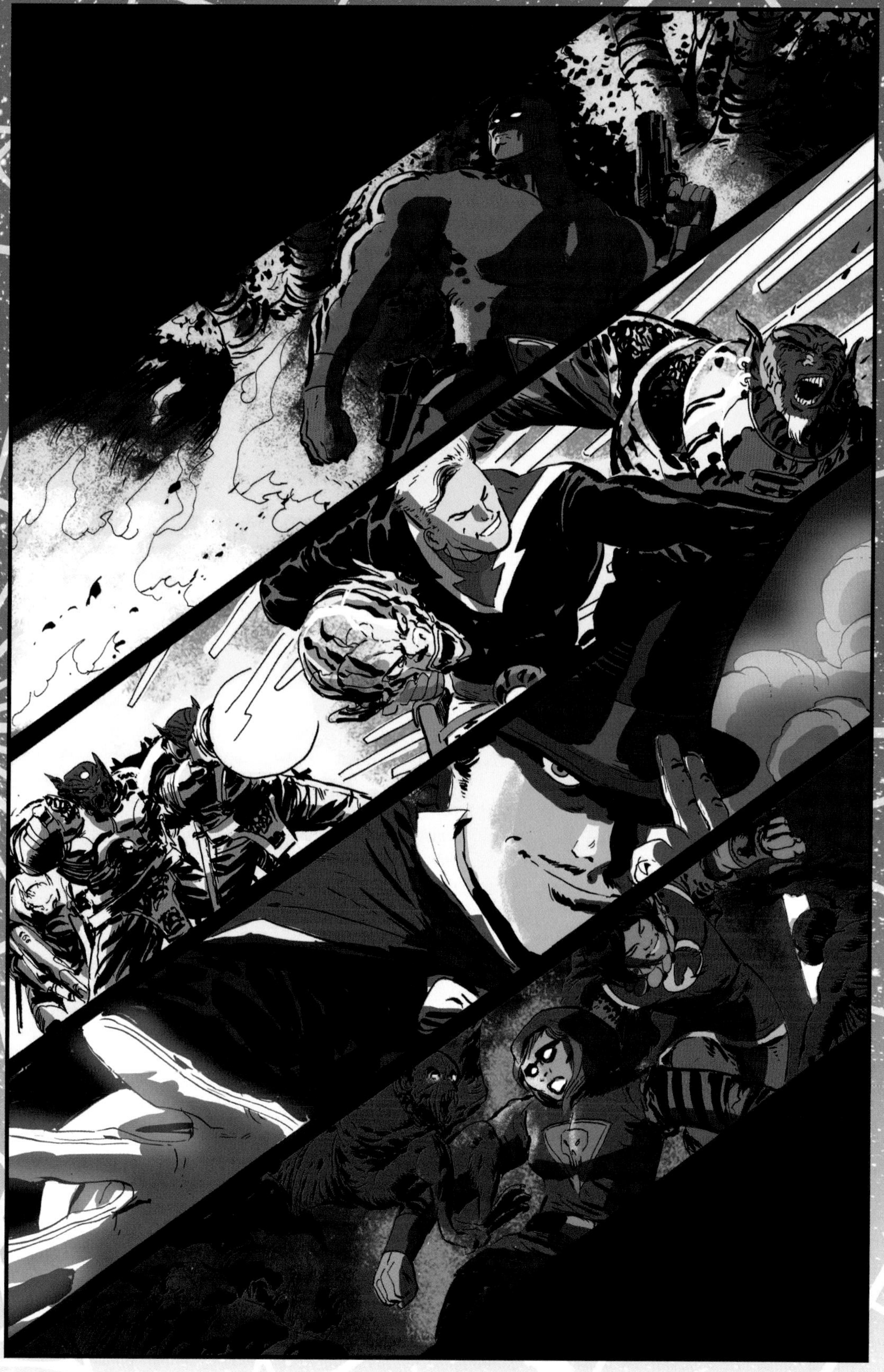

Issue #1 alternate cover
Art by **DAN McDAID**

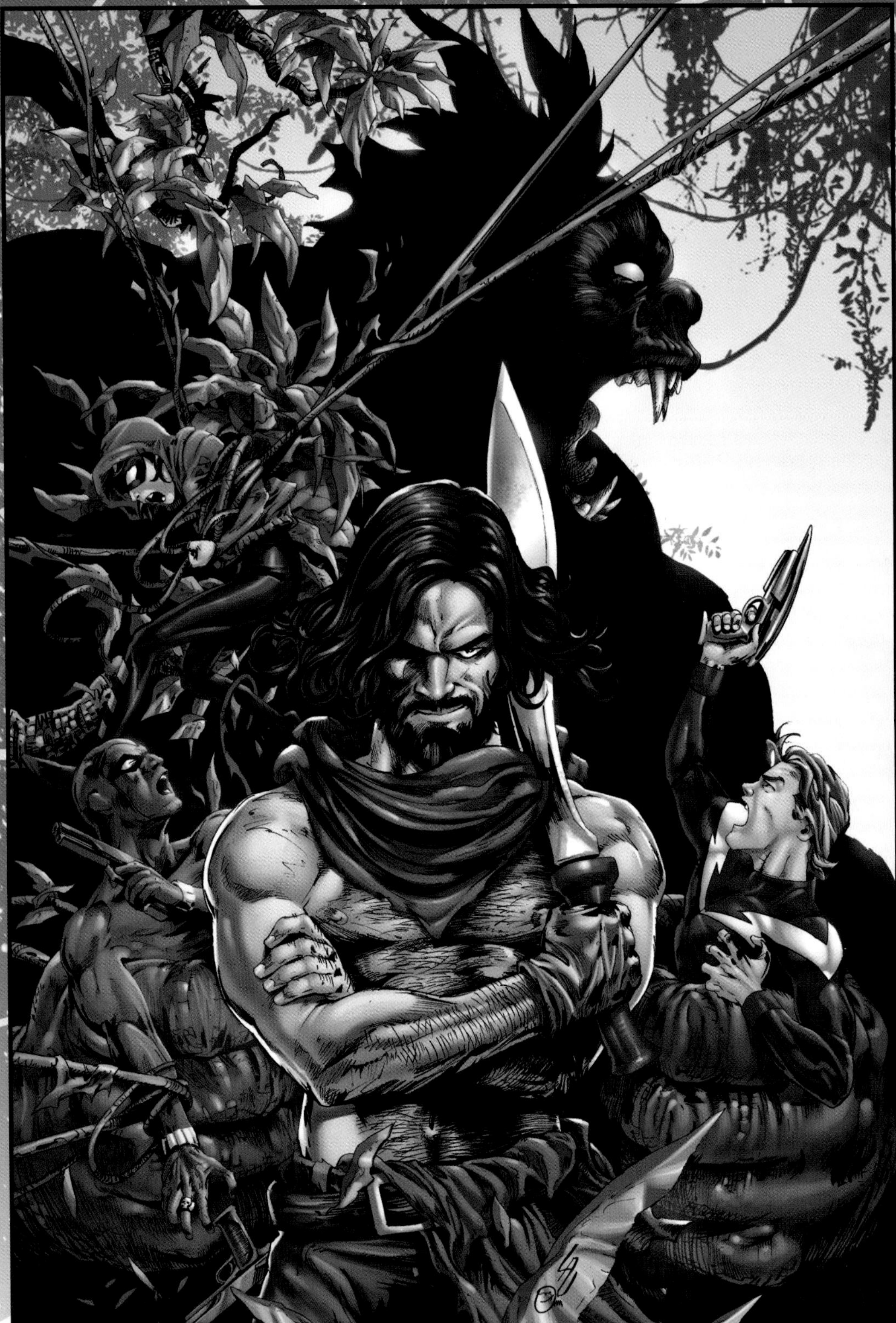

Issue #1 alternate cover
Art by **JONATHAN LAU**
Colors by **OMI REMALANTE**

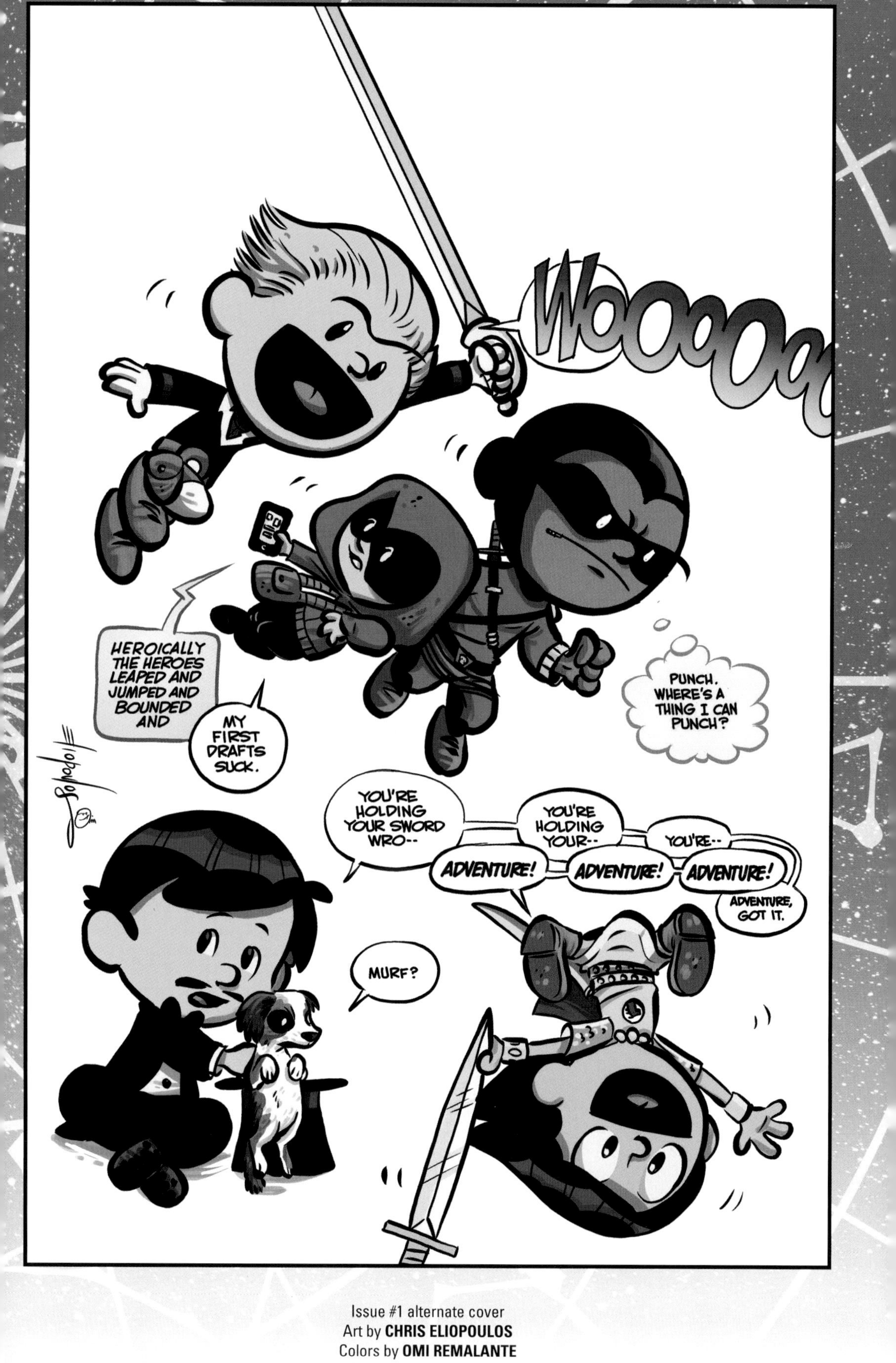
WOOOOOA
HEROICALLY THE HEROES LEAPED AND JUMPED AND BOUNDED AND
MY FIRST DRAFTS SUCK.
PUNCH. WHERE'S A THING I CAN PUNCH?
YOU'RE HOLDING YOUR SWORD WRO--
ADVENTURE!
YOU'RE HOLDING YOUR--
ADVENTURE!
YOU'RE--
ADVENTURE!
ADVENTURE, GOT IT.
MURF?

Issue #1 alternate cover
Art by **CHRIS ELIOPOULOS**
Colors by **OMI REMALANTE**

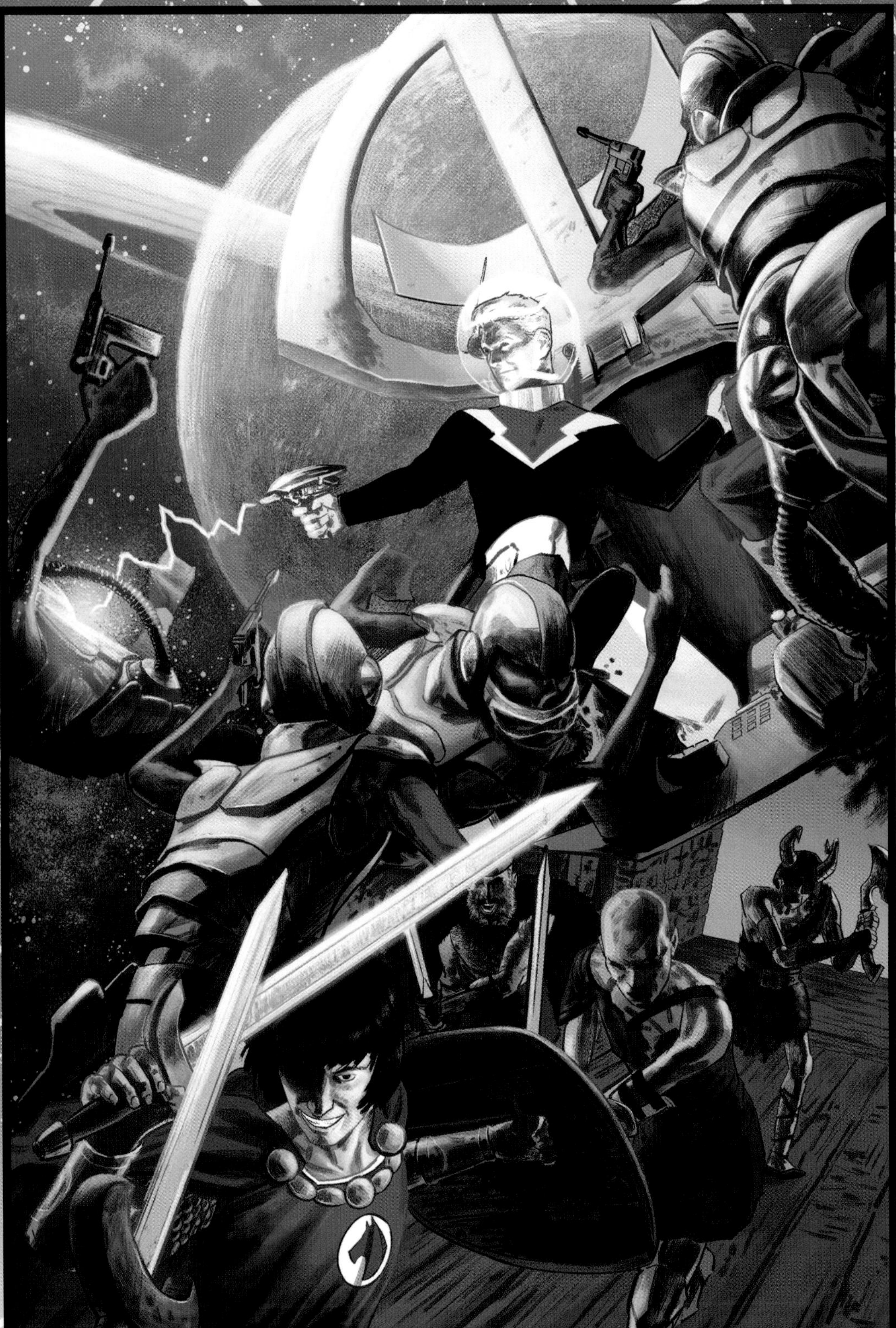

Issue #1 alternate cover
Art by **COLTON WORLEY**
Colors by **RON SALAS**

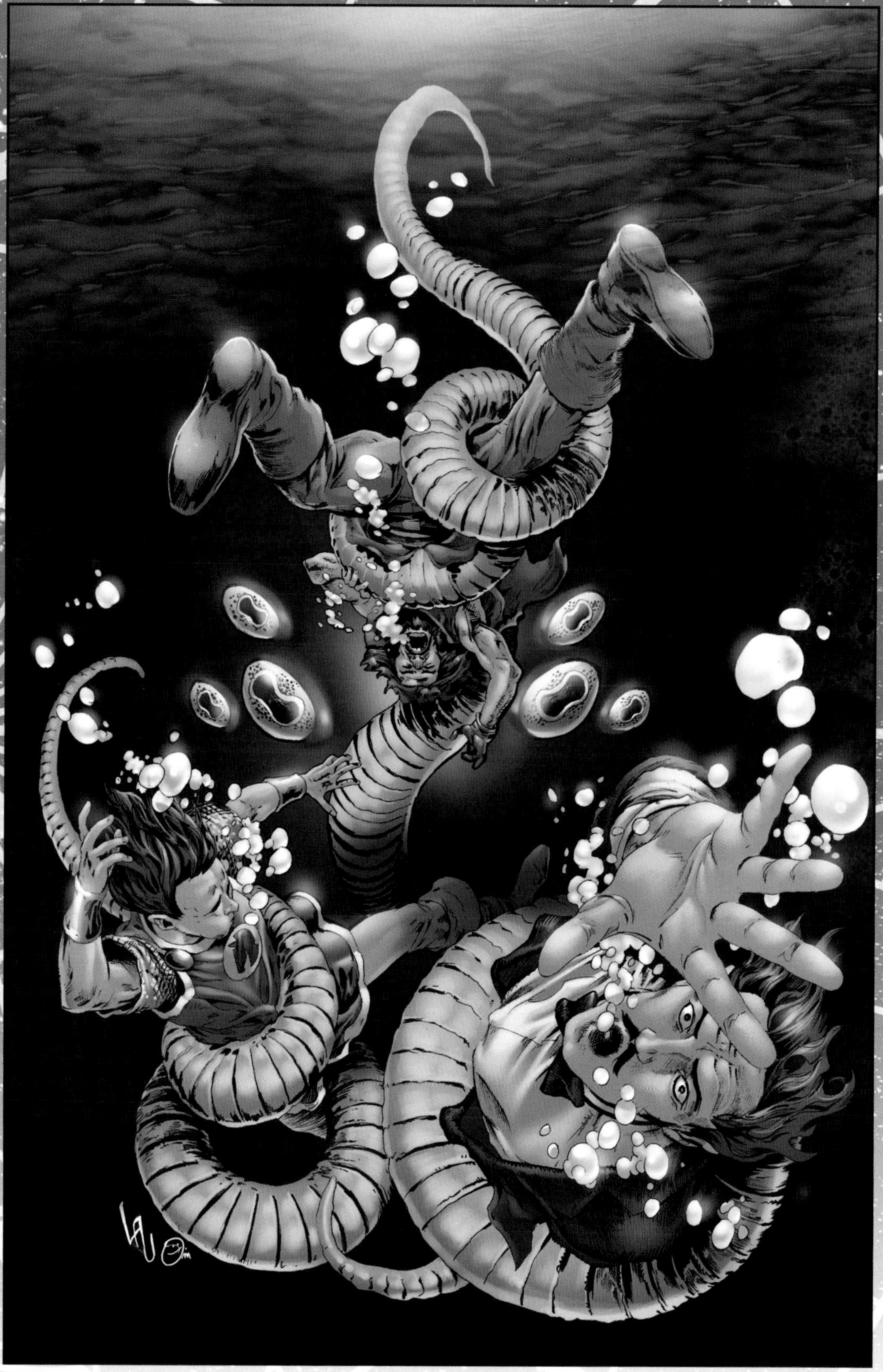

Issue #2 alternate cover
Art by **JONATHAN LAU**
Colors by **OMI REMALANTE**

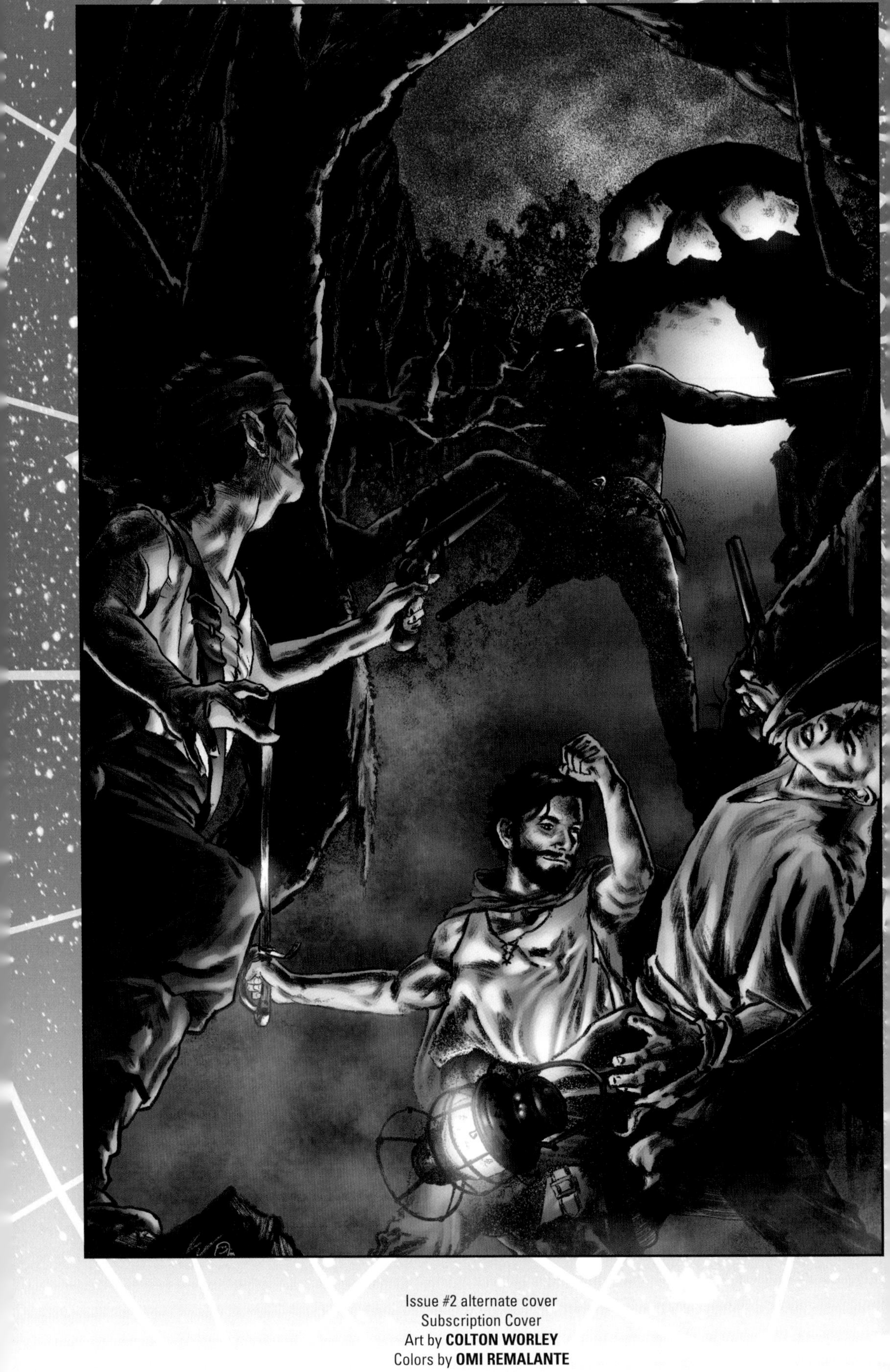

Issue #2 alternate cover
Subscription Cover
Art by **COLTON WORLEY**
Colors by **OMI REMALANTE**

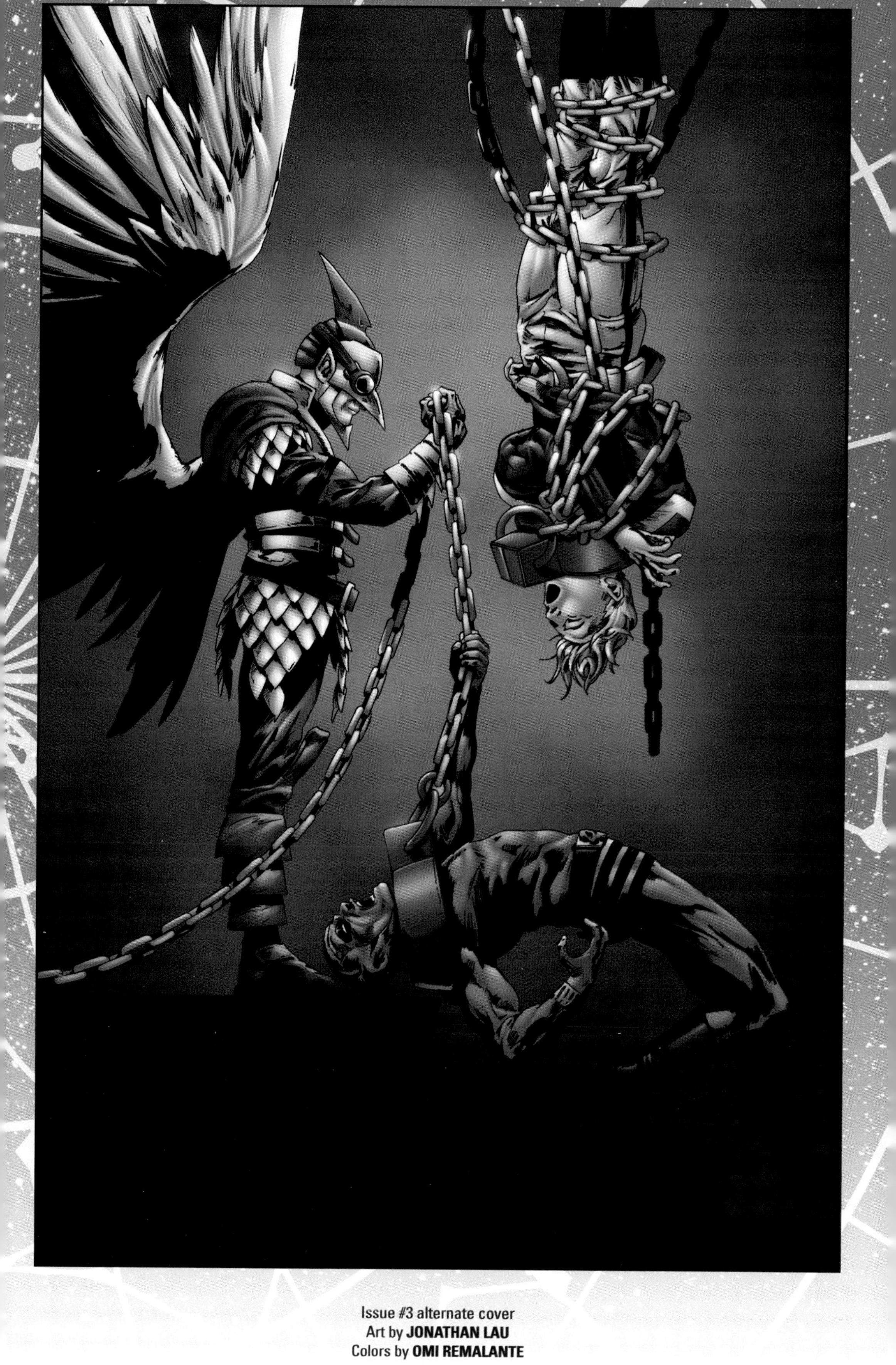

Issue #3 alternate cover
Art by **JONATHAN LAU**
Colors by **OMI REMALANTE**

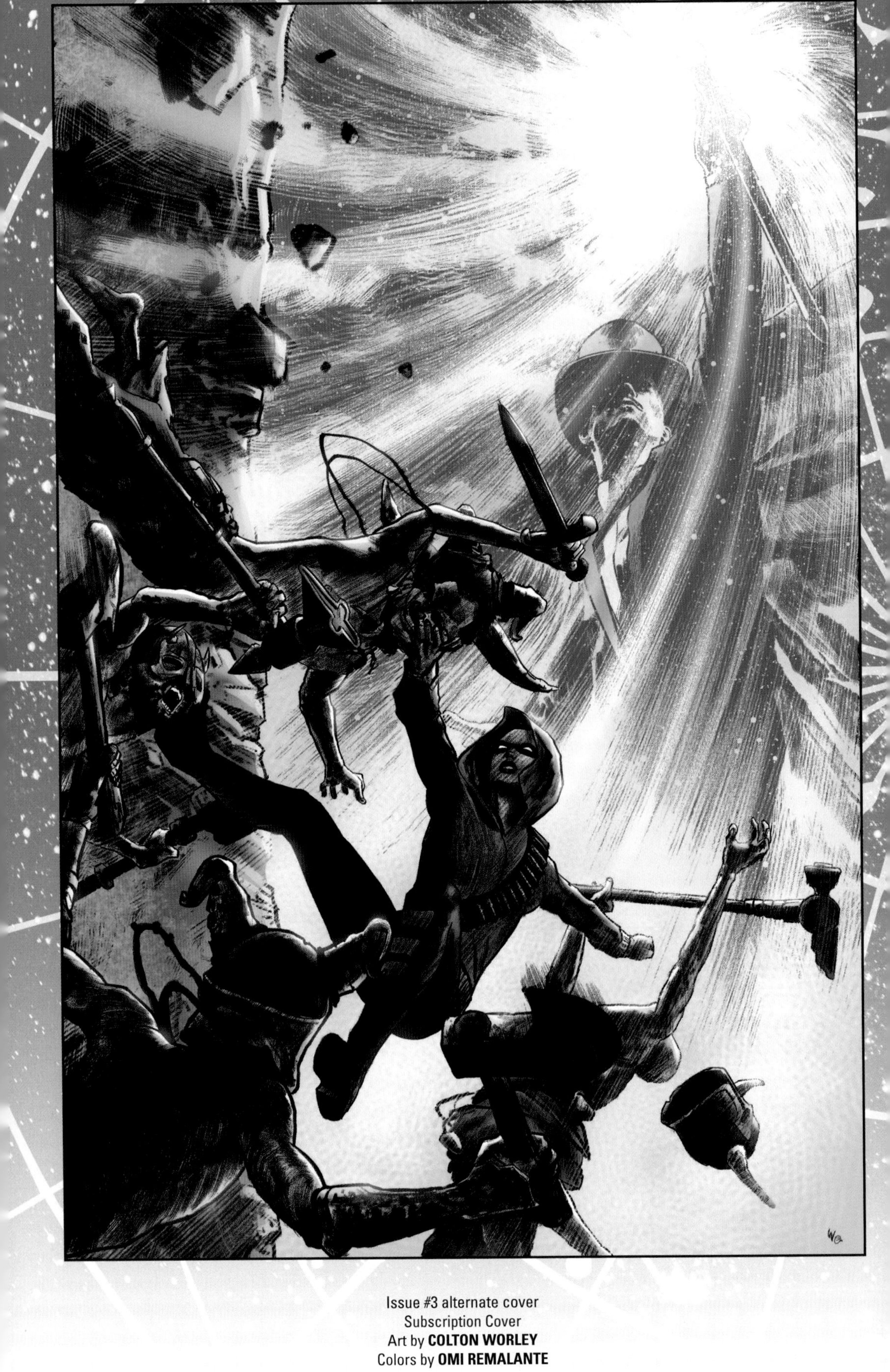

Issue #3 alternate cover
Subscription Cover
Art by **COLTON WORLEY**
Colors by **OMI REMALANTE**

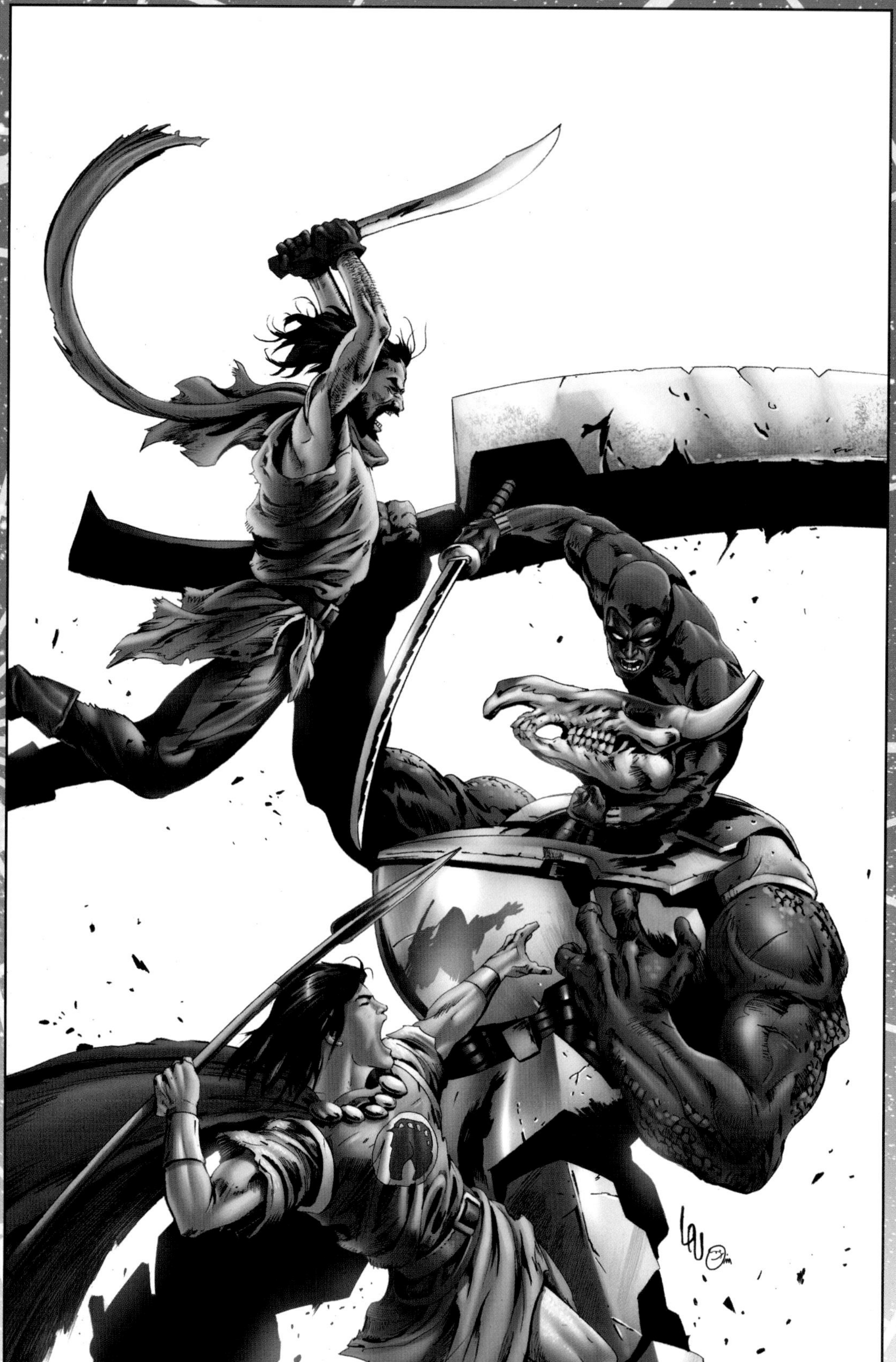

Issue #4 alternate cover
Art by **JONATHAN LAU**
Colors by **OMI REMALANTE**

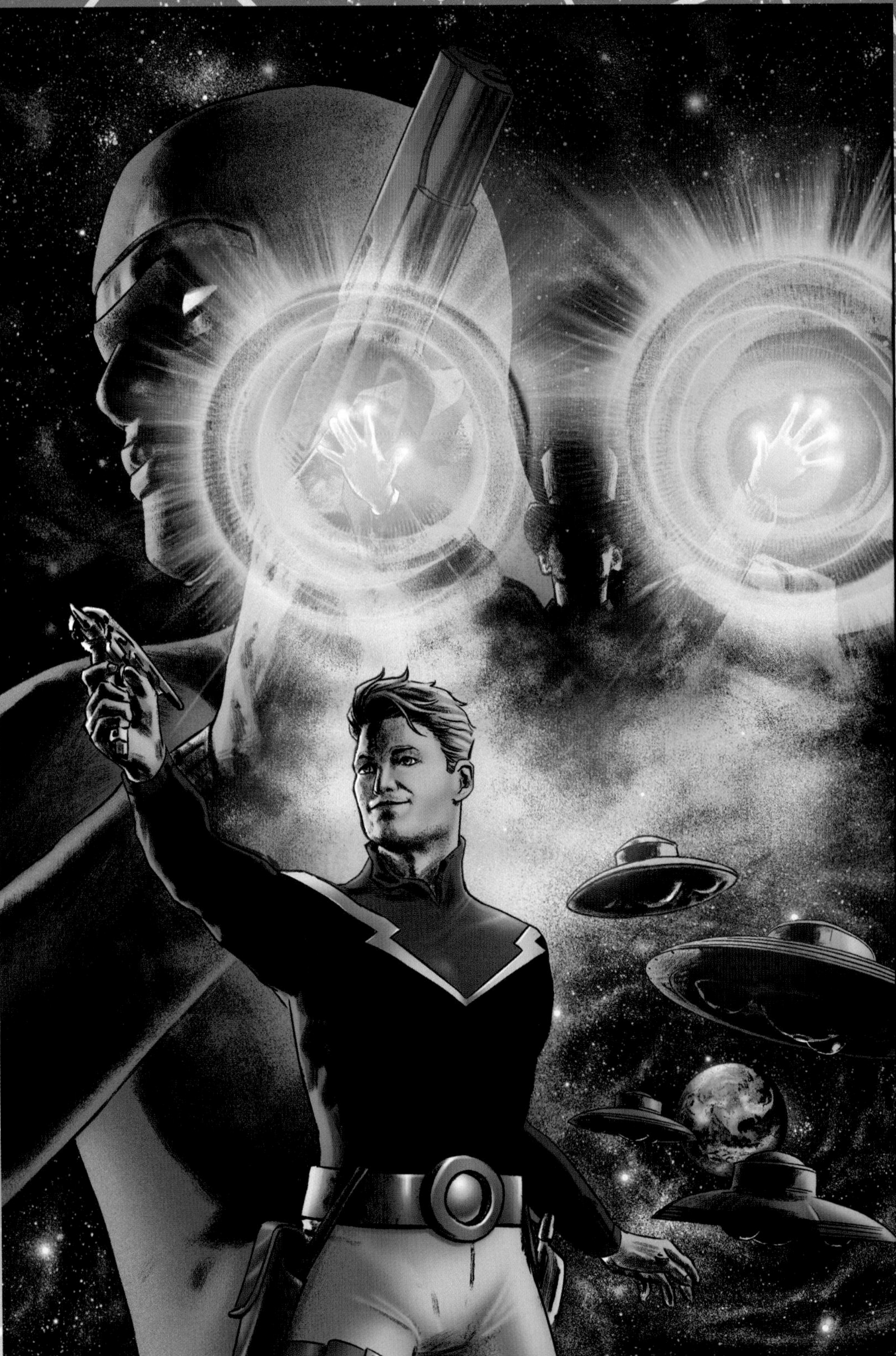

Issue #4 alternate cover
Subscription Cover
Art by **COLTON WORLEY**
Colors by **OMI REMALANTE**

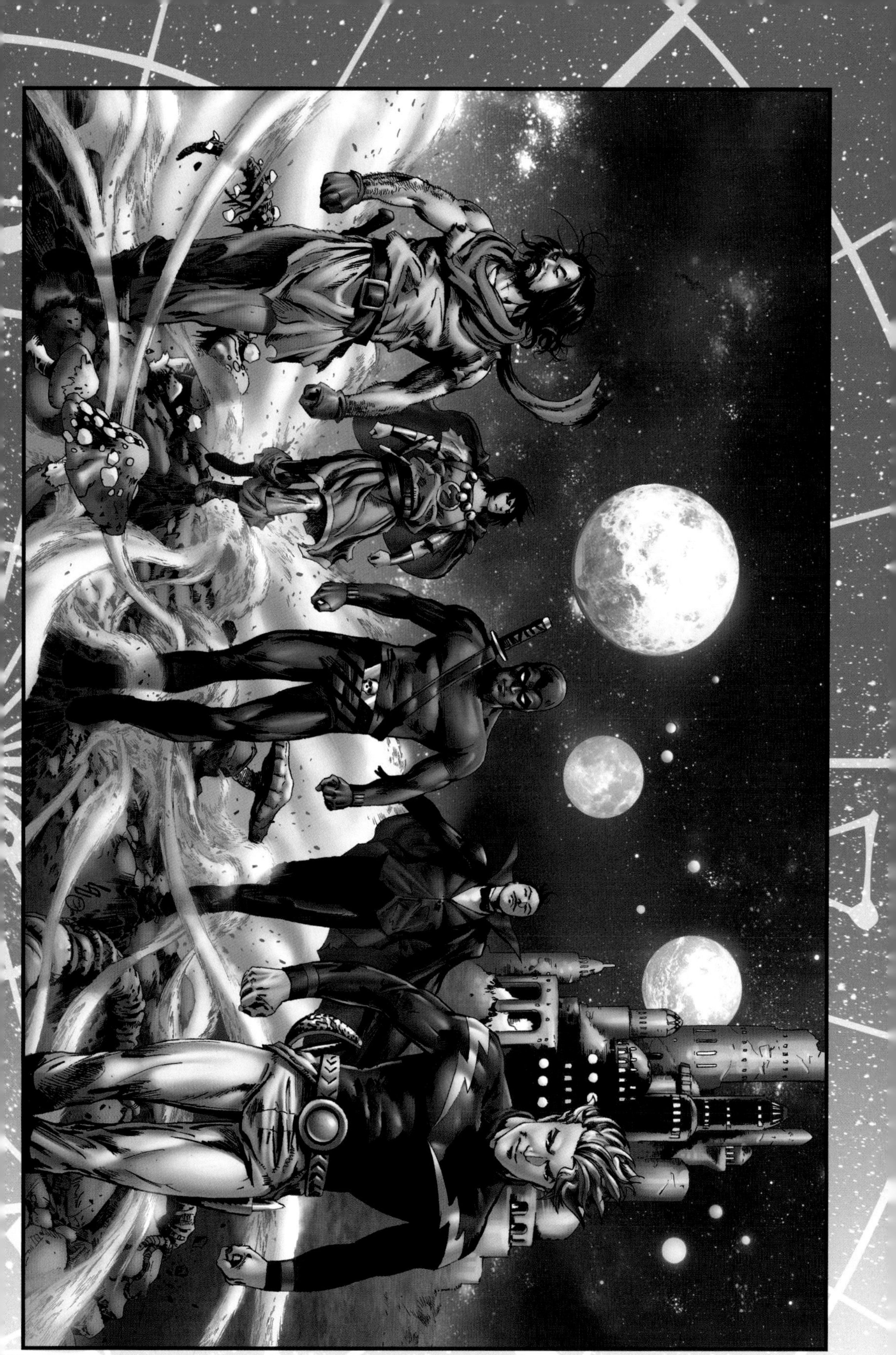

Issue #5 alternate cover
Art by **JONATHAN LAU**
Colors by **OMI REMALANTE**

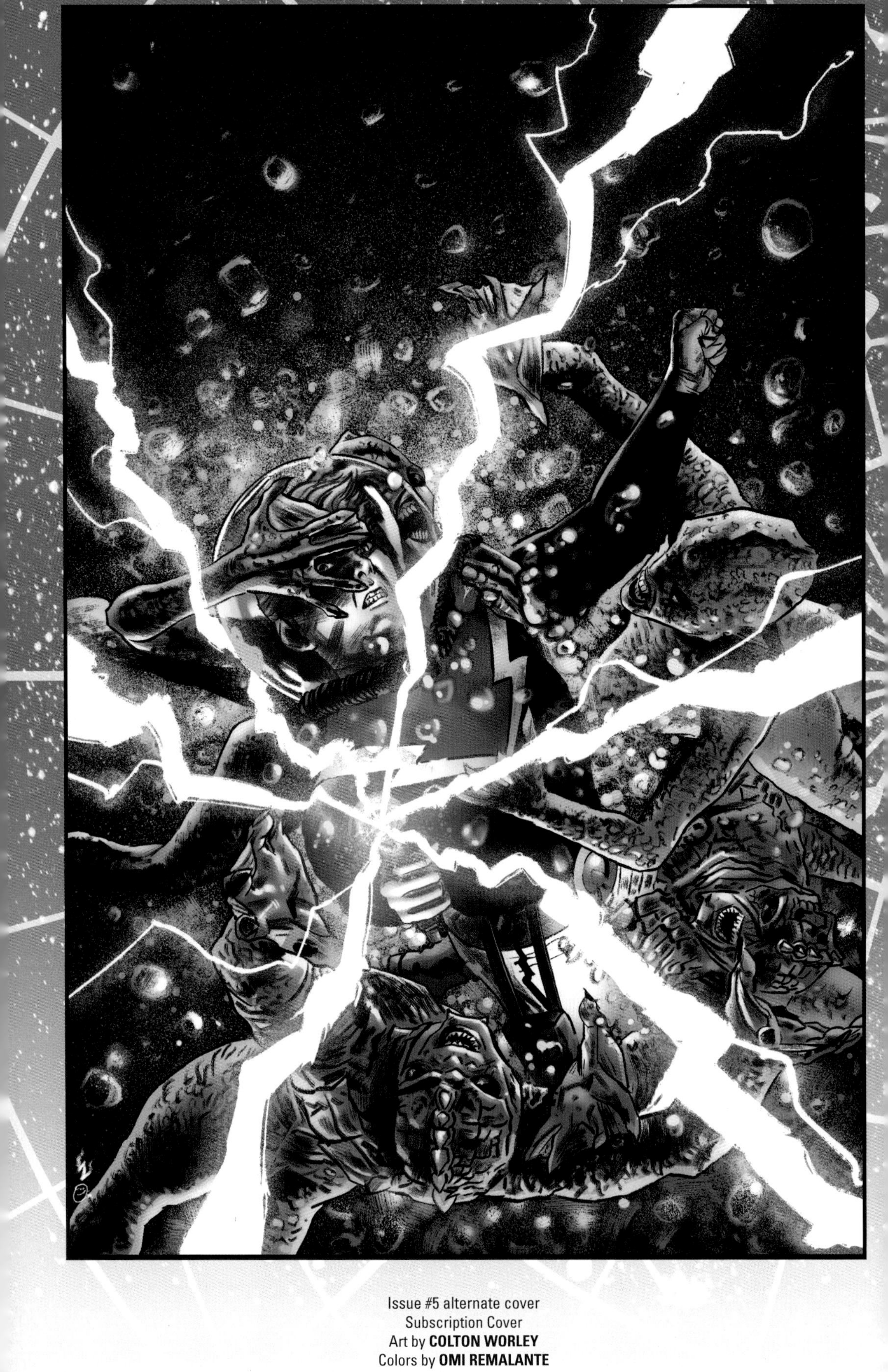

Issue #5 alternate cover
Subscription Cover
Art by **COLTON WORLEY**
Colors by **OMI REMALANTE**

TO BE
CONTINUED IN...

FLASH GORDON™

KINGS CROSS

BY JEFF PARKER,
JESSE HAMM,
AND GRACE ALLISON.

KING
DYNAMITE